Encountering Images
of Spiritual Transformation

Encountering Images of Spiritual Transformation

The Thoroughfare Motif within the Plot of Luke-Acts

James M. Morgan

WIPF & STOCK · Eugene, Oregon

ENCOUNTERING IMAGES OF SPIRITUAL TRANSFORMATION
The Thoroughfare Motif within the Plot of Luke-Acts

Copyright © 2013 James M. Morgan. All rights reserved. Except for brief quotations in critical publications or reviews, no part of this book may be reproduced in any manner without prior written permission from the publisher. Write: Permissions, Wipf and Stock Publishers, 199 W. 8th Ave., Suite 3, Eugene, OR 97401.

Wipf & Stock
An Imprint of Wipf and Stock Publishers
199 W. 8th Ave., Suite 3
Eugene, OR 97401
www.wipfandstock.com

ISBN 13: 978-1-61097-980-1
Manufactured in the U.S.A.

All scripture quotations, unless otherwise indicated, are taken from the Holy Bible, New International Version®, NIV®. Copyright ©1973, 1978, 1984 by Biblica, Inc.™ Used by permission of Zondervan. All rights reserved worldwide.

Scripture quotations in Greek are from *Novum Testamentum Graece*. 27th ed. Stuttgart: Deutsche Bibelgesellschaft, 1993. Used by permission. All rights reserved.

With heartfelt thanks to our parents:
Jim and Margaret Morgan
and
Hansruedi and Annemarie Bärtschi

Contents

List of Tables and Figures / ix
Preface / xi
Foreword xiii
List of Abbreviations / xv

Part One: Motifs and Plot for the Study of Luke-Acts

1. **How Can Motifs Contribute to the Study of Luke-Acts?** / 3
   Reading Luke-Acts through Motifs and Plot
   Why Such Interest in Thoroughfares in Luke-Acts?
   The Power of Motifs: Definition, Identification, and Evaluation
   Thoroughfare Expressions in Luke-Acts: How and Where do They Appear?
   Thoroughfare Motif's Performance: What Narrative and Theological Value?

2. **The Plot of Luke-Acts: the Reader's Encounter with Spiritual Transformation** / 36
   Definition of Plot from the Reader's Perspective
   Theophilus as the Real and Implied Reader
   Plot Theory and the Analysis of Nonfiction
   The Plot of Luke-Acts
   Questions for the Thoroughfare Motif within the Plot of Luke-Acts

Part Two: Analysis of the Thoroughfare Motif's Performance within the Plot

3. **First Encounters: Portraits of the Hero and the Forerunner** / 61
   (Luke 1:5—3:38)
   Proleptic Portraits of John and Jesus via Zechariah's Canticle (Luke 1:76, 79)
   John the Baptist and the Way for the Lord (Luke 3:4–5)
   Summary of the Thoroughfare Motif in the Initial Orientation

4. **Contrasting Encounters: Thoroughfare Imagery for and against the Hero** / 76
   (Luke 4:1—23:56)
   On the Road Transition from John the Baptist to Jesus' disciples
   Pictures of the Plot: Thoroughfare Imagery and Responses to the Hero

Contents

Thoroughfare Reception Scenes from Jericho to Jerusalem
Jesus: the Teacher of the Way of God (Luke 20:21)
Summary of the Thoroughfare Motif in the Raveling Sequence

5 **Pivotal Encounter: An About-face on Emmaus Road / 117**
    (Luke 24:1—Acts 2:13)

Jesus and Disciples on Emmaus Road (24:32, 35)
Summary of the Thoroughfare Motif in the Pivot Sequence

6 **Expanding Encounters: From Roads to "the Way" / 123**
    (Acts 2:14—28:15)

Spotlight on Peter's Extension of Jesus' Mandate in Jerusalem
Highlighted Thoroughfare Reception Scenes for the Jews and the Nations
Paul and Missionary Entourage: Teachers of "the Way(s) of God/the Lord"
Paul: Protagonist for the Collective Character, "the Way"
Summary of the Thoroughfare Motif in the Unraveling Sequence

7 **Final Encounter: "The Way" in Rome via Paul / 179**
    (Acts 28:16–31)

Paul and "the Way" before the Jewish Leaders in Rome
Summary of the Thoroughfare Motif in the Final Orientation

PART THREE: THE THOROUGHFARE MOTIF'S NARRATIVE AND THEOLOGICAL VALUE FOR LUKE-ACTS

8 **The Thoroughfare Motif's Narrative Performance / 183**

Preliminary Remarks
Thoroughfare Motif within the Plot's Sequences
Thoroughfare Motif's Efficacy via Freedman's Five Criteria
Synthesis of the Thoroughfare Motif's Narrative Value
Additional Literary Contributions

9 **The Thoroughfare Motif's Theological Contribution / 198**

Preliminary Remarks
The Value of Plot and Motif Analysis for Theological Studies
Theological Implications from a Christocentric Plot and Motif
Conclusion: The Divine Way and Human Response in Plot and Explotment

Bibliography / 221
Subject Index / 233

List of Tables and Figures

Table 1.1: Statistics on Thoroughfare Terms in Five Narrative Sequences 27

Table 2.1: Five Major Narrative Sequences in Luke-Acts 51

Figure 2.1 Emplotment and Plot: The Story from External and Internal Perspectives 37

Figure 2.2 Emplotment, Plot, Explotment in Historical Narrative Applied to Luke-Acts 38

Figure 8.1 Symbolic Correlation between Thoroughfare Motif and Passage to Salvation 193

Preface

This book represents a significant revision of my dissertation successfully defended at the Evangelische Theologische Faculteit (Leuven, Belgium) in 2010. I would like to indicate here the major changes that have been made, explain the background of this book, and mention key people who have encouraged me (a nomadic researcher) *along the way*.

I have updated my research as well as included works that were not available to me while writing my dissertation in Niger. I have highlighted the analysis of the motif in Part Two and extended the final chapter on the motif's theological contribution. Therefore, certain parts have been significantly reduced, especially the literature review, plot theory, and plot analysis of Luke-Acts. Concerning my approach, it is still narratological, but I now give more emphasis to the reader's presence and participation in plot theory and, consequently, also in the analysis.

This book is primarily for teachers and students of the Bible, in particular for those who have a keen interest in Luke's writings (Luke and Acts). In order for the book to be more accessible to a broader audience, I have translated all quotations from the Bible and other foreign languages. Most of the technical points on the Greek text have been placed in parentheses or footnotes. Knowledge of Greek is helpful but not necessary to appreciate the major contribution of the work. Yet, this research is also for those interested in literary or narrative theory applied to biblical and other ancient narratives. Narratives deserve the attention they have received in the past forty years, and, hopefully, this project makes a small contribution especially concerning motif and plot theory.

Concerning background and key persons in this endeavor, aspects of this research began in 1998 when I first taught a class on Christianity and World Religions at the Istituto Biblico Evangelico Italiano (Rome). While preparing my notes, my curiosity was sparked by designations of faith in the Bible. One of these was "the Way" in the Acts of the Apostles. Since those discussions with my students, I had the opportunity to explore the notion of a *divine way* in my Master's thesis at ETF supervised by Prof. Dr. Hendrik

Preface

Koorevaar. This paved the way for further research, which moved into the area of New Testament since I was teaching increasingly in that field. My curiosity in expressions of paths, roads, and ways did not fade (perhaps due to my first degree in Geography and Geology!), so I set out to study the narrative value of thoroughfare expressions in Luke and Acts following the capable guidance of Prof. Dr. Martin Webber. In the meantime, my family and I returned to Niamey (Niger) for ministry at the Ecole Supérieure Privée de Théologie and the Foyer Evangélique Universitaire (SIM). It was a pleasure to work with the staff and students in both institutions. However, doctoral work was extremely difficult and required several trips to Belgium for research, guidance, and writing. I am particularly thankful to Lilian, Daniel, Melinda, Christina, and our families for their support during this time of intense activity. I'm now trying to make up for some of the time lost . . .

I am thankful for the readers' constructive critiques of my dissertation at ETF and for the permission and encouragement to publish my research. Many thanks also go to the staff at Wipf & Stock who provide expertise and guidance to publish dissertations. Their commitment to research is commendable. I wish also to thank our mission family, SIM Niger and Switzerland, and our faithful supporters who allow me to do academic research as a part of my ministry. Finally, many thanks to Prof. Dr. Luc Devillers and colleagues in the Biblical Studies department of the University of Fribourg for their encouragement and solidarity. Conditions for doing research are optimal here and have allowed me to finish this project in peace and good health.

Foreword

The study of New Testament books as narratives has been a welcome development in recent times, and I am delighted to introduce and commend this careful narrative-based study of the thoroughfare motif in Luke-Acts by James Morgan. What will readers gain from his well organized and clearly written study?

First, they will gain a well-grounded understanding of how *plot* works in narrative, and have Luke's plot illuminated. Dr Morgan shows a solid grasp of theoretical discussions of this topic, enables his readers to see the key ideas clearly, and then leads his readers carefully through Luke and Acts from this perspective, sketching the plot of the double-work well. He thus sensitizes readers to how Luke's overall plot works and develops, and equips them to continue reflecting themselves, on Luke-Acts and other narratives.

Secondly, Dr Morgan's careful study of *the thoroughfare motif* will enable readers to see just how much Luke communicates using this motif, and in what ways he communicates. Again, Dr Morgan is on top of the theoretical discussion of motifs, and guides his readers with a light touch through it, so that they are not overwhelmed by abstract theory, but have sufficient grasp of the theory to understand how to apply it to Luke-Acts. Dr Morgan shows clearly how this motif touches many of the major themes of Luke-Acts, and thus his study leads readers into the heart of the two books. To read this book is not only to gain a fuller appreciation of Luke's message and means of communication, but also to see a model of an approach which has the potential to be applied to other Lukan motifs—and motifs in other biblical books, too.

Thirdly, in the body of this book (Part Two) Dr Morgan provides thoughtful exegetical study of Luke and Acts, and readers will gain helpful insights and perspectives on particular passages and issues. He has read and engaged with Luke-Acts enough for it to enter his bloodstream and, after being filtered through his clear mind, to emerge in readable and lucid prose on the page.

Fourthly, throughout, Dr Morgan shows a keen grasp of scholarly discussion of Luke-Acts and demonstrates the ability to sift this discussion

Foreword

wisely to find the grain and reject the chaff. His judgements are generally sure-footed, demonstrate careful thought, and lead to better understanding.

Finally, this study enhances Christian theological understanding through Dr Morgan's engaging development of the theological contribution of the thoroughfare motif (especially in Chapter 9, after being introduced in Chapters 1 and 2). Having argued that Luke aims to confirm and enhance his readers' faith in Jesus, here we learn specific ways in which their faith is to develop—and are ourselves invited to participate in the Christian journey along which Luke encourages his first readers to go. He identifies Luke's understanding of Jesus, salvation, and the believing community as key themes on which greater light is shone by the thoroughfare motif—core themes of Luke-Acts indeed!

We are indebted to Dr Morgan for the care and hard work which has gone into this study. In it he enriches our understanding of Luke's writings and Luke's methods.

Steve Walton
Professor of New Testament,
London School of Theology

List of Abbreviations

AASF	Annales Academiae scientarum fennicae
AB	Anchor Bible
ABRL	Anchor Bible Reference Library
AnBib	Analecta Biblica
ANLEX	Friberg, Barbara, Timothy Friberg, and Neva F. Miller. *Analytical Lexicon of the Greek New Testament.* Baker's Greek New Testament Library. Electronic ed. Grand Rapids: Baker, 2000.
ANTC	Abingdon New Testament Commentaries
Apg.	Apostelgeschichte (German, "Acts of the Apostles")
BA	Bauer, Walter. *Griechisch-deutsches Wörterbuch zu den Schriften des Neuen Testaments und der frühchristlichen Literatur.* Edited by Kurt Aland and Barbara Aland. 6th ed. Berlin: Walter de Gruyter, 1988.
BAFCS	*The Book of Acts in Its First-Century Setting.* Edited by Bruce W. Winter. 6 vols. Grand Rapids: Eerdmans, 1993-1997.
Bailly	Bailly, Anatole. *Le Grand Bailly. Dictionnaire Grec Français.* Edited by L. Séchan and P. Chantraine. Rev. ed. Paris: Hachette, 2000.
BBB	Bonner biblische Beiträge
BDAG	Bauer, Walter, Frederick W. Danker, W.F. Arndt, and F.W. Gingrich. *A Greek-English Lexicon of the New Testament and Other Early Christian*

List of Abbreviations

	Literature. 3rd ed. Chicago: University of Chicago Press, 2000.
BDB	Brown, Francis, S.R. Driver, and Charles A. Briggs. *The New Brown, Driver and Briggs Hebrew and English Lexicon of the Old Testament*. Grand Rapids: Baker, 1987.
BDR	Blass, Friedrich, and Albert Debrunner. *Grammatik des neutestamentlichen Griechisch*. Edited by Friedrich Rehkopf. 18th ed. Göttingen: Vandenhoeck und Ruprecht, 2001.
BECNT	Baker Evangelical Commentary on the New Testament
BETL	Bibliotheca ephemeridum theologicarum Lovaniensium
BIRS	Bibliographies and Indexes in Religious Studies
BIS	Biblical Interpretation Series
BSL	Biblical Studies Library
BTB	*Biblical Theology Bulletin*
BTNT	Biblical Theology of the New Testament
BTS	Biblical Tools and Studies
CBQ	*Catholic Biblical Quarterly*
CBSS	Continuum Biblical Studies Series
CNT	Commentaire du Nouveau Testament
CP	Culy, Martin M., and Mikeal C. Parsons. *Acts: A Handbook of the Greek Text*. Waco, TX: Baylor University Press, 2003.
CPS	Culy, Martin M., Mikeal C. Parsons, and Joshua J. Stigall. *Luke: A Handbook of the Greek Text*. Waco, TX: Baylor University Press, 2010.
DJG	*Dictionary of Jesus and the Gospels*. Edited by Joel B. Green and Scot McKnight. Downers Grove, IL: InterVarsity, 1992.
EKKNT	Evangelisch-katholischer Kommentar zum Neuen Testament

EQ	*Evangelical Quarterly*
GBS	Guides to Biblical Scholarship
HNT	Handbuch zum Neuen Testament
HTKNT	Herders theologischer Kommentar zum Neuen Testament
IBT	Interpreting Biblical Texts
ICC	International Critical Commentary
JBL	*Journal of Biblical Literature*
JETS	*Journal of the Evangelical Theological Society*
JSNT	*Journal for the Study of the New Testament*
JSNTSup	Journal for the Study of the New Testament: Supplement Series
KEK	Kritisch-exegetischer Kommentar über das Neue Testament
LCBI	Literary Currents in Biblical Interpretation
LD	Lectio Divina
LEH	Lust, Johan, Erik Eynikel, and Katrin Hauspie. *Greek-English Lexicon of the Septuagint*. Rev. ed. Stuttgart: Deutsche Bibelgesellschaft, 2003.
LkEv	Lukasevangelium (German, "Gospel of Luke")
LN	Louw, Johannes P., and Eugene A. Nida. *Greek-English Lexicon of the New Testament: Based on Semantic Domains*. 2nd ed. Vol. 1 Introduction and Domains. New York, NY: United Bible Societies, 1989.
LNTS	Library of New Testament Studies
LXX	*Septuaginta*. Edited by Alfred Rahlfs and Robert Hanhart. Rev. ed. Stuttgart: Deutsche Bibelgesellschaft, 2006.
MM	Moulton, J.H., and G. Milligan, *The Vocabulary of the Greek New Testament Illustrated from the Papyri and Other Non-Literary Sources*, London: Hodder and Stoughton, 1949.

List of Abbreviations

NA²⁷	Nestle-Aland; *Novum Testamentum Graece*. 27th ed. Stuttgart: Deutsche Bibelgesellschaft, 1993.
Neot	*Neotestamentica*
NICNT	New International Commentary on the New Testament
NIGTC	New International Greek Testament Commentary
NovT	*Novum Testamentum*
NTD	Das Neue Testament Deutsch
NTL	New Testament Library
NTOA	Novum Testamentum et Orbis Antiquus
NTS	*New Testament Studies*
ÖTKNT	Ökumenischer Taschenbuchkommentar zum Neuen Testament
PBM	Paternoster Biblical Monographs
RSR	*Recherches de science religieuse*
Rusconi	Rusconi, Carlo. *Dizionario del Greco del Nuovo Testamento*. 2nd ed. Bologna: EDB, 1997.
SBF	Studium Biblicum Franciscanum
SBL	Studies in Biblical Literature
SBLMS	Society of Biblical Literature Monograph Series
SNTSMS	Society for New Testament Studies Monograph Series
SNTV	Studies of the New Testament and its World
SP	Sacra Pagina
ST	*Studia theologica*
TF	Theologische Forschung
TPINTC	Trinity Press International New Testament Commentaries
TWNT	*Theologisches Wörterbuch zum Neuen Testament*. 10 vols. Edited by Gerhard Kittel and Gerhard Friedrich. Stuttgart: Kohlhammer, 1932–79.
WBC	Word Biblical Commentary

PART ONE

Motifs and Plot for the Study of Luke-Acts

1

How Can Motifs Contribute to the Study of Luke-Acts?

LUKE-ACTS WAS AN AMBITIOUS project: a two-volume narrative seeking to convince and engage readers regarding the spiritual impact of Jesus of Nazareth on the Jewish people and other nations.[1] The author, "Luke," portrays a movement that extends through Jesus and his disciples from Jerusalem to Rome.[2] He selects and portrays examples of this spiritual transformation on individuals and groups, some of which are quite unexpected. Yet, Luke also highlights significant opposition to Jesus' mandate on human and spiritual planes. Indeed, this is not a story of a blissful pilgrimage. Rather, a pattern of reception and rejection among the Jewish people and "the nations" pervades the entire work. Luke aims to bring

---

1. The present research assumes the narrative unity of the Gospel of Luke and the Acts of the Apostles, but it also provides evidence for this position. See these now classic contributions underlining the literary unity of Luke-Acts, Cadbury, *Making of Luke-Acts*; Unnik, "'Book of Acts," 34–38; and Talbert, *Literary Patterns*. For recent defenses of the unity of Luke-Acts, see Verheyden, *Unity*, 3–56; Marguerat, "Luc-Actes," 57–81; Spencer, "Unity of Luke—Acts," 341–66; Green, *Luke-Acts*, 101–19; and Morgan, "Luc-Actes," forthcoming. For opposing positions, see Parsons and Pervo, *Rethinking*; Rowe, "History," 131–57; Bockmuehl, "Why not Let Acts be Acts?," 163–66; Pervo, *Acts*, 18–20; and Walters, *Assumed Authorial*. The results of Walters's study have been recognized as convincing by Pervo and unconvincing by Green in their book reviews (*RBL* [December 2009] http://www.bookreviews.org). For this question in relation to the reception history of Luke and Acts, see Gregory, "Reception," 459–72.

2. The author is anonymous in the two scrolls dedicated to Theophilus. According to early church tradition, "Luke the beloved physician" (Col 4:14), Paul's co-worker, produced these writings (cf. 2 Tim 4:11; Phlm 1:24). Based on these verses, church tradition, and the close ties with Paul in Luke-Acts, this proposal remains the most plausible; hence, I use "Luke" and "narrator" interchangeably to designate the author of Luke-Acts. For a recent creative profile of Luke (son of an elite, Hellenized Jewish family), see Kuhn, *Elite Evangelist*, 102–6.

his audience to a greater certainty of faith by exploring central questions related to God's plan accomplished through Jesus and his disciples despite opposition. Therefore, the two long scrolls, Luke and Acts, represent above all a narrative with a theological *point* and a specific pragmatic aim. Luke is not interested in merely conveying information about God; his aim is to provide certainty, assurance through instruction, about the difference that God's revelation in Jesus brings (Luke 1:4).

In fact, not only was Luke's project ambitious from a literary perspective, it was also audacious from a theological outlook. Internal evidence supports the idea that Luke intended his writings to be read within the tradition of Israel's Scriptures. Through his work, he sought to extend what had already been written about Israel's God. While something new happened—the Messiah has come—Luke's intent was to connect the new with the old, to underline continuity in God's interventions for Israel and all of humanity. This is the theological and pragmatic force of this two-volume work. It reflects Luke's concern for his readership, namely, that they might live according to the reality of God's continued activity through Jesus and his disciples.

Reading Luke–Acts through Motifs and Plot

To achieve these aims, rather than abstract or speculative theological argumentation, Luke provides theological interpretation through episodes, speeches, quotations, as well as, of course, through description and asides. Nonfictional narrative in fact has its own rhetoric: the "rhetoric of the real."[3] In this sense, Luke-Acts is perhaps as theological as Paul's letter to the Romans. Yet, rather than much explicit commentary, Luke develops his theology through an impressive arsenal of narrative and literary techniques. The present work focuses mainly on one of these narrative techniques: the motif. More specifically, it explores the thoroughfare motif as a part of this literary, theological and pragmatic masterpiece.

Yet, what do motifs have to offer to the study of an ancient text such as Luke-Acts? As repetitive elements, motifs have interpretative value since they progressively draw the audience's attention and have a cumulative effect on them pointing to what is meaningful in the narrative. Therefore, the present work examines a motif that contributes to the encounter of this world of spiritual transformation that Luke describes with great flair.[4] The

3. Abbott, *Narrative*, 44.
4. "Theophilus" is the only specific addressee mentioned in the four canonical

thoroughfare motif includes those figurative and concrete expressions involving ways, roads, city streets, and country paths. Why, for example, does Luke seem to take pleasure in describing transformational events on thoroughfares or in relation to them? Is there a connection between expressions like "the way of peace," "the way of salvation," "the way of God," and "the Way"? In fact, why does Luke use such an unusual expression like "the Way" to describe Jesus' followers? Moreover, does thoroughfare imagery appear in key moments of the plot? How does the thoroughfare motif perform within the plot of Luke-Acts? In other words, how does the thoroughfare motif enhance the reader's encounter with the hero's mandate of spiritual transformation through thoroughfare imagery? How do such expressions contribute to the *spiritual landscape* of Luke-Acts, the intermingling of concrete and figurative uses of physical imagery?[5]

This study suggests answers to these questions and indicates how this motif might have been important for Theophilus and the broader audience, from the perspective of "sympathetic readers" of the first century who sought to understand the story of Jesus and his disciples in light of Israel's theological and literary history. In fact, Luke-Acts is a story within a larger story, which is told in the Jewish Scriptures. Luke portrays God as accomplishing his plan of redemption through the Jewish people, not only for them but also for every nation on earth. For this reason, this study also examines explicit and implicit intertextual cues—"the function and impact of a text or texts in a focal text"— to shed further light on the above questions.[6]

Like an instrument in an orchestra or a pattern within an elegant tapestry, the thoroughfare motif works together with other motifs and themes to create a captivating exploration of spiritual transformation, both received and resisted. The exploration of this motif's performance will be done within the unfolding plot. It asks what difference the motif makes, progressively and cumulatively, to the reader's encounter with the story's main questions

---

gospels (Luke 1:1; Acts 1:1). We only know Theophilus through the few details in these verses. Various proposals have been made about his identify, but no consensus has been reached. I provide some general details about his profile in Chapter 2 based on inferences from the text of Luke-Acts.

5. I borrow James Resseguie's term *spiritual landscape* from his book of the same name. Two chapters have some common ground with the thoroughfare motif: "Topography: The Landscape of Spiritual Growth" and "Journeys: The Itinerary of Spiritual Formation." Resseguie, *Spiritual Landscape*, 9–27; 29–44.

6. Charlesworth, *Intertextuality*, 200. Charlesworth provides a sensible discussion on intertextuality for biblical studies in the same volume (pp. 199–206) in which he defines this term as ". . . the attempt to appreciate the meaning of a text by focusing on the text (or texts) within it; that is, quoted in it or echoed in it." Ibid., 218.

working toward some degree of closure. Reading the motif as a participant in the plot sheds light on its pragmatic and theological value.

The intent of this work is to make the results from previous research more accessible to a wider readership. I explain terms and concepts that often occur in the study of New Testament literature and theology, the Gospel of Luke, and the Acts of the Apostles. English translation accompanies the Greek text that contains thoroughfare expressions. In addition, I describe key terms from narrative theory (*narratology*)[7] and its application to biblical texts.[8] Of course, some knowledge of the above fields will make reading this book easier. Yet, it is hoped that readers will enjoy exploring the above questions and not be overwhelmed by technical discussion.

Since scholars have long recognized the value of thoroughfare expressions in Luke-Acts, the next section indicates key contributions with which I interact, build on, and extend. First, I wish to clarify here that this study explores a motif, and not a concept or a theme. These terms can be a source of confusion. For example, some scholars use the word "way" or *hodos* to describe a general concept that covers various elements. Furthermore, this discussion does not focus on well-known themes such as journey, travel, or divine movement themes in biblical and other literature. This follows the view that motifs and themes are not identical. Themes are abstract entities (e.g., violence, peace, etc.) that are composed of multiple elements including motifs, which are tangible entities (e.g., swords, doves, etc.). Thus, journey and divine movement themes are broader and require, for example, the analysis of verbs of movement and biblical place names. On the other hand, the thoroughfare motif, being smaller, contributes to those themes, but especially to the theme of salvation. I will elucidate the distinction between motifs and themes further below.

---

7. Among others, the present study has benefited particularly from these works: Aristotle, *Poetics*; Chatman, *Story and Discourse*; Abbott, *Narrative*; Herman, *Basic Elements*; Scholes et al., *Nature of Narrative*; Ricoeur, *Temps et récit*; and Baroni, *La tension narrative*.

8. This work is particularly indebted to the works of biblical scholars who have applied narrative theory to these ancient texts. Generally known as *narrative criticism* in biblical research, I have found these introductions particularly helpful: Sternberg, *Poetics of Biblical Narrative*; Bar-Efrat, *Narrative Art*; Powell, *What is Narrative Criticism?*; Fokkelman, *Comment lire le récit biblique* (original Dutch ed. *Vertelkunst in de bijbel. Een handleiding bij literair lezen*; Marguerat and Bourquin, *Pour lire les récits bibliques* (Eng. ed. *How to Read Bible Stories*); and Resseguie, *Narrative Criticism*.

Why Such Interest in Thoroughfares in Luke-Acts?

Recent studies demonstrate that thoroughfare expressions continue to enjoy scholars' attention.[9] Yet, why has there been so much interest in roads, paths, and ways in the Gospel of Luke and the Acts of the Apostles? An obvious response might be that since traveling permeates both volumes, there must be an extensive use of such vocabulary. Their usage would seem inevitable. Some literal uses are present, but not as much as one would expect. In fact, figurative uses have attracted the most attention. They have sought value in thoroughfare expressions to shed light on various questions such as early Christian communities, Luke's theology, and linguistic and theological connections with earlier texts. These five words for thoroughfare occur with various nuances in Luke-Acts: *hodos* (ὁδός way, road); *tribos* (τρίβος path); *plateia* (πλατεῖα broad street); *rumē* (ῥύμη narrow street); and *phragmos* (φραγμός a path along a fence, wall, or hedge). Yet, research has focused predominantly on *hodos* due to its greater frequency (forty of the forty-nine occurrences) and its significant meanings, especially the intriguing idiom "the Way" (*hē hodos*) in Acts.[10] Consensus has not been reached about the referents, origins, and sources for this expression. This explains the continued curiosity in it and its pragmatic force even on modern readers. Consequently, the literary review below is limited to research on uses of *hodos*.

Scholars have had broad interests in using occurrences of *hodos* as evidence. I use four categories here to present their research: *mimetic, expressive, objective,* and *pragmatic*.[11] These categories describe four main interests that drive literary research and correspond considerably to those of biblical research.[12] Mimetic and expressive approaches may be considered referential due to a literary work's assumed value for revealing something beyond the text, that is, as a means to an end (what they refer to). Thus, mimetic describes *context-centered* studies that seek to understand an aspect of the

---

9. For example, Paul Trebilco dedicates a chapter to "the Way" in his book *Self-designations*, 247–71, as does Darrell Bock, "The Church and the Way in Luke-Acts in his *A Theology of Luke and Acts*, 303–10. E.R. Urciuoli explores the relationship between *hodos* and *hairesis* (as a philosophical school) in his article "'Quella ὁδός," 117–36. Moles, "Luke's Preface," 476 and "Time and Space," n.p., *passim*.

10. For an extensive literature review on thoroughfare expressions, see Morgan, *Thoroughfare Motif*, 3–32. Other reviews are in Nötscher, *Gotteswege*, 7–8; Bovon, *Luke the Theologian*, 42, 362–64; and Baban, *On the Road*, 27–71.

11. These categories are borrowed from Abrams, *Glossary*, 51–52.

12. Cf. Mark A. Powell who applies Abrams's categories to biblical research in *Narrative Criticism*, 6–21.

historical context by means of the literary work. Studies labeled expressive are *author-centered* in that the research explores some aspect of the author (sources, theology, etc.). Conversely, objective and pragmatic studies are *poetic* because of their interest in a work's value for its intrinsic qualities or for the effects that it seeks to evoke in the reader.[13] Thus, objective studies are *text-centered* since their *final* interest is in the literary work itself and its components. Finally, pragmatic literary research focuses on the response that the text seeks to evoke in the reader; thus, it is *reader-centered*.

Mimetic value. Studies that focus particularly on the referential value of *hodos* have explored the expression "the way" (ἡ ὁδός *hē hodos*) due to its peculiar form, nuanced meaning, and puzzling origin. These questions almost dominate the history of research on uses of *hodos*. Most discussions of *hodos* focus on six occurrences in Acts, five preceded by the article ("the Way" in 9:2; 19:9, 23; 24:14, 22) and one with the demonstrative pronoun "this way" (ταύτην τὴν ὁδόν *tauten ten hodon*, 22:4). The general assumption is that the pronoun does not change the essential meaning of *hodos* in Acts 22:4. Since no other qualifying elements occur (e.g., adjectives, nouns, etc.), I refer to these six occurrences simply as *hē hodos*, or the unmodified *hodos*.[14]

Three main lines of inquiry regarding the historical value of this expression are discernible: (1) its early Christian usage and identity, (2) its sources and tradition history, and (3) its meanings corresponding to similar Hebrew and Greek expressions in biblical and non-biblical literature. Due to its elusive nature, the majority of scholars have used extrinsic data to shed light on the above questions.

Regarding its referents, many scholars view the unmodified *hodos* as a window to the religious context, that is, that Luke appropriated a term that was already in use among the followers of Jesus.[15] Henry Cadbury describes it as "the most unusual of the names for Christianity."[16] Lake and Cadbury suggest that the unmodified *hodos* was probably used in Greek-speaking Jewish circles to identify a heretical group.[17] Most scholars, however, suggest

---

13. Cf. Powell et al., *Bible and Modern Literary Criticism*, 5–6.

14. Interestingly, the authors of *The Vocabulary of Luke* indicate that this expression does not occur in Mark or Matthew, but they do not indicate it as "characteristic of Luke." Denaux and Corstjens, *Vocabulary*, 427.

15. Although Vittorio Fusco discusses the term *hairesis* (sect), he does not refer to Luke's description of early Christian communities through *hodos* (e.g., Acts 24:14). Fusco, *Premières communautés*, 18, 54, 244.

16. Cadbury, *Names*, 391.

17. Lake and Cadbury, *Beginnings*, 100.

How Can Motifs Contribute to the Study of Luke-Acts?

that followers of Jesus from Jewish origin first used the term for themselves.[18] For example, these followers claimed to represent the correct teaching, as opposed to a sect or faction holding another doctrine (*hairesis*, cf. Acts 24:5, 14).[19] For Jesus' followers, this expression was honorable (contra Cadbury and Lake) in contrast to the derogatory "Nazarenes" used by their opponents.[20] It designates a messianic Jewish group that claimed to be "the Way" for Jews as well as for others, as the continuation of the true Israel.[21] Paul Trebilco echoes many of the points above (and below) attempting to demonstrate that "the Way" reflects a historic usage among Christians and that it is not Luke's literary invention. Luke appropriated it from Christian sources (probably Mark and Q) and not from Qumran, inspired by "the way of the Lord" in Isa 40:3.[22] Already in use at the time of Paul's encounter with Jesus, John the Baptist might have already used the expression.[23] Trebilco does not deny the theological emphasis of Luke's use, an example of Luke's "theological shorthand" for "the Way of Jesus."[24] However, he claims that the position that Luke coined the expression is weakened by several elements: sparse usage, only eight times (he includes "way of Lord/God in Acts 18:25–26)[25]; no occurrences after Acts 24:14; no explicit link between the self-designation and Luke's theology of the journey; and limited locations connected to the expression (Damascus, Jerusalem, Caesarea, and Ephesus).[26] Trebilco recognizes the main obstacle for his argumentation: this particular usage of "the Way" has not been found outside of Acts. Therefore, perhaps it was

---

18. See Minear, *Images*, 149–50; Fitzmyer, "Jewish Christianity," 236; and Bauckham, "James," 56.

19. Michaelis, "ὁδός," 93.

20. Pritz, *Nazarene*, 14–15.

21. Witherington, *Acts*, 302. Similarly, Repo argues that early Christians resembled the Essenes in that they considered themselves the community of the new covenant and representatives of the true Israel. Repo, *Der 'Weg'*, 130.

22. Trebilco, *Self-Designations*, 256–57.

23. Ibid., 263–65.

24. Ibid., 266.

25. Since Trebilco uses quotes around "the Way," it would be better to include only those specific occurrences and not "the way of the Lord" and "the way of God" in Acts 18:25–26. Ibid., 261. Furthermore, it is an overstatement that the six occurrences of "the Way" are sparse, since *hodos* occurs forty times in Luke-Acts. They represent a significant part of similar, figurative expressions with *hodos* (e.g., "way of peace," "ways to life," and "way of salvation").

26. He mistakenly attributes the occurrence in Acts 24:14 to Jerusalem; it should be Caesarea, as with the occurrence in Acts 24:22. Ibid., 261.

Encountering Images of Spiritual Transformation

not actually used by Christians.[27] He justifies his position by pointing to evidence that this expression was only used in Jewish Christian circles in which the metaphor was readily understandable, especially in connection with Isa 40:3. In the Greco-Roman context, Christians would not have found this self-designation appropriate, because it "does not say enough and is potentially confusing."[28] Trebilco's defense of the historical usage behind "the Way" is plausible, but it is not the only possibility. As will be seen, Luke uses omitted elements in expressions (*ellipsis*) quite often, especially with words placed in relation to "God" and "Lord." Moreover, Trebilco places too much emphasis, as do others, on the connection with Isa 40:30 (in Luke 3:4) and "the Way." Other important figurative uses of *hodos* should be taken into consideration as a part of Luke's overall characterization of Jesus and his disciples (e.g., Luke 20:21; Acts 18:25–26).

Concerning sources for *hē hodos*, S.V. McCasland claims that Christians might have received the idiom through contact with the Qumran community.[29] Based on affinities with expressions containing *derek* (דֶּרֶךְ way, road, path) in the *Manual of Discipline* (1QS 8:13–16 and 9:16–21) and *hē hodos* in Acts, McCasland argues that "the Way" is an abbreviated form of "the way of the Lord" from Isa 40:3, the same prophetic source claimed by the community in Qumran. Eero Repo, however, traces the idiom further back to the Essenes in Syria, which then passed from John the Baptist or his disciples to the earliest Christians.[30] Repo suggests that the original form would be *hē hodos*, which was expanded later by qualifiers such as nouns and adjectives.

Although these sources and tradition histories remain possible, the author's knowledge of the Jewish Scriptures in Greek (the Septuagint or LXX) is a sufficient source for the idiom.[31] Furthermore, the meaning of "way" in the Qumran documents differs from the uses in Acts since the expression based on the community's interpretation of "Prepare the way of the Lord" meant the study of the Torah, and, literally, "in the wilderness."[32] Michaelis's

---

27. Ibid., 267.

28. Ibid., 268.

29. McCasland recognizes that both groups could have received this usage of *hodos* independently, but he claims that there was probably "a real contact in ideas and persons between Qumran and early Christianity." McCasland, "The Way," 229.

30. Repo, *Der 'Weg'*, 160–61.

31. Cf. Hengel, Review of *Der 'Weg'*, 364 and Dreyfus, Review of *Der 'Weg'*, 292.

32. Hengel and Schwemer, *Jesus*, 303n36. Charlesworth describes the Qumranites' application of Isa 40:3: "They were in the wilderness to prepare the Way of Yahweh through worship (thus the Rule of the Community ends with a hymn of praise) and

How Can Motifs Contribute to the Study of Luke-Acts?

conclusion still stands: "The results can therefore only be that the origin of this peculiar usage, which is limited within the NT to Acts and subsequently initially found no imitation, cannot be explained with certainty."[33] This supports the hypothesis that the unmodified *hodos* may be an example of Luke's literary art.

Concerning meanings, some scholars find one definition for all occurrences assuming that *hodos* has one referent and that the meaning of one occurrence (e.g., 9:2; 24:14) reveals the meaning of the others. One finds definitions such as "teaching" ("doctrine")[34], "church"[35], and "religion" as in religious movement or a technical term for "Christianity."[36] For example, Max Wilcox asserts that the idiom is "probably simply a surviving trace of the old name for the Christian religion."[37]

"Way of life" is a common definition, based on the link with the *ethical walk* or *halakah* from Jewish literature.[38] Similarly, certain occurrences might exemplify how early Christians understood their faith as experienced internally by the individual.[39] Others suggest that there might be more than one meaning among the six occurrences, for example, both "group" and "teaching."[40] Wilfried Eckey demonstrates the difficulty of encapsulating the expression, by wrapping up various nuances through a string of words: "'The Way' is in early Christianity and especially in Luke a symbol for faith-, teaching-, and life direction [orientation] of Jesus' disciples . . . ."[41] This might capture the comprehensive nature of the expression. Yet, the idea that the

---

study: It was *in the wilderness*—not in the Holy City, the center of the earth—that they were to study Torah (מדרש התורה). Charlesworth, *Intertextuality*, 220–21.

33. Michaelis, "ὁδός," 95. My translation. Unless indicated otherwise, all translations in this book from biblical and non-biblical texts are mine. Cf. Haenchen, *Apg.*, 268

34. Michaelis, "ὁδός," 93–94. He concedes that the occurrences in Acts 9:2 and 22:4 may be closer to the designation of Christians as a group. Ibid., 93n174.

35. Lake and Cadbury, *Beginnings*, 100.

36. McCasland, "The Way," 222. Repo, *Der 'Weg'*, 10, 14. Interestingly, Pervo translates the unmodified *hodos* as "the Movement" in his commentary (*Acts*, 230).

37. Wilcox, *Semitisms*, 106.

38. E.g., Malina and Neyrey, "First-Century Personality," 92; and Pathrapankal, "Christianity," 533.

39. Cf. Brown, *Apostasy*, 141; and Lyonnet, "'La voie'," 158, 162.

40. E.g., Riesenfeld, "La voie de charité," 146–57; Brox, *Der Glaube*, 103–4; and Geiger, "Der Weg," 670. Filson mentions briefly that this expression designates "the Christian faith and group." Filson, "Journey Motif," 77.

41. "'Der Weg' ist in der frühen Christenheit und besonders auch bei Lukas Chiffre für die Glaubens-, Lehr- und Lebensrichtung der Jünger Jesu . . . ." Eckey, *LkEv. 11,1– 24,53*, 829.

idiom might be the quintessence of all ancient nuances of "way" is unlikely.[42] In fact, the two most common definitions for its mimetic value are a self-designation for Jesus' followers and their teaching.

Several scholars have evaluated the meanings of *hodos* and related terms in Luke-Acts in light of data from biblical and non-biblical literature in order to compare and contrast their uses, often in relation to motifs and themes (e.g., way, walking, journey). The prime example is Friedrich Nötscher's *Gotteswege und Menschenwege in der Bibel und in Qumran* (*God's Ways and Men's Ways in the Bible and in Qumran*). This major survey of a *way* terminology (*Weg-terminologie*) in the Old and New Testaments also includes the then new evidence in the Dead Sea Scrolls. In addition to thoroughfare terms, he includes activities that take place on thoroughfares (e.g., verbs of movement and leading, etc.). His study shows nuances of *way* imagery in various phases of biblical literature. For example, Christians, including Luke, appropriated certain meanings through their Christological interpretation. However, Nötscher's broad coverage of expressions and texts limits his treatment of occurrences in Luke and Acts. This diachronic method occurs in other works such as the *migration* concept (*Wanderung*, e.g., in Wingren, Kuschke, and Geiger).[43] I note this because it is symptomatic in research to use "way" as an umbrella term, often without a thorough analysis of occurrences of *hodos*. It raises the question about the selection of words or expressions that construct a "way terminology," a "Way concept," or a "way motif." This ultimately depends on the scholar's interests and his or her definition of such terms.

Expressive value. Concerning the *expressive* value of *hodos*, scholars have employed certain uses to shed light on Luke's theology, in particular the notion of a history of salvation.[44] William Robinson uses "way" as a concept, expressing the idea of movement toward a goal (i.e., salvation). Robinson is interested in the various uses of *hodos* throughout Luke-Acts as long as they fit his notion of "way" as a course of events. His thesis is this: "Luke seems to have visualized the continuity of the history of salvation as a course (δρόμος) or a way (ὁδός)."[45] Hence, certain uses of *hodos* and related terms

---

42. Göllner, "'Weg,'" 207.

43. Wingren, "'Weg,'" 111–23; Kuschke, "Die Menschenweg," 106–18; and Geiger, "Der Weg," 663–73.

44. Robinson, *Way of the Lord* and "Luke's Travel Narrative." His dissertation was published in German in 1964 as *Der Weg des Herrn. Studien zur Geschichte und Eschatologie im Lk-Evangelium*.

45. Robinson, *Way of the Lord*, 61.

would function as "stage markers" in Luke's expression of various phases of God's salvation coming to the Jews and the nations through Jesus. Positively, Robinson demonstrates how certain uses of thoroughfare terms contribute to the paramount theme of salvation in the Gospel of Luke. Moreover, he mainly uses intrinsic data to do this, making his approach more synchronic than previous works. However, his argument would be stronger with clearer terms for his overarching concept and more exegetical attention to thoroughfare expressions in Luke and Acts.

Extending Robinson's work to Luke and Acts, Schuyler Brown proposes a different framework by which to understand occurrences of *hodos* and the concept of "way" in Luke-Acts, namely, the relationship between the "the Way of the Lord" and apostasy and perseverance in Luke-Acts.[46] His divisions of Luke-Acts create discontinuity in the narrative and affect his interpretation of *hodos* and the "way" motif.[47] For example, the eight *hodos* occurrences, which he defines as individual, internalized Christian religion, all seem, in contrast, to have to do with Christian teaching or community. He arrives at this definition through a spiritualizing hermeneutic, which exaggerates the individual and spatial "way" relationship in Luke's Gospel and reduces its value for the collective identity of Jesus' disciples in Acts.[48]

David Pao suggests that Luke uses *hodos*—especially *hē hodos* and "the way of the Lord" in Luke 3:4—as "identity markers." This would reflect the literary influence of the Exodus theme in Isaiah on Luke's hermeneutical framework.[49] Octavian Baban has shown how the literary technique *mimesis* and the journey theme in Hellenistic literature might have influenced Luke in his composition of the post-Easter *on the road* encounters. The journey theme was popular in literature and the use of journeys in geographical works promoted ideologies.[50] This sparks interest in Luke's use of literary elements to support his theological and pragmatic project.

Recently Darrell Bock has examined briefly the relationship between the uses of *ekklēsia* ("church" or "assembly") and *hodos* from a biblical

---

46. See Brown, *Apostasy*, 131–45. John Navone has explored the universal extent of the "way of the Lord" in Luke's theology of history. However, his discussion on thoroughfare terms mainly confirms previous research. Navone, "Three Aspects," 115–32; "The Way of the Lord," 24–30; and "The Way," 99–105.

47. See also Bovon's critique of Brown's contribution in *Luke the Theologian*, 364.

48. Brown, *Apostasy*, 141.

49. Pao, *New Exodus*, 68.

50. Baban, *On the Road*, 139–40.

theological perspective.[51] Besides the many references from Jewish Scriptures already noted in previous works, his contribution highlights the sense of continuity and newness of Jesus' movement communicated through expressions involving these terms. Positively, he notes *hodos* expressions that are often neglected in discussions about *hē hodos* in Acts (e.g., Luke 1:78; 20:21). Generally, "the Way" refers to the movement of Jesus' disciples as a whole, whereas "church" indicates local communities of believers.[52] Bock summarizes how Luke might have understood "the Way" in relation to Israel's spiritual heritage: "The community's message teaches that if that promise of Israel's God is appreciated, those who respond will be a part of the new movement that is faithful to the old promises. In other words, if one were a good Jew following what God has done in Christ, one would join the Way. This summary reflects the complexity of how the church emerges according to Acts."[53]

Objective value. Under the *objective* category, scholarly contributions examine uses of *hodos* as evidence for intrinsic motifs or themes in Luke-Acts. Georg Geiger, for example, using *motif* as a synonym for *theme*, demonstrates that occurrences of *hodos* contribute to a "way motif" (*Wegmotiv*).[54] More accurately, Geiger traces a broader, *divine movement* theme, a red thread through Luke-Acts based on three points of evidence: (1) the semantic field of movement, (2) a biblical theological geography-topography, and (3) intrinsic and extrinsic uses of *hodos*.

Octavian Baban demonstrates how the post-Easter *on the road* encounters with Jesus contribute to the journey theme, specifically its emphasis on individual salvation, and serve as a major transition in Acts from the mission among the Jewish people to the nations. The significance of these thoroughfare (or *on the road*) encounters will be explored in Part 2.

Returning to the unmodified *hodos*, various scholars have noted its poetic value. Its unique abbreviated form (*ellipsis*, with an omitted element) and its repetition are indeed both literary techniques that add aesthetic quality to the text. This ellipsis is supported by other examples in Luke-Acts, which often omit the possessive constructions "of God" or "of the Lord" (e.g., "the law"; "the Spirit"; "the word"). Moreover, Luke uses the idiom in some relation to Paul, in episodes of conflict, and it would appear to function as an "identity marker" in order to make a clear distinction between

---

51. Bock, *Theology*, 303–10.
52. Ibid., 308.
53. Ibid., 304.
54. Geiger, "Der Weg," 663.

How Can Motifs Contribute to the Study of Luke-Acts?

Jesus' followers and other religious groups. Thus, Pao perceives a strategic use: "The term is not a remnant of Luke's source accidentally appearing in Acts (and nowhere else in early Christian literature). In the narrative of Acts, it is a term that functions as a symbol that defines the identity of the early Christian movement over against the competing claims of the majority culture."[55]

Pragmatic value. Under the *pragmatic* category, Paul Borgman explores how a first-century audience would have reacted to an expressive reading of Luke-Acts. He includes comments on *hodos* as evidence suggesting that the repetition of "way" in various expressions might have functioned as a "signal word" to enhance the listening experience in a public reading of Luke-Acts.[56] Because it is repeated, it was meant to be heard like other important expressions such as "believe," "kingdom," "Jesus as Lord," "repentance," and "resurrection." Borgman identifies the early introduction of the *way* motif in Zechariah's prayer (1:76–79) and its contribution to the overall narrative. Nevertheless, he does not identify the image of the "dawn from on high" in Luke 1:78 as a reference to Jesus, which would increase its potential pragmatic impact on an audience. Instead, he understands "God's mercy" as the agent through which this will happen.[57] This key foreshadowing device will be discussed in Chapter 3.

Classicist John Moles provides an original suggestion that links the pragmatic aim of Luke-Acts and its road imagery.[58] Moles argues that a spatial pattern begins to develop already from the opening paragraph. Luke seeks to provide assurance (ἀσφάλεια, literally "security from falling," but also used in relation to roads), through a narrative (διήγησιν, literally "leading through") having "closely followed" (παρηκολουθηκότι) other sources. The significance for Luke's audience is intriguing: "Thus ἀσφάλειαν conveys the 'security' or 'safety' that Theophilus or any reader derives from the truth

---

55. Pao, *New Exodus*, 65.
56. Borgman, *The Way*, 11, 31.
57. Ibid., 36.
58. Moles, "Luke's Preface," 461–82. Moles has developed this proposal in another article, "Time and Space Travel in Luke-Acts." He envisages the whole of Luke-Acts as a narrative road that leads to the Christian Road (i.e. "the Way"). Clearly, when he speaks of road imagery, he does not restrict this to the five thoroughfare terms in Luke-Acts. On the contrary, Moles develops a theme, similar to *divine movement* in previous studies. Yet, Moles's project is broader, working equally on the discourse level, making use of a variety of lexical, etymological, syntactical, and narrative links (especially in the prefaces and the ending) to highlight Luke's use of time and space. This is a refreshing, creative construction; yet, some of the links might drift from the narrative road that Luke actually had in mind.

both of the Christian narrative as related by Luke and of the True Christian Road which that narrative describes, prescribes and instantiates. Hence yet another vital link between Preface and narrative."[59] Moles's observation on these words' spatial relationship is creative. He acknowledges that only a reading of the whole narrative allows one to understand fully the significance of Christian *asphaleia* (usually rendered "certainty" or "assurance").[60] Although in a different manner, the present research also explores the link between Luke's pragmatic aim and thoroughfare imagery.

Regarding the unmodified *hodos*, Cadbury perceived its emphatic nature. The idiom serves to attract readers' attention, similar to the use of capital letters and italics in modern languages to emphasize a particular expression, for example, "the Way" or "*the way*."[61] Consequently, one of the questions to be explored is what did Luke wish to evoke in his audience through this emphatic technique?

In addition to these pragmatic features, scholars have also explored certain uses of *hodos* as fertile expressions for contemporary Christian thought and practice: collective and individual liturgical practice[62], faith[63], ethics[64], missiology[65], and religious instruction.[66]

In light of the literary review, it is evident that scholars have long noticed the presence of thoroughfare expressions in Luke-Acts, especially the intriguing unmodified *hodos* in Acts. Indeed, uses of *hodos* have been studied for various questions on Luke-Acts using a variety of sources. Luke-Acts presents a rich display of literal and figurative uses of thoroughfare expressions to communicate concrete and abstract thoughts, some of which are similar to uses in the New Testament, Hebrew Bible, and the Dead Sea Scrolls. Given the presumed knowledge of the Jewish Scriptures by first century readers, it is plausible that they could recognize various values mentioned above, for example, interxtextual allusions and emphasis.

---

59. Ibid., 476. He explains this further: "For his part, Luke promises proof of the truth of Christianity and of the consequent 'safety' of the Christian Road. What, precisely, is that 'safety'? The security of the truth, of course, meaning, as we have seen, both that this truth is securely true and that it provides security." Ibid., 480.

60. Ibid.

61. Cadbury, *Names*, 392.

62. Gros, *Je suis la Route*, 133–38.

63. Brox, *Der Glaube*, 156–57

64. Wingren, "'Weg,'" 111.

65. Pathrapankal, "Christianity," 533.

66. Göllner, "'Weg,'" 215.

Interest and Approach of This Research

What then is missing thus far in research on *hodos* and related terms in Luke-Acts? Although several studies have given attention to particular uses of *hodos* and related terms and expressions, some even speaking of a "way motif," a "way concept" or a "way theology," no study has demonstrated comprehensively how Luke uses thoroughfare expressions to form a literary motif in Luke-Acts as part of its literary and theological project. This research seeks to fill this gap by exploring the implied reader's encounter with the story through this motif together with other motifs and themes. In other words, how does this motif help tell the story about Jesus and his disciples? Is the motif meaningful to the implied reader? What responses might it seek to elicit? How does it enhance Luke's theological project? Thus, with respect to the four categories used to classify previous research, this study investigates first the *objective* and *pragmatic* values of thoroughfare expressions and then relates them to the *expressive* for a theological reading of Luke-Acts. In reality, of course, these categories are inseparable in actual texts since they are woven together in one tapestry for readers. Luke, for example, uses literary devices to express his theologically grounded and motivated story in order to achieve certain pragmatic aims. Thus, this research traces the motif's narrative and theological performance for the implied reader.

More specifically, compared to previous research, the following methodological guidelines will be followed:

1. *The focus of interest will be narrower (one motif) as well as one primary field of data (Luke-Acts).* Broader interests and fields of data have been the norm in studying occurrences of *hodos* in Luke-Acts. It is profitable to narrow down both. While recognizing the value of diachronic interests and approaches, I employ primarily a synchronic approach with the aim of identifying and evaluating one literary motif (the thoroughfare motif) in a single literary work (Luke-Acts).[67] Following William Freedman's theory on motifs, the motif will not be analyzed on *hodos* alone, but on the associational cluster composed by words of the semantic field of *thoroughfare*.[68] Accordingly,

---

67. Norman Petersen sets forth the principle that underlies my approach: ". . . The text itself must be comprehended in its own terms before we can ask of what it is evidence, whether in relation to the time of writing or in relation to the events referred to in it." Petersen, *Literary Criticism*, 20.

68. See LN, "Geographical objects and features. 1. P. Thoroughfares: roads, streets, paths, etc. (1.99–1.105)."

the data are primarily limited to these expressions in this two-volume narrative.

2. *The narrative connections between the various expressions involving thoroughfare terminology will be underlined more fully.* Positively, scholars have shed some light on several individual occurrences, especially those of the idiom *hē hodos*. Yet, it is still necessary to explore the relationship between the expressions. In addition, some occurrences have not been adequately studied for their contribution to the motif, for example, the description of John the Baptist and Jesus in Zechariah's prayer (Luke 1:78–79), the cluster of terms in the Parable of the Great Supper (Luke 14:21, 23), and Jesus as the teacher of the way of God (Luke 20:21).

3. *The narrative performance of the thoroughfare motif will be explored within the plot's gradual development.* A unique contribution of this work is the use of plot theory to evaluate a biblical motif. When scholars use literary terms like *theme*, *motif*, or *plot*, it is not always clear what they mean by them or what value they add to the analysis of a given work. This study attempts to fill that gap by explaining clearly, and exploiting more fully, literary and narrative theory. In order to determine the narrative value of the thoroughfare motif, it is constructive to analyze *hodos* and related expressions within the plot of Luke-Acts. Plot has to do with the reader's progressive encounter with the story's main questions. Thus, this study provides a summary of the plot of Luke-Acts and then analyzes both literal and figurative uses of thoroughfare expressions to determine whether they work together to form a motif within the construction of the plot and how the motif might be meaningful to readers and evoke a particular response.

At this point, we turn to a brief description of motifs. Following that, the study focuses on the plot of Luke-Acts within which the thoroughfare motif performs.

The Power of Motifs: Definition, Identification, and Evaluation

When discussing books and films, we often speak of "motifs" and "themes" whose meanings seem clear on the surface. Yet, popular and professional definitions often lack clarity and the two terms are frequently used as synonyms. This study considers them separate, yet complementary. In addition to providing a definition, the following section will explore questions about how to identify a motif and evaluate its performance in a literary work including its pragmatic effects.

Literary Motifs: A Definition

What are motifs and how do they perform in a literary work? The terms *motif* and *theme* are the two most common forms of narrative repetition.[69] François Jost informs that no consensus exists as to their nomenclature: "One critic may call *motif* what another designates as *theme*."[70] Sometimes these terms are used as synonyms.[71] Whatever the choice, most literary scholars often explain one term over against the other. Thus, they agree that, though closely related, motifs and themes are distinct. In recent narrative theory, motifs tend to be viewed as concrete entities and themes as abstract ones. Abbott, for example, describes motif as "a discrete thing, image, or phrase that is repeated in a narrative. Theme, by contrast, is a more generalized or abstract concept that is suggested by, among other things, motifs. A coin can be a motif, greed is a theme."[72] Other examples illustrate their complementary relationship: "Beauty, nature, violence, and love can be themes; roses, gardens, fists, and the phrase 'Barkis is willin'' can be motifs. Themes are implicit in motifs, but not the other way around."[73] Narratologists Natascha Würzbach and Gerald Prince also make this distinction. Würzbach defines motif as "the concrete realization of a fixed abstract idea, often spanning a complete narrative unit."[74] Similarly, Prince writes, "A minimal thematic unit . . . [that] should not be confused with a theme, which constitutes a more abstract and more general semantic unit manifested by or reconstructed from a set of motifs: if glasses are a motif in *Princess Brambilla*, vision is a theme in that work."[75]

---

69. Abbott, *Narrative*, 242.
70. Jost, "Introduction," xvii.
71. E.g., Bock, *Theology*, 303–4 and Baban, *On the Road*, 1–2.
72. Abbott, *Narrative*, 237. So Hawthorne, *Glossary*, 299.
73. Abbott, *Narrative*, 95.
74. Würzbach, "Motif," 322.
75. Prince, *Narratology*, 55.

Abbot's definition above is a good working definition of motif. This concerns a motif in a single work, not multiple works (a diachronic motif).[76] William Freedman provides two valuable clarifications; a motif can be an associational cluster and have symbolic value:

> ... a family or associational cluster of literal or figurative references to a given class of concepts or objects, whether it be animals, machines, circles, music, or whatever. It is generally symbolic—that is, it can be seen to carry a meaning beyond the literal one immediately apparent; it represents on the verbal level something characteristic of the structure of the work, the events, the characters, the emotional effects or the moral or cognitive content.[77]

Thus, the motif is not necessarily limited to a single, unchanging element (the repetition of a phrase, an object, etc.), but may include a variety of literal and figurative references whose collective function is to act symbolically, revealing to the reader—with cumulative effect—"subtly what the incidents perhaps tell him bluntly."[78] Freedman clarifies, however, that a motif should be distinguished from a *symbol* which may occur singly, while the motif is "necessarily recurrent and its effect cumulative."[79] The symbol is an event or thing described, whereas the motif, "although it may appear as something described, perhaps even more often forms part of the description. It slips, as it were, into the author's vocabulary, into the dialogue, and into his imagery, often even at times when the symbolized referent is not immediately involved,"[80] and is thus "a complex of separate parts subtly reiterating on one level what is taking place on another."[81] In this sense, this study explores how the thoroughfare motif performs within the unfolding story.

Freedman explains further that the motif generally contributes to one or all of three aspects of a literary work: cognitive, affective, and structural.[82] Cognitively, it might reveal something about the minds of the characters (understanding, morals, etc.) and of the general setting. Affectively, it might contribute to the emotive content of the work, seeking to elicit certain re-

---

76. Scholars also use term *leitmotif* to describe this literary device in a single work. When used in this sense *leitmotif* is distinguished from *motif* a diachronic figure found in various literary works. Cf. "motif" in Baldick, *Oxford Dictionary*, 215–16.

77. Freedman, "Motif," 127–28.

78. Ibid., 124.

79. Ibid.

80. Ibid., 125.

81. Ibid., 129.

82. Ibid., 125.

sponses from the reader. Structurally, the motif might help describe the action of the story. Regular appearance of the motif adds to the narrative's coherence and unity. Freedman concludes, "Most motifs, however, relate to more than one of these aspects, although one may be of paramount importance."[83] Würzbach elucidates the motif's part in the structural aspect: "A motif usually builds around a nuclear action sequence which can take different forms and cover more than a single event. Plot-intensive motifs stand at the centre of the logic of action, while less intensive motifs such as 'rose' or 'spring' remain peripheral and do not significantly affect a text's narrative progression or plot."[84] The analysis below shows that the thoroughfare motif contributes to this aspect by enhancing or intensifying the plot, since, as Freedman summarizes, "The motif, then, may become a part of the total perspective, pervading the book's atmosphere and becoming an important thread in the fabric of the work."[85]

Criteria for the Identification of a Motif

Yet, how does one actually identify a motif? Freedman presents two main criteria for establishing the presence of a motif in a single literary work: frequency and avoidability (or unlikelihood). A motif is necessarily recurrent; however, no specific number of occurrences justifies the presence of a motif. This depends on the work and its length. The motif must recur often enough to suggest a purposeful use rather than mere coincidence or necessity, and "pervade the atmosphere sufficiently to assure that they will be at least subliminally felt."[86] Some motifs are so subtle that one might notice and appreciate them only in successive readings or viewings.

The second factor, *avoidability*, is complementary to the first in that "the contexts in which the references appear or the uses to which they are put (extra literal uses, for example) do not *demand* references from the field of the motif."[87] For example, automobiles in a story about a mechanic are difficult to avoid especially if the main setting is a garage. References, however, to automobiles and automobile-like things, or sayings or images having to do with automobiles in contexts where they are avoidable, could be evidence

83. Ibid.
84. Würzbach, "Motif," 322.
85. Freedman, "Motif," 125.
86. Ibid., 126.
87. Ibid.

of an automobile motif. The discussion of the motif's efficacy will clarify this aspect. Having established the presence of a motif, how can one evaluate its performance in a literary work and its potential pragmatic effects?

Criteria for the Evaluation of a Motif's Efficacy

Freedman provides constructive criteria for evaluating the efficacy of a motif as a literary technique toward the work and the reader: (1) frequency of recurrence, (2) avoidability or unlikeliness of appearance, (3) significance of contexts, (4) coherence, and (5) symbolic correlation. In addition to these qualities, I will also point out the motif's intertextual value. This is particularly important for biblical literature because of the frequent borrowing of motifs and themes from other sources. Biblical writers use them to make a point, portray a character, or highlight a scene, because their readers were able to recognize these allusions. Consequently, I will point out those uses of thoroughfare imagery that appear to allude to other texts.

Frequency and avoidability add to the work's aesthetic value and make a deeper impression on the reader when the motif occurs frequent and extensive enough in the work in a way that the contexts do not necessarily demand it. In short, an effective motif is neither too obvious nor too discrete. Freedman explains, "There would seem to be a law of diminishing returns here, the efficacy of the motif beginning to decline at the point where unlikelihood begins to shade into unsuitability or frequency into tedious repetition. Maximum power will therefore probably be achieved at the degree of frequency and improbability just short of this negative tendency, a point that varies from work to work."[88]

The third factor concerns the significance of the contexts in which the motif occurs. The potency of the motif increases when it appears in climactic points of a work. This is particularly strengthened "if the symbolized referent of the motif is in the fore at these points."[89] In other words, in relation to the plot, the cumulative force of the motif is enhanced when it appears in moments where narrative tension is particularly felt, either increasing or decreasing.

The fourth factor regards the coherence of the various elements of the associational cluster that make up the motif. In other words, do they fit together? Are they relevant to the principal end of the motif as a whole?

---

88. Ibid.
89. Ibid., 126–27.

Alternatively, do they ramify into a variety of unrelated purposes? Freedman provides this principal: "the closer the association between the components of the cluster the more unified their effect."[90] Hence, the motif's aesthetic quality and its cumulative effect depend in part on the degree to which the motif coheres.

The fifth factor concerns the motif's symbolic function. Is the motif appropriate to the referent that it symbolizes? A motif of circularity is more appropriate to a book about circular, repetitive fortune than a story about a love triangle.[91] Therefore, the pragmatic force of the motif depends also on its appropriate correlation to the referent, since the reader needs to make the connection between the two in order to grasp and appreciate more fully its function in the narrative.

Thus, this approach evaluates the thoroughfare motif by employing Freedman's criteria, along with the intertextual factor. It traces the motif's performance—as a rhetorical actor on the reading level—within the narrative's progression, the plot, as a part of the reader's encounter both cognitive and experiential. Chapter 2 provides additional information about plot theory. With these fundamental points on the literary motif, we now turn to background information on thoroughfare expressions that compose the motif in Luke-Acts.

Thoroughfare Expressions in Luke-Acts: How and Where do They Appear?

In order to identify and evaluate the thoroughfare motif, it is crucial to know what to look for, and since this is an exegetical study, necessarily based on the Greek text, this section provides background data on thoroughfare terminology. To this end, some technical discussion is unavoidable, and for those readers interested, finer points can be found in the footnotes. Moreover, I indicate narrative usage of these expressions in Luke-Acts as well as initial observations that require attention in the analysis of the thoroughfare motif.

Lexical and Syntactical Data for Thoroughfare Terminology

Following the principle that literal and figurative uses of an entity can form an associational cluster of a motif, this analysis includes primarily five terms

---

90. Ibid., 127.
91. Ibid.

of the *thoroughfare* semantic field in Luke-Acts: *hodos* (way, road); *tribos* (path); *plateia* (broad street); *rumē* (narrow street); and *phragmos* (a path along a fence, wall, or hedge).⁹² Two other terms for thoroughfare in the New Testament, *amphodon* (city street) and *diexodos* (street crossing, outlet), do not occur in Luke-Acts.

This section provides definitions of the five terms and their number of occurrences in the New Testament and in Luke-Acts.⁹³ As stated, the most important term for this study is *hodos* since it represents forty of the forty-nine occurrences.⁹⁴ Louw and Nida define it as "a general term for a thoroughfare, either within a population center or between two such centers."⁹⁵ Consequently, it is translated variously in English translations as "road," "highway," "street," and "way." It occurs forty times in Luke-Acts (twenty in Luke and twenty in Acts) of the 101 times in the New Testament.⁹⁶ Although not included in the statistics of the explicit uses of *hodos*, I indicate here two expressions that assume *hodos* and are evidence for the thoroughfare motif. The word for thoroughfare is understood through particular grammatical expressions: the adjective ellipsis "straight" (εὐθείαν *eutheian*) for "straight road"⁹⁷ (Luke 3:5) and the expression "that" (ἐκείνης *ekeines* Luke 19:4) for "by that road."⁹⁸

---

92. LN, 18–19. The words *eisodos* (εἴσοδος) and *exodus* (ἔξοδος) are not included with the five words for thoroughfares in Luke-Acts. Both occur only once in Luke-Acts: *eisodos* in Acts 13:24 as a reference to John the Baptist's "entrance," that is, his manifestation as Jesus' forerunner (BDAG, 294–95), and *exodus* in Luke 9:31 as a euphemistic reference, in the transfiguration pericope, to Jesus' "departure," that is, his death (BDAG, 349–50).

93. Statistics on the Greek text are based on *Novum Testamentum Graece*, Nestle-Aland 27th ed. (Stuttgart: Deutsche Bibelgesellschaft, 1993) in BibleWorks, version 9.0.011g.1, Norfolk, VA: BibleWorks, 2012.

94. Denaux and Corstjens indicate three expressions with *hodos* that are "characteristic of Luke": κατὰ τὴν ὁδόν, ἡμέρας/σαββάτου ὁδός, and ὁδὸς (τοῦ) κυρίου. It is not clear to me why they omit the unmodified *hodos* as uniquely Lukan. Denaux and Corstjens, *Vocabulary*, 427.

95. LN, 18. Likewise, BDAG (p. 691) provides this basic, literal notion: "a way for traveling or moving from one place to another; *way, road, highway*, used by personal or impersonal entities."

96. In the Gospel of Luke: 1:76, 79; 2:44; 3:4, 5; 7:27; 8:5, 12; 9:3, 57; 10:4, 31; 11:6; 12:58; 14:23; 18:35; 19:36; 20:21; 24:32, 35. In the Acts of the Apostles: 1:12; 2:28; 8:26, 36, 39; 9:2, 17, 27; 13:10; 14:16; 16:17; 18:25, 26; 19:9, 23; 22:4; 24:14, 22; 25:3; 26:13.

97. BDR (§241.4) understand this as an example of an ellipsis through an adjectival attribute (ὁδός as εἰς εὐθείας). They indicate other examples where *hodos* is understood: ποίας (Luke 5:19); ἐκείνης (Luke 19:4); μακραν (with the fossilized accusative, Luke 7:6; 15:20; Acts 2:39; 17:27; 22:21).

98. One of the two examples of the "genitive of place" in the NT in which ὁδοῦ is

How Can Motifs Contribute to the Study of Luke-Acts?

Concerning the term *tribos*, Louw and Nida define it as "a well-worn path or thoroughfare;" hence, the translations, "path" or "beaten path."[99] It occurs once in Luke-Acts (Luke 3:4) of the three times in the New Testament (all three in the quotation of Isa 40:3; cf. Matt 3:3; Mark 1:3).

Two terms, *plateia* and *rumē*, describe thoroughfares in urban contexts. Louw and Nida define *plateia* as "a wide street within a city;" hence, an "avenue" or simply "wide street."[100] It occurs four times in Luke-Acts (Luke 10:10; 13:26; 14:21; Acts 5:15) of the ten times in the New Testament. The counterpart for *plateia* is *rumē*: "a city thoroughfare which is relatively narrow;" thus, "narrow street," "lane," or "alley."[101] It occurs three times in Luke-Acts (Luke 14:21; Acts 9:11; 12:10) of the four times in the New Testament.

The term *phragmos*, on the other hand, describes thoroughfares in rural contexts: "a path or area along a fence, wall, or hedge (where desperately poor people might stay);" hence, the meanings "byway" or "path."[102] *Phragmos* occurs once in Luke-Acts (Luke 14:23) of the four times in the New Testament.[103]

Additionally, I provide here some brief comments on how these words function in sentences, namely, their syntactic value. Words for thoroughfare never occur as the subject of a verb. None of the words occurs in the nominative case (indicator of *subject*), or in other constructions that would indicate their use as the logical subject. They mostly occur in a description for circumstantial information (real or illustrative, thirty times) responding to questions such as whence? (ἐκ), whither? (εἰς, ἐπί, κατά), where? (παρά, ἐν, κατά), and how far? (with the accusative case).

---

to be understood (instead of the classical ἐκείνῃ) BDR (§186.1). The other example is with ποίας (also for the classical ποίᾳ) in Luke 5:19, which does not make a particular contribution to the thoroughfare motif. Cf. also the genitive of place or space in Wallace, *Greek*, 124 and Nolli, *Luca*, 619.

99. LN, 19.

100. Ibid. The word *plateia* is the feminine form of the adjective πλατύς (*platus* "wide") in which *hodos* is assumed, consequently "wide street."

101. Ibid.

102. Ibid.

103. Not all lexicons mention that *phragmos* is a type of thoroughfare (e.g., Bailly, 2095 and Thayer, *Greek-English*, 657. Rusconi (p. 361) grants that it is a possibility: "a way between the hedgerows." This is plausible in light of the parallelism with ὁδός, which is preceded by another parallelism, *plateia* and *rumē* (14:21). BDAG (p. 1064) indicates *fence, wall, hedge*, and mentions what kind of people might gather there: "Vagabonds and beggars frequent the hedges and fences around houses Luke 14:23." So, also ANLEX (s.v.φραγμός).

In the figurative uses, they occur as direct objects (responding to the question, what?), but also as complements (in conformity to what? concerning what?). They are direct objects of verbs indicating transmission of knowledge (διδάσκω "teach"; γνωρίζω "make known"; κατηχέω "instruct"; ἐκτίθεμι "explain"), communication (καταγγέλλω "proclaim"; κακολογέω "speak evil") and perception (οἶδα "know"), but also "distort" (διαστρέφω) and "persecute" (διώκω). In these cases, *hodos* always occurs and it denotes either humans or things. In fact, one perceives a sense of opposition through three verbs—"speak evil against," "distort," and "persecute"—which underlines the conflict in the storyworld. Perhaps surprisingly, Luke uses *hodos* only one time in a circumstantial phrase to qualify a verb of movement related to Jesus (πορεύομαι, Luke 9:57).

Having presented some general lexical and syntactical data for these terms, I indicate below some brief observations on their narrative usage within the progression of the plot.

Narrative Data for Thoroughfare Terminology

This step indicates in a preliminary way where and how theses expressions occur within the progression of the plot. It justifies the focus on certain occurrences over others. In this analysis, I employ five narrative sequences: initial orientation, raveling, pivot, unraveling, and final orientation. They represent various phases in the reader's encounter with the story in relation to the increase and decrease of narrative tension. I discuss this further in Chapter 2. The textual limits of these sequences in Luke-Acts appear under the sequence titles. Table 1.1 below indicates four elements: (1) the distribution of the occurrences in the five narrative sequences; (2) literal and figurative uses; (3) the objects that they describe (actions, persons, etc.); and (4) the *voices* that use the terms (e.g., the narrator; Jesus, etc.). I discuss the data in the four subsections to point out those occurrences or patterns that merit particular attention in the analysis of the motif in Chapters 3–7. This table will useful for consultation when reading later chapters.

Table 1.1: Statistics on Thoroughfare Terms in Five Narrative Sequences[104]

Sequence	Initial orientation Luke 1:5—3:38	Raveling Luke 4:1—23:56	Pivot Luke 24:1—Acts 2:13	Unraveling Acts 2:14—28:15	Final orientation Acts 28:16–31
Number of occurrences	6 occurrences hodos: 5 tribos: 1	18 occurrences hodos: 13 plateia: 3 rumē: 1 phragmos: 1	3 occurrences hodos: 3	22 occurrences hodos: 19 plateia: 1 rumē: 2	No occurrence
Literal or figurative	- Literal: 0 - Figurative: 6 (3 in biblical citation)	- Literal: 15 - Figurative: 3 (once in biblical citation)	- Literal: 2 - Figurative: 1	- Literal: 10 - Figurative: 12 (once in biblical citation)	NA
Description of persons, items, and actions	Characters/items: 5 [John the Baptist (4); Jesus (1)] Circumstantial: 1 [distance covered by Mary and Joseph (1)]	Characters/items: 2 [John the Baptist (1); Jesus (1)] Circumstantial: 16 [events involving: Jesus (would-be disciples, beggar, crowd (3); instructions to disciples (4); in Jesus' teaching illustrations (9)]	Characters/items: 0 Circumstantial: 3 [events involving: Jesus and Emmaus disciples (2); distance covered by disciples (1)]	Characters/items: 12 [Resurrection (1); Jesus' disciples and teaching (9); Elymas (1); Nations (1)] Circumstantial: 10 [events involving: Peter (2); Philip (3); Paul (5, with Jesus 3)]	NA
Voice: Who uses these words?	- Narrator: 4 (3x in citation of Isaiah 40:3–4) - Zechariah: 2	- Jesus: 14 - Narrator: 3 - The "spies": 1	- Narrator: 2 - Emmaus disciples: 1	- Narrator: 12 - Paul: 5 - Peter: 1 (in biblical citation) - An angel of the Lord: 1 - Jesus: 1 - Ananias: 1 - Possessed servant girl: 1	NA

104. This table does not include the two occurrences, already noted, that assume *hodos* (*eutheian* in Luke 3:5 and *ekeines* in Luke 19:4). [See End Note of Chapter 1]

Encountering Images of Spiritual Transformation

Thoroughfare Expressions in the Five Narrative Sequences

This first question helps to understand where the expressions occur in the narrative's progression. Do they appear more often in some places than others? Is there a decrease or increase as the narrative progresses? How might their presence affect the reading in those particular moments? Table 1.1 indicates occurrences in four of the five sequences: six times in the initial orientation, eighteen times in the raveling, three times in the pivot, twenty-two times in the unraveling, but not once in the final orientation. In the two symmetrical pairs (initial and final orientations; raveling and unraveling), there is some imbalance since there are six occurrences in the initial orientation, but no occurrences in the final orientation. It is reasonable to ask whether this affects the overall force of the thoroughfare motif. As far as the raveling/unraveling pair, though there is only a slight difference in occurrences, eighteen and twenty-two respectively, there is a significant increase in the occurrences of *hodos* in the unraveling sequence (19) compared to the raveling sequence (13). This increase is primarily due to its figurative use in the portrayal of the disciples and their teaching, therefore these occurrences receive particular attention in the analysis. Finally, all of the terms except *tribos* occur in two parallelisms in the Parable of the Great Supper (Luke 14:21–23). This cluster of terms merits attention due its symbolic value for the plot.

Literal and Figurative Uses

The question whether thoroughfare expressions occur literally or figuratively is extremely important because it explores their various nuances, especially when circumstances do not require their use. *Literal* indicates the primary, concrete meaning of thoroughfares, either on the action level (i.e., in the description of narrated events, e.g., "the road from Jerusalem to Gaza") or in the embedded level as in illustrations (e.g., "a man was going down a road").[105] Thus, a word for thoroughfare may be considered as having literal value even if it is not actually portrayed as an existent road (e.g., in a parable). Conversely, *figurative* describes nonliteral meanings in real or imaginary contexts that express another sense (e.g., "journey" or "the way of the Lord").

The terms occur in a literal sense (real or illustrative) twenty-seven times and in a figurative sense twenty-two times.[106] Regarding the literal

---

105. For a discussion on literal and figurative meanings, see Abrams, *Glossary*, 96–97.

106. Literal (27 occurrences): Raveling: 8:5 (*hodos*), 12 (*hodos*); 9:3 (*hodos*), 57 (*hodos*); 10:4 (*hodos*), 10 (*plateia*), 31 (*hodos*); 12:58 (*hodos*); 13:26 (*plateia*); 14:21 (2x *plateia*

meanings, the narrator uses these terms only twelve times to describe eight different episodes on the action level: five with Jesus, two with Peter and one with Philip. Given the importance of journeying in Luke-Acts, it is significant that thoroughfares have a small role in expressing movement on the action level.[107] Moreover, six of these eight episodes describe encounters centered on Jesus. Jesus meets (1) the would-be followers (Luke 9:57); (2) the blind beggar (Luke 18:35); (3) the crowd (Luke 19:36); (4) the Emmaus disciples (Luke 24:32, 35); and (5) Paul (Acts 9:17, 27; 26:13); and (6) Philip and Ethiopian (Acts 8:36, 39). As stated, Zacchaeus's encounter with Jesus is included in the discussion of the five other encounters because of the ellipsis assuming *hodos*.[108] These encounters warrant attention due to their part in the portrayal of Jesus and their presence in decisive moments of the plot.

As regards figurative meanings, many of them are not required by the context and seek to draw the reader's attention. Interestingly, *hodos* occurs twenty-one of the twenty-two times when thoroughfare terms occur with a figurative meaning. The exception is *tribos* in Luke 3:4 where it is parallel with *hodos*. The figurative uses of *hodos* become more important than the literal uses in the progression of the narrative, especially in the unraveling sequence.[109] This is equally true for the beginning of the narrative in which all six occurrences of these terms occur figuratively in the initial orientation (five of which are *hodos*). They appear almost entirely in the characterization of John the Baptist and Jesus.[110] The narrator uses these images in this initial

---

and *rumē*), 23 (2x *hodos* and *phragmos*; 18:35 (*hodos*); 19:36 (*hodos*). Pivot: 24:32 (*hodos*), 35 (*hodos*). Unraveling: Acts 5:15 (*plateia*); 8:26 (*hodos*), 36 (*hodos*), 39 (*hodos*); 9:11 (*rumē*), 17 (*hodos*), 27 (*hodos*); 12:10 (*rumē*); 25:3 (*hodos*); 26:13 (*hodos*).

Figurative (22 occurrences): Initial orientation: 1:76 (*hodos*), 79 (*hodos*); 2:44 (*hodos*); 3:4 (2x *hodos* and *tribos*); 3:5 (*hodos*). Raveling: 7:27 (*hodos*); 11:6 (*hodos*); 20:21 (*hodos*). Pivot: Acts 1:12 (*hodos*). Unraveling: 2:28 (*hodos*); 9:2 (*hodos*); 13:10 (*hodos*); 14:16 (*hodos*); 16:17 (*hodos*); 18:25 (*hodos*), 26 (*hodos*); 19:9 (*hodos*), 23 (*hodos*); 22:4 (*hodos*); 24:14 (*hodos*), 22 (*hodos*).

107. Thoroughfare terms directly qualify verbs of movement on the action level only in Luke 9:57 (Jesus, πορεύομαι); Acts 8:36 (Philip and the Ethiopian, πορεύομαι); 8:39 (the Ethiopian, πορεύομαι); 12:10 (an angel of the Lord and Peter, προέρχομαι). Thoroughfare terms qualify other actions in main clauses and verbs of movement occur in subordinate clauses: (1) the beggar sitting while Jesus draws near (ἐγγίζω Luke 18:35); (2) the crowd spreading their cloaks while Jesus was going along (πορεύομαι 19:36); (3) the people carrying the sick when Peter came by (ἔρχομαι Acts 5:15).

108. Inferred through ἐκείνης which assumes ὁδός as a local genitive (Luke 19:4) and circumstantial information.

109. The increase in figurative uses from the raveling to the unraveling is three to twelve.

110. Except for once where ὁδός occurs in an adverbial phrase for the distance of

part of the narrative to stimulate Theophilus's interest and prepare him to explore and experience the story's central questions and narrative connections between initial figurative uses and later ones.

In addition, the terms occur with a figurative meaning five times in biblical citations: Isaiah 40:3-4 (Luke 3:4-5), Malachi 3:1 (Luke 7:27), and Psalm 16:11 (Acts 2:28). These occurrences merit some attention because of their part in the intertextuality of the text recalling to the reader's mind images that he might have known from the Jewish Scriptures in Greek.

What do These Terms Describe?

Do these terms describe characters, actions, or things? Here I present some general observations that indicate a particular focus. My intention is not to construct a barrier between description of characters and events; indeed narrators use physical settings to portray individuals or groups. Rather, this step indicates when thoroughfare expressions occur circumstantially to describe actions and when they help portray characters or other elements (e.g., objects or concepts via metaphor or metonymy). For these reasons, I employ two main categories in the table: "characters and things" and "circumstantial information for actions," followed by the total sum for all of the sequences. In most cases, the figurative meanings describe characters and the literal meanings the actions. There are, however, three occasions where a figurative use of *hodos* means "journey" (by extension) that describe actions (Luke 2:44; 11:6; Acts 1:12).

First, thoroughfare terminology occurs nineteen times in the description of characters and other entities.[111] As regards Jesus, *hodos* appears twice, once in the initial orientation (Luke 1:79) and once in the raveling sequence (Luke 20:21). Both are significant descriptions of Jesus. Second, fifteen occurrences help portray other protagonists closely associated with Jesus such as John the Baptist, and those who follow Jesus, including Paul at a certain moment in the story. Paul appears in the general category "Jesus' followers and teaching," since after the first use of the unmodified *hodos* in Acts 9:2, he becomes one of the disciples. As noted above, there is a great increase of characterization of the disciples via thoroughfare terms in the unraveling sequence (twelve times) compared to the other sequences. These occurrences

---

Joseph and Mary's journey.

111. John the Baptist (Luke 1:76; 3:4 (2x); 3:5; 7:27); Jesus (Luke 1:79; 20:21); the resurrection (Acts 2:28); Jesus' followers and message (all in the unraveling sequence; Acts 9:2; 13:10; 16:17; 18:25, 26; 19:9, 23; 22:4; 24:14, 22); and the nations (14:16).

merit particular attention because of what they reveal about their relationship with Jesus. Fourth, the word *hodos* occurs once in the description of an idea (the resurrection) which is found in a biblical quote (Acts 2:28). Finally, the word appears twice to describe an entity outside those closely associated with Jesus: Elymas (13:10) and the nations (14:16).

As regards thoroughfare terminology in circumstantial description, the narrator uses these terms to describe episodes on the action level and in illustrations for a total of thirty occurrences: twelve for the physical setting of eight episodes on the action level;[112] seven for commanded or planned actions;[113] two in adverbial phrases;[114] and nine in Jesus' illustrations.[115]

Do any of these occurrences have particular relevance to the plot's development? First, as stated, eight occurrences of *hodos* describe encounters with Jesus (whom I will also designate as *hero*), in three different sequences (raveling, pivot, and unraveling). These occurrences are a part of a pattern of thoroughfare encounters, due to their description of Jesus and their appearances in decisive moments of the plot. Second, three occurrences related to Jesus' disciples concern instructions about their mission, thus not occurring in the description of encounters. Some discussion is justified because they qualify the continuity and closure of the thoroughfare motif in relation to John the Baptist's mandate.

Third, the uses of *hodos* and related terms in Jesus' illustrations (embedded narration) make up almost one fifth of the total occurrences. Most of these merely provide circumstantial information for the parables. Some occurrences, however, have significant value for the plot's development (e.g., the Parable of the Great Supper).

---

112. The would-be followers (Luke 9:57); the blind man (Luke 18:35); the crowd (Luke 19:36); Emmaus disciples (Luke 24:32, 35); Paul (9:17; 9:27; 26:13); the sick and Peter (Acts 5:15); Philip and the Ethiopian (Acts 8:36, 39); Peter and an angel of the Lord (12:10).

113. Six commanded actions: Jesus and the disciples' mission (Luke 9:3; 10:4; 10:10); Jesus regarding reconciliation (Luke 12:58); an angel of the Lord to Philip (Acts 8:26); Jesus' instruction to Ananias (Acts 9:11). One planned action: the plot to murder Paul (25:3).

114. The distance of journeys by Mary and Joseph (Luke 2:44) and the disciples (Acts 1:12).

115. The parables of the Sower (Luke 8:5, 12), Good Samaritan (Luke 10:31), Narrow Door (Luke 13:26), Great Supper (Luke 14:21 (2x), 23 (2x), and perseverance in prayer (Luke 11:6).

Which Narrative Voices use These Terms?

This question seeks to identify those who uses these terms in the narrative (the *voices*), as well as patterns and points of view that affect the occurrences. It is evident that the voices of the narrator and Jesus use thoroughfare expressions the most (respectively twenty-one and fifteen times, which combined are thirty-six out of the forty-nine occurrences). The narrator's use is the only one present in the four sequences, beginning with the description of John the Baptist (through the biblical citation of Isa 40:3–4 in Luke 3:4–5) and ending with the description of the planned ambush of Paul's adversaries (Acts 25:3).

Of the fifteen occurrences, Jesus uses nine in his illustrations, five in his instructions (four for his disciples, and once for Ananias), and once in a biblical citation (Mal 3:1 in Luke 7:27). Some of these uses help understand Jesus' perception of his mandate and anticipate certain scenes in which he is protagonist.

Apart from these two main voices, various characters use thoroughfare expressions throughout the story: beginning with Zechariah (Luke 1:76, 79), the "spies," the Emmaus disciples, Peter (citing a biblical citation), an angel of the Lord, Ananias, a possessed servant girl, and ending with Paul (Acts 26:13). Two are voices of antagonists, the "spies" in Jerusalem and the demon possessed girl in Pisidian Antioch. Since both occurrences convey a sense of irony, the study seeks to understand if the point of view of the voice adds a particular nuance to their usage. Finally, the voices of the narrator and Paul in the unraveling sequence are particularly important for exploring meaningful nuances of *hodos*.

The above discussion provides a general lexical, syntactical, and narrative overview of thoroughfare terminology against the backdrop of five progressive narrative sequences. Additional observations were also explained in order to justify a particular focus on certain occurrences. Before turning to the plot of Luke-Acts, I discuss the value of motifs and plot for the study of narratives, in particular biblical literature.

Thoroughfare Motif's Performance: What Narrative and Theological Value?

As stated, this study intends to extend research on the uses of thoroughfare expressions in Luke-Acts by asking questions that are different than those of previous studies and by using methods that have not been fully exploited.

In short, this motif merits further study in order to appreciate its value for Luke-Acts. In light of the technical and statistical information above, is there really enough evidence to identify a thoroughfare motif? If so, do the expressions occur in significant moments of the plot? Do they call attention to the reader both on literal and figurative levels? How does it perform as a literary figure? Fundamentally, what does the motif contribute narratively and theologically? What difference does it actually make pragmatically in the implied reader's encounter of the Luke's two-volume work? To answer these and other questions, it is necessary to have an understanding of the progressive development of Luke-Acts as a narrative construction for the analysis of the thoroughfare motif.

Yet, someone might rightly ask the very practical and valid question: "So what?" Indeed, what difference does it make to do further work on this literary motif in Luke-Acts? A final answer can only be offered at the end of the study. However, its relevance lies fundamentally in the aesthetic and interpretative value of motifs. Freedman's discussion of motifs argues that it is not sufficient for an interpreter to indicate the presence of a motif, rather he or she must demonstrate its value for literary research:

> If the reader can show satisfactorily that the presence of the motif is at least sometimes quite easily avoidable, that its overall frequency is greater than sheer coincidence or necessity might produce, that the separate members of the family or cluster operate together to a common end, and that they are singularly appropriate to a given aspect of the work in hand, he has, I think, shown both the existence and efficacy of a motif in that work.[116]

Thus, the interpreter who not only identifies a motif but also demonstrates its efficacy for a given literary work performs a useful task in helping other readers to have a greater appreciation for it. This is the primary concern of this study for the field of Luke-Acts.

Yet, what intrinsic qualities does an effective motif actually have so that it enhances a literary work in the eyes of the reader? Our interest in and appreciation of the motif is based on two premises: its synecdochic function and its ability to express subtlety, richness, and complexity in a literary work. Based on Kenneth Burke's notion that the synecdoche is the basic figure of speech,[117] Freedman claims that the motif's symbolic function is a subtle and elaborate variation of it. As a microcosmic part representing the whole, the motif also

---

116. Freedman, "Motif," 127.
117. See Burke, *Philosophy*, 22–23.

plays a role in this indispensable, human manner of viewing and communicating some aspect of the literary work. In other words, the motif can have interpretative value for the overall work not only for isolated contexts.

The second premise concerns the general consent that the qualities of subtlety, richness, and complexity are desirable qualities in a work of art and that the effective motif has the capacity to express these qualities for the reader. Based on these two premises, Freedman suggests certain pragmatic effects that a motif can have on readers. First, it enhances the reader's respect for the work and, consequently, also for the author. Second, as an expression of the above intellectual qualities, it is a source of literary enjoyment and appreciation. Third, for those with analytical interests, it becomes a delight to observe how a literary technique functions "both on its own and as a spoke in a well-oiled wheel."[118] Finally, he concludes, "Affectively ... it follows that the reinforcement of those effects on various levels, particularly the enrichment of the overall effect by means of a part, can only add scope and depth to the reading experience."[119]

Similar to Freedman's first premise, H. Porter Abbott highlights the interpretative value that a motif can have for a literary work. The interest in the thoroughfare motif is based on the presupposition that repetition is often an indicator of what is *meaningful* in the literary work. Abbott explains the importance of repetition: "The recurrence in narrative of images, ideas, situations, kinds of characters. Repetition is one of the surest signs of the meaningful. If you are stuck trying to interpret a text, one good question to ask yourself is: What is repeated in this narrative? Theme and motif are terms commonly used for kinds of repetition in narrative."[120] Since a motif is necessarily a repetitive element, it calls for an evaluation of its efficacy in illustrating what is meaningful in the work. Thus, Abbott recognizes the motif's potential value and limits for interpretation: "Identifying themes and motifs cannot in itself produce an interpretation: since the same themes and motifs can lend themselves to any number of different interpretations. But identifying themes and motifs can help enormously in establishing what a work is about and where its focus lies, and that in turn can be used to eliminate some interpretations and to lend support to others."[121]

Therefore, in view of Freedman and Abbott's considerations, the task of demonstrating how an effective motif functions and how it enhances the

118. Freedman, "Motif," 131.
119. Ibid.
120. Abbott, *Narrative*, 241.
121. Ibid., 95.

appreciation of the work is a beneficial activity. This research attempts to demonstrate that the thoroughfare motif plays a significant part in the plot of Luke-Acts as a part of a rich literary work in which many threads are woven to form a fine tapestry. The thoroughfare motif, as one of the threads, has a peculiarity of its own and emphasis that merits more attention, for its unique contribution, but also for its interaction with other motifs and themes. In short, the author of Luke-Acts had pastoral concerns for his audience and attempted to satisfy them through a finely crafted narrative about God's plan for humanity, which is enhanced by a variety of literary features. In fact, literary and theological aspects are naturally intertwined in the narration and reading experience of Luke-Acts, whose storyworld has been described as a "world under divine sovereignty," thus a "theocentric literary world."[122] Given this overlap between literary and theological description, the interests of this book correspond to recent narrative and theological readings. For example, on the pragmatic level of narrative, there is much affinity with Marguerat and Wénin's *Saveurs du récit biblique*.[123] In addition, due to this work's interest in the relationship between thoroughfare imagery and the theme of salvation, it also has much in common with Brenda Colijn's *Images of Salvation in the New Testament*.[124] Putting these two interests together, one could describe my approach as *rhetorical narratology*, because it explores how the narrative works, with its various literary components, and how it seeks to persuade readers regarding the central questions investigated. Furthermore, the narrative itself seems to desire a *passionate* reading, because of the sympathetic reader it implies and seeks to inspire. For these reasons, it is constructive to trace the rhetorical force of the motif within the plot, the reader's encounter with the storyworld, its questions and explicit and implicit values. Thus, we turn now to the plot of Luke-Acts.

---

122. Brawley, *Centering*, 25, 33.
123. Cf. Marguerat and Wénin, *Saveurs du récit*, 13–18.
124. Cf. Colijn, *Images of Salvation*, 17–23.

2

The Plot of Luke-Acts: the Reader's Encounter with Spiritual Transformation

ALTHOUGH PLOT THEORY IS at least as old as Aristotle's *mythos* in his *Poetics*,[1] literary scholars have not reached consensus about its definition. Hilary Dannenberg's conclusion is accurate: "Despite its apparent simplicity of reference, *plot* is one of the most elusive terms in narrative theory."[2] One of the factors for this ambiguity is its location: whether in the causal structure of story, on the level of action, on the level of discourse, in the production of the narrative, or in its reception. Due to the complexity of plot theory, I describe below this concept and its value for the study of fiction and nonfiction, whether ancient or contemporary. As stated, the main distinction between this definition of plot and others lies in the reader's perspective since a receiving consciousness is necessary for plot to happen. The objective here is to provide a progressive rhetorical framework of the two-volume work within which the thoroughfare motif can be identified and evaluated. For those who have not read the Gospel of Luke and the Acts of the Apostles as one narrative with two parts, this chapter will be particularly useful.

Definition of Plot from the Reader's Perspective

Like *motif* and *theme*, scholars use *plot* and *story* interchangeably. For this reason, some clarification is necessary. In this research, these terms are distinct and complementary. The following description and illustration

---

1. See, for example, Malcolm Heath's explanation of Aristotle's use of *mythos* in *Poetics*, xxii–xxviii.
2. Dannenberg, "Plot," 435.

summarizes this. *Story* concerns the narrative viewed from the outside, while *plot* describes the reader's encounter within the storyworld (see fig. 2.1).

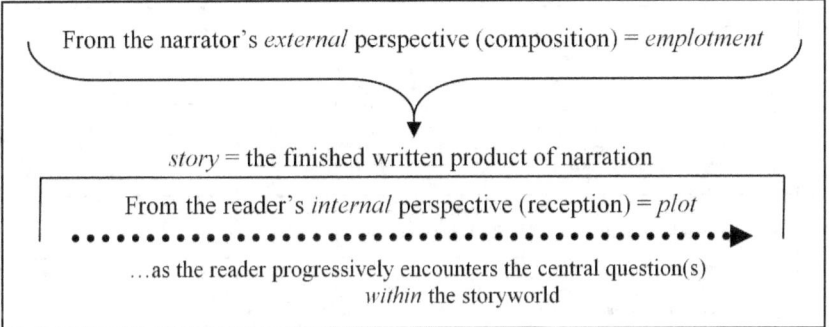

Figure 2.1: Emplotment and Plot:
The Story from External and Internal Perspectives[3]

Plot is the reader's progressive encounter—cognitive and emotive—of the storyworld, exploring one or more central questions toward some degree of closure. This encounter is what intrigues readers and leads them to seek satisfaction to their expectations and questions. This progressive, explorative encounter can vary from one representation to another depending on how the narrator has *emplotted* the story. In other words, narrators choose certain material and omit others. They emphasize certain points and conceal others. Narrators can also rearrange the temporal order, revealing things to the reader that the characters in the story do not know. Conversely, the reader can become aware of certain information only much later in the narrative. *Plot*, as understood here, can be better grasped when compared to two related concepts: *emplotment* and *explotment*.[4] These distinct processes are intricately related because of the relationship between explored questions and readers in the composition phase, *reading* phase, and the *post-reading* (and eventually *re-reading*) phase. The subsequent sections explain their similarities and differences. Figure 2.2 applies these three terms to Luke-Acts.

---

3. This illustration is taken from Morgan, "Emplotment," 71.

4. For a detailed discussion of these terms, see Morgan, "Emplotment," 64–98. Because of this emphasis on exploration and intrigue through reading, I also suggest the possibility of three alternative terms: *intriguement*, *intrigue*, and *ex-intriguement*. Ibid., 98.

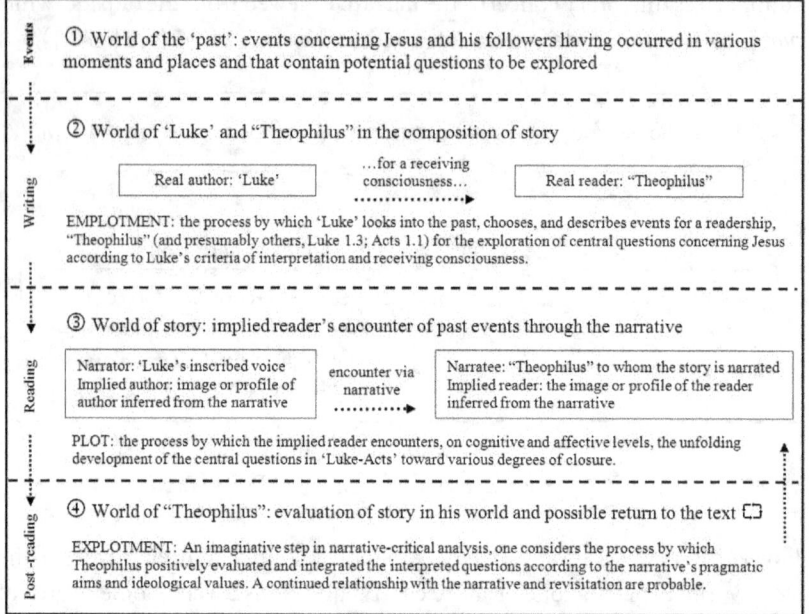

Figure 2.2: Emplotment, Plot, Explotment
in Historical Narrative Applied to Luke-Acts[5]

First, *emplotment* describes the narrator's work of producing the narrative in view of a receiving consciousness like "Theophilus." The author of Luke-Acts, it can be deduced, wrote according to Theophilus's interests and needs as well for the broader intended audience. *Plot*, on the other hand, is the process that describes the audience's progressive encounter with the text, for example, when Theophilus and others (with him) actually read or listened to the narrative. This process concerns their interpretation (cognitive level) and experience (emotive or pragmatic level).[6] Finally, explotment can be useful in describing the process by which readers evaluate and integrate or reject the story's interpretation and its explicit and implicit values into their lives. It describes the effects of the story on the reader after the reading and a possible return to the same narrative for further exploration and experience. The present study focuses principally on the second phase (plot). Nonetheless, the three phases are intrinsically connected by the notion of

5. This illustration is taken from Morgan, "Emplotment," 86.

6. My definition of *plot* is similar to James Phelan's *narrative progression*, which underlines the dynamic rapport between narrative and audience, the synthesis of two dynamic systems, that is, the internal logic of the narrative and the audience's developing interests and responses to it. Cf. Phelan, "Narrative Progression," 359–60.

The Plot of Luke-Acts: the Reader's Encounter with Spiritual Transformation

exploring certain questions with the presence of a receiving consciousness (reader, listener or viewer). These terms illustrate the pragmatic aspect that exists from one phase to another.

A key feature in this type of analysis is the identification of the *hero* in a story.[7] The hero is the main protagonist, who may be one person or a group, even a nation. The point is that the story's main questions revolve around someone or some group. On the action level, the hero accomplishes actions or endures them, which imply some change or transformation in him or her (or others or things). How this change happens and how it is described produces curiosity and suspense (even in a repeated reading or viewing). This focus on an individual or a group's existence or destiny provides continuity in the narration and the reader's exploration of certain questions for which he or she seeks entertainment, enlightenment, edification, etc. Further below, I will justify my choice for identifying Jesus as the hero of Luke-Acts, thus not only of the first volume but also of the second.

Theophilus as the Real and Implied Reader

Given that I emphasize the role of reader in plot theory and in the analysis of the thoroughfare motif, an explanation of the *reader* of Luke-Acts is necessary. First, due to the importance of oral performance of narratives and simply reading aloud in Antiquity, the designation reader will also represent here *auditor* (or *audience*).[8] This question about reader continues to be debated in literary theory (e.g., real, implied, ideal, etc.). These labels can be helpful but also confusing. In this study, I use reader principally for *implied reader* following this distinction: the real reader is the individual or audience (Theophilus and others) to whom the real author ("Luke") wrote the narrative.[9] The implied reader is the image of the real reader that can be reasonably, but not completely, constructed from the text and its assumptions, namely, its explicit and implicit elements. Consequently, this concerns an implied reader in historical context. Admittedly, this is not a simple or

---

7. Prince defines "hero" as "the protagonist or central character in a narrative. The hero (or heroine) usually represents positive values." Prince, *Narratology*, 40.

8. Several studies have demonstrated the interaction between oral and written performance in Greco-Roman rhetoric and its value for studying biblical literature. See, for example, Mack and Robbins, *Patterns*; Rothschild, *Luke-Acts*; Shiell, *Reading Acts*; and Maxwell, *Hearing*.

9. Moving from Theophilus to audience in the description becomes somewhat awkward when referring to them by pronouns "him" and "them" and similar. Yet, it recalls the fact that Theophilus and certainly others listened to this narrative together.

perfect task. However, what helps avoid complete randomness in this construction is to keep one's focus on what the reader encounters progressively, that is, the information and the literary and narrative devices that the narrator gradually allows the reader to interpret and experience.

Luke-Acts is unique among the narrative literature in the New Testament in that the narratee (Theophilus) is specifically named. Despite the sparse details in the text about this personage, I will use "Theophilus," along with "reader(s)" and "audience" to refer to the intended reader(s).[10] In fact, most certainly Luke had a broader audience in mind as the *real reader* (or *authorial audience*).[11] Again, we are working with an image of the audience provided by the author. Of course, this also has some difficulties since, besides the evidence in Luke-Acts, we have no further information in extant literature about Theophilus. Therefore, it is necessary to work with a provisional, general description of this personage and the broader audience that Luke sought to inform and influence.[12] Based on the evidence in Luke-Acts, Theophilus and the general audience can be described in this way:

- The length and quality of the Greek text imply readers with a knowledge and appreciation of the Greek language and rhetorical techniques of that period. Yet, this does not necessarily exclude an

---

10. Concerning the identity of "Theophilus," scholars have various opinions on three main points: whether "Theophilus" was a historical person, a follower of Jesus or another type of reader, and a representative of a wider audience. Alexander argues for a real person and suggests various social relationships to Luke: social superior; patron; an outsider; or publisher (*Preface*, 188–200). Some suggest "Theophilus" as a fictitious title, "friend of God," for an unspecified Christian reader or at least a sympathetic reader (cf. Bonz, *Past as Legacy*, 131–32). Nolland (*Luke 1—9:20,5*, xxxiii) indicates the possibility of a real recipient identified via this pseudonym (perhaps for protection or discretion?). Regarding the second point above, J.C. O'Neill suggests an educated public who is intended to embrace the Christian faith (*Theology of Acts*, 177; cf. also Larkin, "Recovery of Luke-Acts," 411–12). For further discussion related to points 2 and 3, cf. Robert Maddox, *Purpose*, 20–22. In Antiquity, a personal dedication in the preface does not preclude a wider audience. Thus, Theophilus could be considered a representative of a broader group (Ibid., 12). Dibelius argues—based on the type of preface in Luke—for a much wider audience outside the community of believers (*Studies*, 88). More convincing is Bock's description that Luke writes not only for Theophilus but for any Gentile who felt the tension of being a part of an originally Jewish movement or any Jew (or Jewish Christian) who might be troubled by Jewish rejection and Gentile openness (*Luke: 1:1–9:50*, 14–15).

11. Cf. Nolland, *Luke 1—9:20*, 5.

12. Minear attempts to discern the historical "social forces" that Theophilus faced (e.g., discouragement leading to skepticism), which also encouraged Luke to provide an appropriate narrative to his reader's needs. He also recognizes the provisional nature of this description given the lack of explicit details. Minear, "Dear Theo," 134–35.

audience with informal education.[13]

- The preface in Luke 1:1–4 implies that readers probably had interest in the author's effort to employ certain methods of history writing in the Greek tradition and at the same time to connect the story of Jesus with the story of the people of Israel. Luke uses the term *diēgēsis* (narrative) to describe his work.[14] In Hellenistic literature, this generic term was used for fiction and nonfiction. It is possible that Luke appropriated this expression in the sense of Theon's definition of narrative: "an expository treatise of events which happened or could have happened."[15] Luke's initial prologue (Luke 1:1–4) and his use of *diēgēsis* instead of "gospel" (Mark 1:1) might suggest that he intends for his work to be read according to the genre of historiography.[16]

- That Theophilus (and broader audience) was from Gentile background and lived in a setting that is predominately Gentile can be inferred from the elements that Luke omits in his narrative: removal of material from his sources containing Jewish preoccupations (e.g., ritual purity, clean and unclean); substitution of Hebrew names with Greek names (e.g., *kurios* "Lord" and *epistatēs* "teacher" instead of *rabbi/rabbouni*; *kranion* "skull" for "Golgotha"; and "Israel" always designates the Jewish people).[17] Finally, given Luke's emphasis on "the nations," Theophilus had a keen interest in non-Jewish individuals and groups who became followers of Jesus.

- On the other hand, the frequent references to Israel's history and religious writings, as well as the imitation of Septuagintal style, suggest that readers were familiar with and appreciated elements of Jewish history and religion, but especially their Scriptures.[18]

---

13. Maxwell, *Hearing*, 125–27.

14. BDAG, s.v. διήγησις: "an orderly description of facts, events, actions, or words *narrative, account*." Compared to a concise description (χρεία), MM (p. 161) suggest that διήγησις "implies some fullness of narrative which suits the use of the word in the Preface of Lk."

15. Theon, *Progymnasmata* 4 as cited in Aune, *New Testament*, 116. Cf. also Cicero, *On Rhetorical Invention*, 1.19.27; Quintilian 4.21.31.

16. Aune, *New Testament*, 116. Cf. Unnik, "Once More," 12–15. For a stimulating article arguing that Luke's preface was a bold and outstanding Christian appropriation of the Greek *decree*, see Moles, "Luke's Preface," 461–82.

17. Fitzmyer, *Luke (I–X)*, 58–59.

18. Cf. Maddox, *Purpose*, 14–15.

- Luke's audience probably appreciated hearing about God's interventions in relation to world history (e.g., Jesus' genealogy goes back to Adam, Luke 3:38; list of nations in Pentecost) and political figures (e.g., Augustus Caesar, Pilate, Felix, Festus, Agrippa and Bernice, etc.). In fact, based on the adjective used to address Theophilus ("most noble," "most excellent," Luke 1:3), he may have occupied some administrative function (perhaps a magistrate).[19]

- The phrase in Luke 1:4, "the things of which you have been taught," suggests that readers had previous knowledge of (at least) the basic elements concerning Jesus and his followers. In addition, the favorable portrayal of Jesus and his disciples as well as polemical asides[20] (Luke 7:30; 16:14) appear to address a sympathetic audience, Christians from pagan background having some contact with Jewish communities. Luke seeks to fill their gaps of knowledge, but equally important, to explain how and why the events are interrelated and what implications they entail for the Jewish people and all other nations.

- The silence concerning the verdict of Paul's trial intimates that the readers probably knew what happened after Paul's two-year sojourn in Rome reported in the conclusion of Acts. Readers were expected to fill in gaps of information like this one based on common knowledge.[21]

This general profile of Theophilus leads to the conclusion that Luke wrote to an individual and a wider audience, which was predominately Gentile Christian, genuinely interested in Jesus and his disciples in relation to Israel's history. Consequently, as a working hypothesis, my reading corresponds well with Gerald Downing's approach:

> I would take as a more important motive for Luke's writing, that of reassuring the hearers of the intellectual and moral—and social—respectability of their group and its beliefs and ethos; and, while still affirming the concern to entertain, I would not now suppose Luke expected to have his work bought by or read to complete

---

19. Ibid., 13. Yet, the epithet κράτιστε is not conclusive evidence that Theophilus was a Roman official or of superior status to Luke. Cf. Cadbury, *The Making of Luke-Acts*, 315 and Alexander, *Preface*, 133. This address could be "a form of polite address with no official connotation" (BDAG, s.v. κράτιστος).

20. For the pertinence of Luke's asides, cf. Sheeley's two contributions, "Narrative Asides," 102–7 and *Narrative Asides*.

21. Marguerat, *Enigma*, 296–97.

outsiders. He is entertaining and reassuring Theophilus and his Christian friends, not least reassuring them that their faith is both entertaining and eminently respectable.[22]

In this sense, I side with those interpreters who understand Theophilus as a follower of Jesus.[23] As Luke writes from the perspective of one of "the Way," Theophilus, I suggest, is also an *insider* of this movement.[24] In fact, this reading attempts to enter this unique narrative situation between two (or more) adherents of this extended group of Jesus' followers. This approach seeks to describe the reception of the text as an experience, and, because of the content that describes God's acts for a believing community, it may be qualified as a religious experience. Consequently, this leads us to the question of plot as an explorative encounter of the past in relation to the present of the reader.

Plot Theory and the Analysis of Nonfiction

Given that most theoretical discussion on plot has been developed for the study of fictional narrative and that the interest of this study in plot is for its value for understanding Luke-Acts (non-fiction from the narrator's perspective), it is appropriate to justify the use of plot theory in the analysis of non-fictional works. A brief comparison of fiction and nonfiction is constructive.

Authors of fiction and nonfiction are faced with choices on the story and discourse levels. What does the reader need to know? Moreover, how should it be expressed for the reader's interest? A fundamental difference is that the author of fiction plays a greater role as designer since he or she is not bound *a priori* by referential information. Such authors can design events and their settings, and characters, even the characters' inner thoughts and motivations. They can move from one setting to another, describing them as precisely as they wish, because they are omniscient within the limits of

22. Downing, "Theophilus's First Reading," 109.

23. In addition to Downing's positive affirmation above, see Minear, "Dear Theo," 133–34 and Bock, *Luke: 1:1–9:50*, 14–15. Unnik finds it is hard to decide whether Theophilus was actually already "inside or outside the Christian fold." Unnik, "Once More," 18. Likewise, Green hesitates to confirm Theophilus as a Christian by pointing to the analogy with Apollos's need for understanding although he had already been "instructed." Green, *Gospel of Luke*, 45–46.

24. As Green describes, "The prologue does, however, communicate Luke's claim to being one of 'us'—that is, a member of the larger community of persons whose lives were being shaped by the events he goes on to narrate. Luke writes as one of the 'people of the Way', a 'Christian.'" Green, *Gospel of Luke*, 36.

their imagination. Authors of nonfictional narrative, on the other hand, are limited to the information that they have been able to recover about the above elements.[25] Yet, they must also make fundamental choices about the material to include and how to organize and express it according to their interpretation and pragmatic aims (e.g., instruction, utility, enjoyment, etc.).

This creative activity in the production of nonfictional narrative is a configurational process between two periods: the past of the events and the present of the narration. Hayden White describes this process as "emplotment" and Paul Ricoeur as *mise en intrigue*.[26] Based on their theories, one may argue that even historians cannot escape the processes of emplotment, conscious or unconscious, in their historical reconstructions. Thus, Ricoeur, interacting with White's theory, summarizes a presupposition concerning a "poetics of history": ". . . that fiction and history belong to the same class as far as narrative structure is concerned."[27] Consequently, the writing of history is rightly considered literature resulting from this creative narrative activity described above.[28]

As regards the pragmatic aspect in nonfictional narrative, the activity of narration is performed for someone's pleasure or utility, even if only for the author's. The textual storyworld in effect provides a bridge for the reader to the temporal sphere of the narrated events. The narrator might seek to give the reader greater comprehension of the causes and effects of an event, or admiration or aversion of certain characters. Consequently, a main function of narrative is to help readers interpret the past and identify implications for the present. Herman explains this human activity: "As accounts of what happened to particular people in particular circumstances and with specific consequences, stories have come to be viewed as a basic human strategy for coming to terms with time, process, and change . . . ."[29] Likewise, Abbott describes narrative as the "rhetoric of the real," and has the effect of *normalization*: "You could in fact argue, and people have, that our need for narrative form is so strong that we don't really believe something is true unless we can see it as a story. Bringing a collection of events into

---

25. The degree of freedom in expressing real events as they "actually happened" depends on multiple factors such as the historian's techniques and ability as well as cultural expectations in historiography.

26. White, *Metahistory*, 7–11 and "Emplotment," 137. Ricoeur, *Temps et récit*, 1:66–104.

27. Ricoeur, *Temps et récit*, 1:287.

28. For the pertinence of these concepts to the study of the Gospel of Luke, see Green, *Luke*, 2.

29. Herman et al., "Introduction," ix.

narrative coherence can be described as a way of normalizing those events. It renders them plausible, allowing one to see how they all 'belong.'"[30]

Donald Juel's comments regarding Luke-Acts and its first readers illustrate the theory of *normalization*: "Luke sought to help his audience make sense of their lives by telling them a story. He provided a framework in which they could locate themselves and in which they could find meaning." Yet, beyond the question of meaning, the first preface of Luke-Acts reveals that the narrator also seeks this explicit pragmatic effect: "so that you might know the certainty concerning the things of which you have been taught (ἵνα ἐπιγνῷς περὶ ὧν κατηχήθης λόγων τὴν ἀσφάλειαν Luke 1:4). As stated above, this serves as a heuristic to explore how Luke-Acts seeks to achieve this desired effect of certainty (or assurance), and whether the thoroughfare motif contributes to it. Thus, the narrator, more than a chronicler, has placed himself in the position of instructor so that his readers, or students, might experience greater certainty regarding their faith in Jesus during the reading and afterwards. Luke-Acts is thus not only a "moving system of information"[31] on the cognitive level; it is also a "system of influence," which attempts to shape readers' beliefs and values.[32] It exemplifies Abbott's *normalization* in that the author attempts to express meaningful and purposeful content, artistically expressed, to provide a coherent, convincing story for his students' experience. In fact, the first passage of Luke-Acts (Luke 1:1–4) can be understood as a pact between the author and reader, since as promises are given by the author, expectations for fulfillment are raised in the reader. Narrative not only has the power to make sense of the past but also to provide an experience, to live and relive the recounted events. It can give a sense of "being there."[33] This is certainly important for a sympathetic audience. In this sense, multiple experiences of these events is possible as long as a return to the narrative remains available.

Moreover, Abbott has raised another question that highlights a potential difference between the pragmatic effects of fiction and nonfiction.[34] He suggests that the degree to which a story makes an impact on readers depends in part on their perception of the narrative as fiction or nonfiction:

---

30. Abbott, *Narrative*, 44.

31. Barthes, "Par où commencer?," 4.

32. Tannehill, *Narrative*, 1:8.

33. This sense of "being there" is referred to as *qualia* in literary theory. It describes those felt, subjective properties related to a given experience. For its application to narrative and mind, see Herman, *Basics*, 143–45.

34. Abbott, *Narrative*, 145.

> Despite the powerful advantages of fiction, nonfiction narratives enjoy one attraction that fiction lacks, and that is that they claim to tell a story that is *factually* true. This is the deep appeal of narratives like history, biography, autobiography, filmed documentaries, and staged monologues representing a real person in her own words (and for that matter all accounts of the way things have actually happened in time, including the narratives of geology, paleontology, astronomy, and other sciences).

This brief description reveals the pragmatic force of nonfictional narrative and that it merits attention in the study of Luke-Acts. In view of this, regardless of the reader's prior knowledge of some elements of the story, it is reasonable to maintain that a narrative can always work toward—albeit to various degrees—pragmatic aims and effects on the reader, whether brief or enduring. In fact, the story can be relived as many times as the reader desires. This is the force of nonfictional narrative rhetoric, which affects plot, the reader's encounter. This guides the following analysis of the plot and the thoroughfare motif as a constituent part. After this lengthy but necessary discussion of plot, we turn now to the plot of Luke-Acts as a unified narrative.

The Plot of Luke-Acts

To describe plot is to describe the encounter and the exploration of central questions undergirded by certain values working toward narrative closure and pragmatic aims. Before turning to my synopsis of the plot of Luke-Acts, I briefly summarize here the results of key studies that have worked with an aspect of plot in Luke-Acts in its entirety, not only on plot in the Gospel of Luke and the Acts of the Apostles.

Previous Research on the Plot of Luke-Acts

Jacques Dupont's seminal study convincingly demonstrates that the ending of Acts provides narrative closure for Luke-Acts regarding the rejection of Jesus by the Jews and the inclusion of the nations.[35] One of the keys lies in the landmarks of Nazareth, Pisidian Antioch, and Rome, which link

---

35. Dupont, "La conclusion des Actes," 457–511. His article brings together years of research on the subject of mission to the Gentiles in Luke-Acts. Cf. Dupont, "Le salut des Gentils," 132–55; and "Je t'ai établi," 343–49.

The Plot of Luke-Acts: the Reader's Encounter with Spiritual Transformation

the apostles with Jesus in his mandate, Jewish reception and rejection, and witness as a light to the nations. Robert Tannehill's article builds on Dupont and other scholars expressing the plot as an outworking of the divine purpose of salvation within the drama of opposing characters, those for it and those against it.[36] This results in tension on the action level. Similarly, Robert Brawley illustrates the antithetical nature of the Luke-Acts narrative, focusing on the narrative schema of God sifting a people for himself among the Jews and the nations.[37] William Kurz, using redaction and narrative-critical methodology, demonstrates how the narrator has plotted Luke-Acts and how the reader is expected to interpret the plot and fill in the gaps of information.[38] Loveday Alexander, applying Gérard Genette's theory of *epitext*, indicates parallels between the "prologue" and the "epilogue," which function as a "paratextual framework" for Luke-Acts, providing an entry and an exit for the reader.[39] These two large sections are debatably too large to be considered paratext.[40] However, the point is that the reader is invited to enter and experience the storyworld of Luke-Acts and then prepared to leave it and return to his or her own world.

Although working with a different understanding of plot, Ju Hur demonstrates the value of evaluating the narrative role of a character (the Holy Spirit) as a part of the causal structure of Luke-Acts.[41] In a similar way, this present study attempts to posit a literary technique, the motif as an inanimate participant, within the narrative progression of Luke-Acts. In addition,

---

36. Tannehill expresses this notion in "Israel in Luke-Acts," 69–85 and in *Narrative*, 1:2.

37. Brawley, *Centering*, 85, 89.

38. Kurz, *Reading Luke-Acts*, 17–36. For this reason, the chapter includes two main sections, "Plotting the Narrative" (pp. 18–31) and a shorter section "Readers and Gaps" (pp. 31–36).

39. Alexander, "Reading Luke-Acts," 411. She refers to Genette's definitions in *Seuils*, 376–77.

40. Genette's theory, strictly speaking, is applicable to that which is not a part of the narrative proper (e.g., prefaces). The "prologue" and "epilogue" that Alexander has identified in Luke-Acts are more likely classified as *text*, an integral part of the storyworld. She justifies this by explaining that in ancient works the equivalent of modern *peritext* could be included in the narrative itself (e.g., prefaces, transitional summaries, and epilogues), especially in the opening and closing scenes. Alexander, "Reading Luke-Acts," 422–23.

41. Hur, *Dynamic Reading*, 278. His description of the plot of Luke-Acts stays on the action level focusing on geographical expansion. Ibid., 191–93. The titles in the outline reflect the story level (i.e., events or what happens) rather than the reader's level as in my plot synopsis that highlights the central questions explored and resulting narrative tension.

like Hur's study, scholars have proposed various types of outlines for Luke-Acts, mostly staying on the level of action.[42] To my knowledge, no proposal has suggested thus far a literary section that overlaps the first and second volumes (see fig. 2.1).[43]

All of the above studies provide examples of literary disclosures, which orient the reader forward (*prolepses*) and backward (*analepses*) in the reading. In the early chapters of Luke, foreshadowing devices are particularly important concerning salvation for the Jews and the nations (e.g., the words of Zechariah, the angels, Simeon, John the Baptist, and then Jesus' discourse at Nazareth). Yet, there are also glimpses of opposition to it (e.g., Luke 2:34–35; 3:16–17). In addition, the ending of the first scroll (Luke) and the beginning of the second (Acts) serve as a *hinge* to connect the two volumes (cf. Luke 24:36–53—Acts 1:11).[44] This technique provides continuity in the story through the presence of the risen Christ, the ascension narratives, as well as the prolepsis concerning the Holy Spirit and reiteration of the disciples' mandate.[45] Furthermore, the authors note how Luke uses Jewish Scriptures to guide the reader's interpretation throughout the narrative. The analysis

---

42. For example, similar to Hur's outline, F. Scott Spencer traces four parallels of geographical expansion of mission in the two volumes. Spencer, *Gospel of Luke*, 95–97. Bonz identifies five main sections (Luke 1–2; 3–12; 13–24; Acts 1–15; 16–28). She begins with the discourse level "The Dramatic Overture: Luke 1–2," then continues with the story level, "Inauguration of the Mission and Initial Opposition: Luke 3–12." Bonz, *Past as Legacy*, 132–83. Bock's narrative outline includes twelve main sequences (five in Luke and seven in Acts). It also remains on the story level. Bock, *Theology of Luke and Acts*, 63–95. Borgman (*The Way*, v–vii) uses the theme of "the Way" in four sections (Luke 1:1—9:5; 9:51—19:44; 19:45–24:53; for fourth section no references provided, but one assumes all of Acts), which begins with the discourse level "The Way: Narrative Preparations," then moves to the action level in the remaining titles.

43. Given the wide consent that Luke and Acts are connected through various literary and narrative elements, it is justifiable to seek a wider portion of text that might form the middle of the two scrolls. Recently, Bonz has suggested—based on textual critical evidence—that the two volumes were one volume and split in two in order to circulate them independently. Bonz, *Past as Legacy*, 153–54. Aune's explanation seems more plausible, namely, that Luke foresaw the necessity for two scrolls and prepared the endings and beginnings accordingly. Similar to other Greco-Roman authors, Luke attempted to maintain the two volumes roughly symmetrical (Luke 19,404 words/2,900 *stichoi* (lines) and Acts 18,374 words/2,600 *stichoi*). Aune, *New Testament*, 117–18.

44. Various proposals delimit the two connecting passages differently. See, for example, the discussions in Walton, "Beginning of Acts," 448–67 and Marguerat, *Actes (1–12)*, 33–34, 36–37.

45. This literary "hinge" reflects an ancient technique: "To knit Luke-Acts together, Luke used the literary techniques of *recapitulation* and *resumption*, also used by Polybius, Strabo, Diodorus, Josephus, and Herodian." Aune, *New Testament*, 117. For the parallels between Luke 24 and Acts 1, see Talbert, *Literary Patterns*, 58–61.

below incorporates some of these results and attempts to bring further elucidations on the plot of Luke-Acts based on plot theory from the reader's perspective.[46]

Plot Synopsis of Luke-Acts as the Reader's Encounter

The plot synopsis attempts to reflect this by expressing two main aspects of plot on the reader's level: cognitive (how the reader is lead to interpret and understand) and emotive (how the reader is lead to experience the narrative). Narratives work on two levels: moving toward some degree of closure as well as "working on" the reader. A plot synopsis then must not be a mere story summary—this happens, then that, and so on—but rather a synthesis that adequately reflects how the reader enters, progresses, and exits the storyworld, as an interpretation and experience of the narrative's main questions. As stated, key to this focus is the identification of the hero, or main protagonist. Following the methodology described above, it is plausible to designate Jesus as the hero, because the whole story depends on his transforming actions (resurrection, ascension, and sending of the Holy Spirit). Without Jesus, Luke-Acts falls apart and other stories must be told. The two volumes describe these actions, their consequences and effects on people, whether received or resisted.

Consequently, this plot summary of Luke-Acts describes the reader's progressive and passionate encounter with the narrator's interpretation of the events that describe or interpret Jesus' works and effects on the world ("accomplished among us" Luke 1:1). It elucidates that sense of being there and witnessing the transformation taking place especially on the spiritual level. In short, it is an exploration of central questions about individuals or groups within certain times and places.

As mentioned in Chapter 1, the narrative scheme model used in this study, commonly known as the "quinary scheme," helps to identify the main sequences of a narrative's development. Initially, the quinary scheme was limited to the action level and as the events occurred chronologically. This was also reflected in the terms used by Paul Larivaille for the five sequences (*initial state, provocation, action, sanction,* and *final state*).[47] My application

---

46. For a fuller description, see Morgan, *Thoroughfare Motif*, 85–120. In the present plot analysis of Luke-Acts, I place greater emphasis on the presence of the reader in plot. In addition, rather than organize the synopsis on the interaction between Jesus and main groups, I emphasize here the progressive exploration of questions and expectations for which the audience seeks enlightenment and satisfaction.

47. Larivaille, "*L'analyse morphologique*," 387.

of this model is on the reader's level as the reader encounters the information of the story.[48] Consequently, this change of focus requires different names for the five sequences: *initial orientation, raveling, pivot, unraveling,* and *final orientation*.[49] The two outer sequences serve to orient the reader to enter and exit the storyworld. One or both may be absent in a narrative. Moreover, it is important to note Jean-Michel Adam's expansion of Larivaille's model. Although he makes subtle changes to the terms, he has added two paratextual sections, a "resume" or "entry/preface" at the beginning of the narrative and a "final evaluation" at the end.[50] When present, both can shape the reader's encounter with the story.

In contrast, the inner sequences generally form the heart of any narrative. They are similar to the reader holding a rope and as the narration progresses the rope begins to ravel producing some felt tension (raveling sequence). The central questions are raised and explored; expectations for illumination and satisfaction are generated, along with a sense of uncertainty that this will happen. At a certain point, the reader may notice that an event or a series of events has caused the story to go in a different direction perhaps causing an initial unraveling and lessening of tension (pivot sequence). If so, normally the main questions continue to find a degree of illumination and expectations are satisfied; thus, tension reduces notably (unraveling). A sense of satisfaction that the main questions have reached some degree of closure and that uncertainty about them has diminished. If the *final orientation* is present, readers typically receive some sort of indication or confirmation about the general gist of the story, the resolution of the story's main questions, and possibly, how the story continues or could continue.

These sequences vary in length and intensity from one narrative to another, and their experience depends on various factors concerning genre, narrator, and audience. Regarding Luke-Acts, studies have shown that Luke has written not only to instruct but also to provide an encounter, so that his specific aim in Luke 1:4 might be realized. In addition, as a sympathetic reader, Theophilus could also be expected to follow the narrative with interest and passion, taking the side of Jesus and his disciples.

In some narratives, the chronological sequence remains essentially linear. In this case, readers encounter the events along with the characters

---

48. My adaptation of the *quinary scheme* from the reader's perspective differs with Marguerat and Bourquin's application in *Pour lire les récits bibliques*, 56–60 and reiterated by Marguerat in *Saveurs du récit*, 87–89.

49. These terms are explained in detail in Morgan "Emplotment," 82–83, 89, 92.

50. Adam, "*Décrire*," 19.

The Plot of Luke-Acts: the Reader's Encounter with Spiritual Transformation

of the story. Despite significant flash-forwards and flashbacks, Luke-Acts is mainly chronological in its development. In plot analysis, the second set of terms—from the reader's view—help to view the story from the inside, as the reader comes across characters and events. In Luke-Acts, the five sequences can be determined by major transitions in the narration (see Table 2.1).[51]

1 Initial orientation Luke 1:5—3:38	2 Raveling Luke 4:1—23:56	3 Pivot Luke 24:1—Acts 2:13	4 Unraveling Acts 2:14—28:15	5 Final orientation Acts 28:16-31

Table 2.1: Five Major Narrative Sequences in Luke-Acts

Jesus' genealogy marks the transition between the initial orientation and the raveling sequences. The stage is now set for the reader to experience the ensuing pattern of reception and rejection of Jesus. Consequently, Jesus' death indicates the end of the raveling and opens the pivot sequence in which the reader encounters three transforming actions: Jesus' resurrection, ascension, and sending of the Holy Spirit.[52] The third transition that opens the unraveling sequence is the sending and reception of the Holy Spirit. Finally, the transition between the unraveling and the final orientation is Paul's arrival in Rome.

In order to express a plausible unifying plot for Luke-Acts, the next step is to put the pieces together, that is, to express in cursory form the primary contribution of each sequence to the reader's encounter. Again, I use here "Theophilus" as the implied reader, who also represents a broader, sympathetic audience.

Initial Orientation Sequence (Luke 1:5—3:38)

After the initial paratext (Luke 1:1-4; "Pn0" in Adam's model) in which the author presents himself as a reliable narrator, an informed instructor, he begins to orient Theophilus in the storyworld proper. The latter is expected to recognize the narrator's style and allusions that hearken to Israel's story as the people of God communicated through Israel's Scriptures. This intertextual

---

51. This delimitation of the sequences does not preclude other types of outlines or the presence of other transitional elements and minor sequences. It attempts to illustrate Luke-Acts in its narrative unity, the *big picture* from the reader's perspective.

52. For the role of one or more *transforming actions* in identifying the *pivot*, see Marguerat and Bourquin, *Pour lire*, 56–60.

background continues until the end of Acts providing the framework of interpretation for actions, quotations, speeches, etc.

The reader gradually becomes aware of the roles of John and Jesus in God's plan through these first chapters of the first volume. It becomes clear that Jesus will be greater than John, who is the forerunner of the Lord and "the prophet of the Most High" (1:76). Yet, Jesus is described as "the Son of the Most High" (1:32); "the Son of God" (1:35); "a dawn from on high" (1:78); the heir of David's throne (1:32–33); "savior" (2:11); "Christ the Lord" (2:11); "the Lord's Christ" (2:26); "a light" for the nations and the Jews (2:32); a baptizer in the Holy Spirit and fire (3:16); a harbinger of judgment (3:17); and God's "beloved son" (3:22). I refer to this collection of descriptions as the hero *proleptic portrait*.[53] Furthermore, Jewish opposition to the hero's mandate is also foreshadowed early in the narrative (2:34–35).

Therefore, the implied reader enters the storyworld having a privileged position as a sympathetic viewer to explore passionately the narrative's main questions about Jesus. Several elements confirm Jesus' identity: God's voice (3:22), John's preaching, and Jesus' genealogy. Yet, Jesus has done nothing thus far to accomplish his mandate. These *potentialities* (or proleptic qualities) will either be realized or averted. How will the hero accomplish his mandate? What transformation will Jesus actually bring? Why will some of the Jewish people reject Jesus?

Thus, the first sequence sets the stage for the audience's exploration of these main questions toward some degree of closure. Pragmatically, the reader grasps the *big picture* by focusing on Jesus as the primary agent of transformation.

Raveling Sequence (Luke 4:1—23:56)

The raveling sequence is extensive in Luke-Acts in which narrative tension develops as the reader becomes aware of the opposition to the hero's mandate on the spiritual and human planes. Satan attempts to sabotage the hero's mandate by proposing to him an alternative plan to rule the nations (i.e., the main *counterplot* on the action level, 4:1–13). Ironically, intense human opposition begins with Jesus' hometown (4:14–30). These two episodes mark the point-of-no-return since opposition and rejection continues unabated until the very end. Equally ironic, opposition continues mainly through the Jewish religious authorities who, among the Jewish people, should be able to

---

53. As a part of characterization, a *proleptic portrait* regards the depiction of a character for the reader's interpretation and experience. See Sternberg, *Poetics*, 337–38.

recognize best his identity. The reader identifies with those who choose to follow Jesus, some of them unlikely candidates as disciples, and he observes and experiences their transformation. Despite Jesus' authoritative teaching, miraculous and compassionate acts, the formation of disciples, and the general favor of the people, he is betrayed, rejected, and brutally executed. The reader learns an interpretative key for understanding the cause of Jewish rejection: their failure to recognize the time of the hero's visitation (19:44). He observes with empathy Jesus' death and the disciples' failures and dejection. The hero's mandate has apparently ended in failure, orchestrated by Satan, and accomplished through those who should have recognized him best. Narrative tension reaches its peak as the reader experiences (or relives) suspense due to a growing sense of uncertainty about the realization of the disciples' mandate and reward (21:12–19; 22:28–30).[54]

The pragmatic effect of this sequence is that Theophilus passionately endures the reception and rejection of Jesus. While in awe of Jesus' actions and teaching, he must also witness the gradual movement toward Jesus' humiliating death, alluded to implicitly and explicitly.

Pivot Sequence (Luke 24:1—Acts 2:13)

The pivot sequence spans both volumes; its focus is completely on the transformation of the disciples from Emmaus road to the day of Pentecost. The reader experiences the disciples' surprise and joy at the reactivation of the hero's mandate through three transformational actions marking the turning point: his resurrection, ascension, and baptizing in the Holy Spirit. Without these events, there would be no more to tell. Through this reversal, the story takes a turn for the better (from the narrator and reader's perspective). The focus here is on the transformation that continues to take place in the disciples who are being prepared to extend Jesus' mandate. Pragmatically, this sequence helps the reader to experience (with the disciples) a dramatic turn from defeat to victory. Some narrative tension remains regarding the question whether others outside this group of disciples will be transformed due to the disciples' slowness to understand (Luke 24:25–27, 37–39; Acts 1:10–11) and their ethnocentric preoccupations for a restored kingdom of Israel (Acts 1:6–7).

---

54. Narrative tension through suspense is not always due to unknown elements in the story. It may be created through expectations of developments already encountered. The degree of suspense depends on memory of and involvement in the story. Suspense can also be generated through exploring how and why events happened.

Encountering Images of Spiritual Transformation

Unraveling Sequence (Acts 2:14—28:15)

The unraveling sequence in Luke-Acts is quite extensive, from the resulting effects of the sending of the Holy Spirit to Paul's arrival in Rome. Although transformation continues in Jesus' disciples, this sequence focuses on the spiritual transformation outside the circle of the disciples. The reader becomes aware of the progressive realization of the hero's mandate despite continued, and often hostile, spiritual and human opposition, among the Jewish people and the nations. Narrative tension develops due to continued internal resistance as some Jewish followers resist their mission to the nations. The disciples from Jewish origin are in need of further transformation. The effects of two highlighted recognition experiences (Cornelius and Saul) lead Jewish believers to realize that they, like Jesus, are a light to the nations. This provides the opportunity for the reader to explore the question of spiritual unity between God, Jesus, and the disciples.

The pragmatic effect of this sequence is that the reader confidently follows the disciples from Jerusalem to Rome. From this point on, narrative tension diminishes in direct proportion to the progress of the hero's mandate, to the point that groups of Jesus' disciples ("the Way") form in various localities from Jerusalem to Rome. The shift in focus from Peter to Paul provides ample instances that clarify the questions concerning Jewish rejection and Gentile inclusion. The reader—probably from pagan background—certainly rejoices and perhaps identifies with certain transformed characters from non-Jewish background. The main questions and expectations are steadily reaching a strong degree of closure. Thus, the reader's faith is strengthened through encountering various events and speeches that demonstrate how the proleptic portrait painted early on has been realized. Jesus has become savior, a light for the Jews and revelation for the nations, reigning in heaven as heir to David's throne.

Final Orientation Sequence (Acts 28:16-31)

The final orientation, symmetrical to the initial orientation, helps Theophilus to make a final interpretation of the story and to reenter his own temporal sphere by observing Paul among the Jews in Rome, the final destination. The story ends in the land of the Romans but among the Jewish community. As the representative of the sect (*hairesis*, i.e., the Way in Acts 24:14, 22), Paul proclaims salvation and the kingdom of God through the "Lord Jesus Christ." In this way, the reader's certainty in Jesus is confirmed through a sense of narrative closure that confirms the proleptic portrait of Jesus, the well-known

The Plot of Luke-Acts: the Reader's Encounter with Spiritual Transformation

pattern of reception and rejection among the Jews, as well as renewed mission toward the nations (28:28). The narrative proper ends here with no final paratext ("PnW" in Adam's model), but with a remarkable *coda* that caps off this work of two scrolls underscoring the reality of the kingdom of God through the spiritual unity between Jesus and his disciples represented by Paul (28:29–30). Pragmatically, the *final orientation* confirms again for Theophilus that Jesus has accomplished his mandate as savior for the Jews and the nations. Consequently, Theophilus is better equipped as a follower of Jesus and prepared to encounter both reception and rejection in his own context.

To summarize, the five sequences work toward the reader's need of certainty as a disciple. Thus, the plot of Luke-Acts targets the reader's interpretation and experience of the realization of Jesus' mandate to bring salvation to the Jews and the nations, foreshadowed so early in the narrative. The reader has had a sense of "being there," participating—as a sympathetic disciple—in the transformational force of the story. Narrative tension develops partly as the reader views the inconsistencies of Jesus' disciples, but especially Satan's counterplot, intense spiritual and human opposition whose aim, conscious or unconscious, is the sabotage of Jesus' mandate. Through the hero's transforming actions and his disciples' participation in the mandate, narrative tension decreases greatly as the *potentialities* of the mandate become *realities*, tangibly illustrated by the formation of groups of Jesus' disciples from the Jews and the nations, even to Rome. With this description of the five sequences, I propose the following general titles from the implied reader's perspective:

Initial Orientation: Perceiving the Aims of the Hero's Mandate (Luke 1:5—3:38)

Raveling: Passionately Enduring Reception and Rejection of the Hero (Luke 4:1—23:56)

Pivot: Experiencing a Dramatic Turn from Defeat to Victory (Luke 24:1—Acts 2:13)

Unraveling: Confidently Following the Expansion of the Hero's Mandate (Acts 2:14—28:15)

Final Orientation: Receiving Final Confirmation of the Hero's Success (Acts 28:16–31)

Observations on the Plot and Closure for Luke-Acts

The plot synopsis can be elucidated further through the following observations emerging from the analysis, which confirms narrative closure for Luke-Acts.

One hero, one mandate. Although other protagonists are easily recognized, the identification of one hero (Jesus) in Luke-Acts through the narrative sequence model provides evidence for a unified plot. Each sequence moves around the reception or rejection of the hero's mandate, foretold, portrayed, and then finally confirmed. Three central transforming actions are enacted or endured by the hero whose effects result in the decrease of narrative tension between the raveling sequence and the unraveling sequence. Without these events involving the hero, there would be no sequel. Spiritual unity between God, Jesus, and the disciples allow for a continuation of the story from Jerusalem to Rome. Viewing Luke-Acts from this perspective argues for greater narrative unity and consequently continuity in the reader's experience.

Spiritual transformation. Evidence for a clear sense of narrative closure concerning Jesus' mandate comes through the identification and comparison of the initial and final orientations (sequences 1 and 5) and the dynamic process of spiritual transformation in the disciples and in those outside this circle (in sequences two and four).[55] The main emphasis of the narrator's portrayal is on Jesus' response to the spiritual need of salvation for the Jewish people and for the nations. The question of the restoration of Israel's kingdom and Jesus as heir of David's throne is secondary to this main emphasis.

One principal counterplot. The identification of one manifest counterplot, Satan's proposal to Jesus to rule the nations, is important evidence that the plot develops around the hero's impact on the Jews and the nations. Its position at the very beginning of the raveling sequence supports this hypothesis. It also functions as a control for the first point.

Narrative tension. On the reader's level, narrative tension develops through a sense of living (or reliving) what Jesus and his disciples experienced, namely their success and failures. The reader experiences a greater sense of certainty and satisfaction as the narrative progresses. Expectations

---

55. Points of non-closure appear in Luke-Acts, but some certainly depend on the reader's knowledge and competence. Narratively, some concern external prolepses, or theologically, prophecies awaiting fulfillment: (1) Jesus' return (Acts 1:11) and "the times of refreshing" (Acts 3:19–21); (2) the restored kingdom for Israel (Luke 1:32–33, 22:30 and Acts 1:6); (3) judgment of the Jews (and the nations)? Recompense and judgment of the people of Israel (Luke 3:17; cf. also 10:10–16; 12:49–51; 19:41–44; 22:30); (4) political deliverance from Israel's enemies (Luke 1:51–55; 68–71, 73–74); (5) Paul's trial in Rome (Acts 28:16, 30–31).

for illumination arise and are satisfied regarding the main questions about Jesus: how he will become what is promised about him in the proleptic portrait and how he will be recognized, received or rejected by various groups and individuals on the spiritual and human planes. Suspense is thus developed based on the anticipations about Jesus and the uncertainty that arises throughout the narrative when his mandate is resisted (Jesus' disciples), opposed (antagonists) or even apparently thwarted (via the crucifixion).

Pragmatic aim reached through normalization. In relation to the pragmatic aim of the narrative (Luke 1:4), the narrator has brought a collection of events about Jesus and his disciples into a coherent whole in accordance with Jewish Scriptures and intrinsic prophecies (internal prolepses) in Luke-Acts. It is plausible to imagine that Theophilus left this meaningful reading experience with a greater sense of certainty regarding the things that he had received about Jesus.

Questions for the Thoroughfare Motif within the Plot of Luke-Acts

This brief section is a bridge between the analysis of the plot and of the thoroughfare motif. It lists various types of questions that guide the analysis in Chapter 4 with the aim of understanding how the thoroughfare motif contributes to the plot's development for the reader's interpretation and experience. Other questions will be formulated using theory on literary motifs. Two general questions direct this analysis: Does the thoroughfare motif contribute to the exploration of the main questions of Luke-Acts (cognitive aspect) and (2) Does the narrator use the motif to elicit some response from the reader (pragmatic aspect)? Additionally, I present here some specific questions related to the five sequences: Does the thoroughfare motif contribute to the reader's understanding of the proleptic portrait of the hero described in the initial orientation? If so, how does it describe what Jesus will be or do? What expectations or questions might be raised in the reader's mind through this motif? Does the narrator use the motif to contribute to the characterization of protagonists or antagonists in the story? How does the narrator use the motif in the raveling, pivot, unraveling, and initial orientation? Is it central to the plot or only peripheral? Finally, what pragmatic response might the narrator seek to elicit through individual occurrences of the motif? And what cumulative effect might the motif have on the reader?

With these questions in mind, the discussion turns to the analysis of the thoroughfare motif in light of the plot of Luke-Acts.

PART TWO

Analysis of the Thoroughfare Motif's Performance within the Plot

3

First Encounters: Portraits of the Hero and the Forerunner

(Luke 1:5—3:38)

THIS DISCUSSION BUILDS ON the comparison between Jesus and John the Baptist in the initial orientation (Luke 1:5—3:38). As a part of the initial orientation, the infancy narratives in Luke 1-2 function as an overture to the rest of Luke-Acts by introducing certain important motifs that will be further orchestrated by the end of the narrative.[1] As Donald Juel states:

> The hymns and prophetic outbursts of various characters in Luke's story have the same function. They are appropriate to the situation, yet they offer an interpretation of events that both foreshadows what is to come and relates them to promises and motifs familiar from Israel's past. The hymns provide an interpretive framework within which the entire story can be understood. That they are unique to Luke only makes these songs all the more significant for interpreting his Gospel.[2]

Indeed, the first chords of the orchestra are struck here and the thoroughfare motif is one of those chords. Therefore, the objective here is to ascertain whether the motif enhances the initial orientation for the reader's entry to the storyworld. Are expectations or questions raised through their usage? How do they help set the stage for the reader's encounter of the story?

The initial orientation contains five occurrences of *hodos* (way) and one of *tribos* (path), used in the description of John the Baptist, Jesus, and

---

1. Cf. Fitzmyer, *Luke (I-IX)*, 163 and Minear, "Birth Stories," 114–18; 129.
2. Juel, *Luke-Acts*, 20–21.

Joseph and Mary's journey from Jerusalem. All six occurrences are figurative in meaning. Their most important contribution is in the proleptic portraits of John the Baptist and Jesus, as well as the portrayal of the fulfillment of John's mandate. Not only does the narrator use them in both portraitures, he also uses them to describe the relationship between the two characters, which extends into the raveling sequence. They are one of the many links deriving from the various doublets characterizing and interconnecting the two individuals.

In order to keep the flow of the discussion below, I indicate here that the occurrence of *hodos* in Luke 2:44 does not require particular attention since it merely indicates the distance traveled by Joseph and Mary ("a day's journey").[3] Although the expression contributes to the theme of journeying, the use of *hodos* here does not make a particular contribution to the plot; thus, it will not be a part of the discussion below.

Proleptic Portraits of John and Jesus via Zechariah's Canticle (Luke 1:76, 79)

The first two uses of *hodos* come through the voice of Zechariah in the passage traditionally called the "Benedictus" (Luke 1:67–79), a canticle containing praises to God and blessings for his son in relation to another individual called "the dawn from on high" (ἀνατολὴ ἐξ ὕψους). The two parts of the blessing have proleptic value, containing anticipations about the future work of the two protagonists. The narrator has already prepared the reader to interpret this passage through Gabriel's birth announcements and the meeting of Elizabeth and Mary. The objective of this discussion then is to understand how the narrator uses *hodos* to characterize further John and Jesus, though the latter is not explicitly mentioned as the referent. The discussion begins with Zechariah's words to John in verses 76–77, but verses 78–79 concerning Jesus are also included for context and ensuing discussion:

> [76] And you, child, will be called prophet of the Most High, for you will go before the Lord to prepare his ways, [77] [and] to give knowledge of salvation to his people through the forgiveness of their sins, [78] because of our God's merciful compassion, by which the dawn from on high will visit us, [79] to bring light to those who are dwelling in darkness and the shadow of death, [and] to lead our feet into the way of peace.

3. That is, in an adverbial qualifier indicating distance.

⁷⁶ Καὶ σὺ δέ, παιδίον, προφήτης ὑψίστου κληθήσῃ· προπορεύσῃ γὰρ ἐνώπιον κυρίου ἑτοιμάσαι ὁδοὺς αὐτοῦ, ⁷⁷ τοῦ δοῦναι γνῶσιν σωτηρίας τῷ λαῷ αὐτοῦ ἐν ἀφέσει ἁμαρτιῶν αὐτῶν, ⁷⁸ διὰ σπλάγχνα ἐλέους θεοῦ ἡμῶν, ἐν οἷς ἐπισκέψεται ἡμᾶς ἀνατολὴ ἐξ ὕψους, ⁷⁹ ἐπιφᾶναι τοῖς ἐν σκότει καὶ σκιᾷ θανάτου καθημένοις, τοῦ κατευθῦναι τοὺς πόδας ἡμῶν εἰς ὁδὸν εἰρήνης.

John the Baptist: Forerunner of the Lord's Ways (Luke 1:76)

After Zechariah praises God (1:68–75), he now speaks directly to his infant son whom he calls "the prophet of the Most High," which is comparable, yet still inferior, to the already announced title of Jesus, "the son of the Most High" (1:32). God sends these two individuals for a common purpose: the spiritual transformation of Israel, namely—in Gabriel's language—Israel's return to their God (cf. 1:16). The people are invited to leave one state and enter a better one, through reconciliation with their God. John has the task to prepare them for this transformation, and Gabriel's announcement has prepared the reader to imagine John as a forerunner before the Lord, similar to Elijah, by going before the Lord to make the people ready for him (1:17).[4] Now the narrator builds on this image: "You will go before the Lord" which is completed by two purpose clauses: "to prepare his ways" (v. 76) and "to give knowledge of salvation to his people through forgiveness of their sins" (v. 77).[5] Again, the image depicts the work of preparation by preceding the Lord so that the people might receive him and the blessings that come through him. As in Gabriel's prophecy, the transformation of the people from one state to another is also the final objective in Zechariah's prophecy, resulting in "salvation." Although Zechariah has already used "salvation" or "deliverance" (σωτηρία) twice in his canticle (vv. 69, 71), it is the first time that salvation is clearly linked to the idea of "forgiveness of sins," which is quite different from the allusions to political deliverance.

---

4. Both verses (1:17 and 1:76) share a similar syntactical structure: a verb of movement followed by two infinitive purpose clauses (the four infinitives are all aorist). The two main notions are clearly expressed: precede and prepare (1:17, προέρχομαι, ἑτοιμάζω, and κατασκευάζω (midd. part.) and 1:76, προπορεύομαι, ἑτοιμάζω).

5. The sense of the plural form here (ὁδοὺς), given its part in the overall picture, does not differ from that of the more common singular form (ὁδός, cf. Luke 3:4; 7:27). The emphasis is still on preparation. Bock (*Luke 1:19:50*, 197) suggests that "the plural is perhaps slightly more descriptive of all that God is doing to save."

Here some ambiguity arises—perhaps intentional?—regarding the referent of "Lord" (κύριος) in the phrases "before the Lord" and "his ways," since the narrator has already used κύριος for the God of Israel (1:15–17) and for Jesus in Elizabeth's exclamation (1:43), then again for the God of Israel (1:45).[6] The immediate context lends support to the referent as God (cf. "the Most High" in 1:76). In this sense, John Hughes is right in describing John the Baptist as being also "the forerunner of God."[7] God sends John to prepare for his intervention. In Luke-Acts, John, as the other characters in Luke's portrayal, must also discover what the exact nature of this divine intervention might be. Yet, John the Baptist is also portrayed as being conscious of preparing for another individual (3:15–17; 7:18–20). Thus, he is preparing for God's arrival, but he discovers later that he is also preparing specifically for Jesus, who is in effect "the Lord's Christ" (2:26).[8] Bock explains, "John goes before the God of Israel, because he goes before the salvation that is tied to the Messiah. In the Messiah, God's plan and design are found, so that when Messiah comes, God comes. John as a prophet will prepare for God's coming by clearing the way for him as he delivers his own in the Messiah."[9] Therefore, Luke uses *hodos*, along with other various elements, to create a picture of a forerunner who prepares the terrain where Jesus will pass by. The image befits John's role as the prophet of the Most High preparing the people to receive the divine visitor, Jesus ("the son of the Most High" 1:32; and "the dawn from on high" 1:78). Thus, the thoroughfare motif depicts an image of relationship between John and Jesus, stimulating the reader's imagination and curiosity. Therefore, this early use of *hodos* enhances the plot by helping to raise expectations and questions in the reader regarding John's role and the people's preparation. How will John prepare the ways of the Lord? What is going to happen when the Lord comes? Who among the people will receive John's message and prepare for the Lord's visitation?

---

6. An important example of the narrator's voice, among others, using κύριος instead of Ἰησοῦς is plainly visible in 7:13 and perhaps also in 7:19 (since the variant κύριον is a more probable reading than Ἰησοῦν). Cf. Bruce M. Metzger, *Textual*, 119.

7. Hughes, "John the Baptist," 191–218. His conclusion, however, that the "historical John" did not understand himself as being *also* the forerunner of Jesus, a specific Messianic figure, is not tenable. To do this, one would have to demonstrate more conclusively that the Lukan evidence (cf. Luke 3:15–17; 7:18–20; Acts 13:24–25; 19:4)—and other canonical material—is not reliable for a historical reconstruction of John's growing self-awareness of his preparation for the coming of another individual sent by God. For example, according to Hughes "the Coming One" refers only to Yahweh. Ibid., 195.

8. The phrase in Luke 2:26 illustrates the use of κύριος for God and χριστός for Jesus.

9. Bock, *Luke 1:1—9:50*, 189. Similarly, Talbert, *Reading Luke*, 30–31.

First Encounters: Portraits of the Hero and the Forerunner

Indeed, the uses of thoroughfare expressions continue in relation to John the Baptist; the voices of the narrator and Jesus will complete this picture. The following section focuses on the second part of Zechariah's blessing that fills in Jesus' proleptic portrait.

Jesus and "the Way of Peace" (Luke 1:79)

The second occurrence of *hodos* (1:79) follows closely the first one. It also helps depict the proleptic portrait of Jesus. Although it is an elliptic prolepsis (i.e., not an explicit referent), most commentators agree that verses 78–79 describe Jesus. Scholarly discussion focuses on the meaning of the expression "the dawn from on high" in Luke 1:78, particularly the uses of *anatolē* (ἀνατολή dawn) in the LXX (cf. Jer 23:5; Zech 3:8; 6:12) and its referent.[10] Many exegetes view *anatolē* in the LXX as a Messianic metaphor,[11] but not all concur that it refers to Jesus. NT evidence outside Luke-Acts is not particularly helpful for identifying the referent.[12] Some understand *anatolē* as a reference to a theophany[13] or to John the Baptist (cf. Mal 3:20 (LXX)).[14] Most scholars, however, interpret the expression as a reference to Jesus due to the Messianic references in the LXX, the qualifier "from on high" (ἐξ ὕψους),

---

10. In the LXX (cf. LEH, 44), ἀνατολή usually indicates the *east* (Nm 3:38) and expressions for eastward direction. Another use is "branch" or "sprout" (LEH, 44). The verb ἀνατέλλω (LEH, 44) mainly expresses the notions: "to make to rise up" (Gn 3:18), "to cause to spring forth" (Isa 61:11); "to rise", "to appear above the horizon (of the sun)" (Gn 32:32). Thus, ἀνατολή renders the Hebrew צֶמַח (branch or shoot), often considered a messianic title (especially Jer 23:5, צֶמַח צַדִּיק LXX ἀνατολὴν δικαίαν).

11. Yet, Bovon overstates the case: "'Ἀνατολή is a messianic metaphor, all exegetes agree on that. In the Septuagint, it can be used for צֶמַח, 'shoot', one of the stereotyped titles of the Messiah." Bovon, *Luc (1,1—9,50)*, 109.

12. The word ἀνατολή occurs ten times [or eleven with Mark 16:8] in the NT. Three main meanings have been identified (cf. BDAG, 74; BA, 123; Rusconi, 26): (1) the rising (of a star) in the singular (Matt 2:2, 9), cf. BDR §141n5 and §253n7; (2) in the plural the notion of *east* (Matt 2:1; 8:11; 24:27; Luke 13:29; Rev 16:12; 21:13; and (3) dawn, the morning star or the sun (1:78), which is the only occurrence that is not the object of a preposition (usually ἀπο or ἐν in Matt 2:2, 9). Cf. 2 Pet 1:19 (φωσφόρος) and Rev 22:16 (ὁ ἀστὴρ ὁ λαμπρὸς ὁ πρωϊνός).

13. Cf. Radl, *Lukas 1,1—9,50*, 127.

14. Fitzmyer, *Luke I–IX*, 387; Klein, *LkEv*, 125; and Vielhauer, *Geschichte*, 40. Vielhauer finds the remark "he was not the light" in John 1:8 as a polemic against the followers of John the Baptist. Yet, Brown (*Messiah*, 381n25) provides more convincing, extrinsic evidence for Jesus as a light (Matt 4:16; John 1:9; 3:19; 8:12; 9:4–5; 12:46; also Matt 2:2 for the star of Jesus).

and the following description of *anatolē* in verse 79.[15] The reader is prepared to interpret this expression as referring to Jesus due to the preceding comparisons in which Jesus is greater than John.[16] In addition, the implied reader may associate this allusion to Jesus through knowledge of its uses in Israel's Scriptures. In fact, Bock suggests that a double entendre may be present; Luke wishes to evoke in the reader associations with the dawn and branch images. Bock, however, consents that the dawn image is the dominant idea.[17] In fact, the meaning of *anatolē* is more likely "dawn"[18] rather than "branch"[19] due to the qualifying prepositional phrase "from on high" and the actions that the *anatolē* will perform, "to bring light" (ἐπιφᾶναι) and "to lead" (κατευθῦναι). Thus, according to Luke's use of the expression, Jesus will be similar to a dawn or sunrise from divine origin.[20] If this interpretation is correct, then Zechariah makes a significant transition in this prophetic utterance, passing from his son to a greater figure still to come.[21]

The blessing of John and the announcement of this dawn are joined by a short causal phrase in 1:78: "because of the merciful compassion of our God", which indicates the source of this initiative, the God of Israel, who had sent Gabriel (1:19, 26). The scene is now set for the reader: the people's miserable state has moved God to intervene and to lead them into a better state. God directs the program behind the scenes. He becomes the unseen, but active, protagonist who assures the forward movement of the recounted events in Luke-Acts, from beginning to end. Next, the relative clause "by which" (ἐν οἷς) introduces how this will happen through the description of Jesus as "a dawn from on high who will visit us." Paradoxically, "dawn" evokes the

15. See, for example, Plummer, *Luke*, 43–44; Schürmann, *LkEv*, 1:92; Tannehill, *Narrative*, 1:159; Bruggen, *Lucas*, 66–68; Johnson, *Luke*, 47–48; Green, *Luke*, 119; Meynet, *Luc*, 94; Eckey, *LkEv*. 1:127; Bassin, *Luc*, 123, 129–30; and Wolter, *LkEv*, 117. Louw and Nida concede the possibility of a Messianic reference, but they also offer an abstract rendering, "the bright dawn of salvation" (LN, 174).

16. These passages compare and contrast the two characters and finally indicate their vital relationship: the announcements of their birth; the meeting of their mothers; their births; the summaries of their growing up; and their respective ministries.

17. Bock, *Luke 1:1—9:50*, 192.

18. See Brown, *Messiah*, 374.

19. Farris recognizes both possibilities but opts for *sprout* or *root* due to "the house of David" in v. 69 and the possible messianic allusions to Jer 23:5 and Zech 3:8; 6:12. Farris, "Zechariah's Song," 895. Yet, the image of shining confirms that Luke is using the metaphor as a rising sun or star rather than branch. Cf. Brown, *Messiah*, 374 and Bovon, *Luc 1,1—9,50*, 109.

20. Cf. BDAG, 74; CPS, 62; Rusconi, 26; and ANLEX: s.v. ἀνατολή.

21. So Farris, "Zechariah's Song," 895–96.

rising movement of the sun and the light that it brings, and "from on high" signifies its divine origin.²² In light of the pattern of comparison between Jesus and John in Luke 1–3, and the description of the "dawn," Bovon's assessment is plausible: "In my opinion, for Luke and his source ἀνατολή is the subject of ἐπισκέψεται, "he will visit", and is not identical with the Baptizer. Otherwise, for whom would John prepare the way? ἐξ ὕψους, "from on high," certainly points to God, the ὕψιστος, the Most High, but is not equivalent. This expression differentiates an ordinary visitor come from earth from the Messiah come from God (cf. 1:32 and 35)."²³

The idea of divine visitation has already been mentioned by Zechariah: "Blessed be the Lord God of Israel, for he has visited and accomplished redemption for his people" (1:68). Now the narrator employs the future tense of the verb "to visit" (ἐπισκέπτομαι) to indicate another divine visitation for the people's benefit ("us" ἡμᾶς).²⁴ Similar to the structure in the description of John, this visitation of "the dawn" also consists of two main actions (expressed through infinitive purpose clauses): (1) to bring light to those who are sitting in darkness and in the shadow of death," and (2) "to guide our feet into the way of peace." This is the first occurrence of the illumination theme in Luke-Acts, and it appears with the beginnings of the complementary thoroughfare motif.²⁵ In the immediate context, the spiritual sense of these foreshadowed actions is justified by the precursor's role: "to give knowledge of salvation through the forgiveness of their sins," and by the poetic language of the two portraits.²⁶ When the descriptions of John the Baptist and Jesus are read together, Zechariah's canticle characterizes the people as being in spiritual need both for the forgiveness of their sins before God and for illumination, because they are in spiritual darkness, so much that they

---

22. Jacoby suggests ἐξ ὕψους as the equivalent of "from Yahweh," thus "the dawn from/of Yahweh." He argues ἀνατολή reflects the LXX translation of צֶמַח (sprout) based on the connection *inter alia* between ἀνατολή ἐξ ὕψους and יְהוָה צֶמַח in Isa 4:2. Jacoby, "ἀνατολή ἐξ ὕψους," 205–14. Yet, this interpretation does not explain Luke's contextualization of the expression with light and darkness imagery.

23. Bovon, *Luc 1,1—9,50*, 109.

24. The variant ἐπισκέψεται, though less supported, is the more natural reading given the parallel structure of verses 1:76–77 and their future verbs (κληθήσῃ, προπορεύσῃ). The aorist ἐπεσκέψατο was probably introduced later to harmonize it with the occurrence at the beginning of the pericope in 1:68. Cf. Bovon, *Luke 1:1—9:50*, 76; and Metzger, *Textual*, 110.

25. The theme of illumination can include sources of light, literal and figurative, and enlightenment, when an individual grasps a spiritual truth or recovers sight.

26. Ancient readers and auditors might have connected this language to Isa 9:1 (LXX). Cf. similar expressions in Psalm 106:10, 14 (LXX).

are under "the shadow of death."[27] The opposite of the illumination theme, "darkness" also appears here and runs through Luke-Acts.[28]

Comparable to a sunrise that closes the night and opens the day, the hero comes to help the people to see what they are now not able to see, that is, how to enter "the way of peace." Consequently, one aspect of the hero's mandate will be to help others to see, to illuminate them by providing God's instruction to the people. This picture is completed by the second notion of "guidance." This "dawn from on high" not only illuminates but also guides them out of this spiritual stupor, "the shadow of death," into a better destination, "the way of peace." The reader will gradually encounter the nature of this "darkness" and "shadow of death" as well as "the way of peace," and, in practical terms, how this will happen. Thus, collectively, this proleptic image depicts a transfer from one domain to another, a potentiality that might become a reality.

How should the expression "into the way of peace" be interpreted (a genitival construction, εἰς ὁδὸν εἰρήνης)? Does it mean, ". . . into the way that leads to peace,"[29] ". . . into the way characterized by peace" or ". . . into a peaceful way"? In keeping with the depicted imagery, the indications are the controlling verb "to guide," its direct object "our feet," which is qualified by the preposition "into" (εἰς) indicating movement into or toward the destination (a thoroughfare, "path" or "way"). Thus, the image is one of guidance toward or into a destination, another place, or, figuratively, another spiritual state. Based on the previous figure of salvation pertaining to John's mandate—to bring the people back to God (1:16) and to give them knowledge of salvation (1:77)—the image describing Jesus should also be understood as a figure of salvation.[30] His mandate is to bring the people into the way that leads to peace with God.[31] Similar to "shadow" coupled with an abstract state

---

27. Cf. LN, 173, 177.

28. The corresponding themes of *seeing* (figurative for understanding or recognizing) and *not seeing* (or *blindness*, figurative for not understanding or not recognizing) are also used throughout Luke-Acts and have interpretative value. Cf. Hartsock, *Sight and Blindness*, 172.

29. Cf. ὁδός occurrences when a qualifying genitive expresses the notion of direction (Matt 10:5 εἰς ὁδὸν ἐθνῶν; Heb 9:8 τὴν τῶν ἁγίων ὁδόν; 10:19 εἰς τὴν εἴσοδον τῶν ἁγίων; and Matt 4:15 ὁδὸν θαλάσσης. BDR (§166.2n2,3)

30. Eckey connects the use of "way of peace" to Isa 59:8, which Paul also cites (Ro 3:17), placing the expression in relation to the theme of salvation in Zechariah's praise. Eckey, *LkEv I*, 129.

31. So Plummer, *Luke*, 44. Moreover, two similar constructions with ὁδός and an abstract idea are "the way (that leads to) salvation" (Acts 16:17) and "the ways (that lead to) life" (Acts 2:28). The imagery of movement ("to guide into") in Luke 1:79 justifies this interpretation.

"death," the thoroughfare image is coupled with the abstract "peace" in order to convey an image of movement from one state to another, a transformation from spiritual darkness to peace with God.[32] Wolter rightly summarizes its narrative significance through the link with "peace": "That Luke certainly thinks of Jesus' preaching through this can be clearly recognized from the use of εἰρήνη ["peace"] in Luke 19:42 and Acts 10:36. Based on this, the "way of peace," which Israel should be led upon, is nothing other than the acceptance of Jesus' preaching."[33]

What is the significance of these occurrences of *hodos* for the plot? This is the only complete image in the initial orientation exemplifying the hero's anticipated transformation of the people.[34] Here Luke clearly portrays Jesus as an agent of spiritual transformation, whose beneficiaries, at this point in the narrative, are the people of Israel ("our feet" via Zechariah's voice). This proleptic image will expand in three ways: (1) its content through illustrations concerning Jesus' mandate (cf. 2:30–35; 3:16–17; 4:18–19); (2) its extent concerning the beneficiaries including the nations (e.g., through the illumination theme, Luke 2:31–32; Acts 26:23); and (3) its protagonists through whom it comes (e.g., Jesus' disciples as a light, cf. Acts 13:47; 26:17–18). The image mainly contributes to the description of Jesus as "savior" (1:69) rather than as heir of David's throne or "son of God." It prefigures Jesus's mandate that is announced by the angels and Simeon, thus adding a nuance to the reader's understanding about the salvation that Jesus would bring (cf. Luke 2:11, 30; 3:6; 5:4; 19:9–10). Spiritual deliverance comes from God to humanity through Jesus (Luke 24:47; Acts 2:38; 4:12; 5:31; 10:43; 13:26; 16:17; 28:28). In summary, the reader has encountered the beginnings of the thoroughfare motif and the broader illumination theme in relation to the hero involving Jesus and his disciples. Indeed, much of the narrative

---

32. If Meynet is correct (*Luc*, 88, 93–95), this image is enhanced by a concentric semantic construction by "ways" (v. 76) and "way" (v. 79), then "give knowledge" (v. 77) and "give light" (v. 79), and "sins" (v. 77) and "death" (v. 79). Syntactically, the structure is closer to A 1 2 c B 1 2 following the independent and dependent clauses (p. 88). This indicates another comparison between John and Jesus.

33. Wolter, *LkEv*, 118. Likewise, Tannehill notes the repetition of "visitation" and "peace" in key moments of Luke-Acts with reference to Jesus and his disciples. Tannehill, *Narrative*, 1:36.

34. Other images of Jesus' proleptic portrait do not provide a complete picture including the protagonist, his actions, and the beneficiaries, for example, his filial relationship with God (1:32, 35; 2:49; 3:22); heir of David's throne (1:32–33); and baptism and judgment (as the Christ 3:16–17).

tension builds on the responses to Jesus' light for their salvation, whether they "see," "know," or "recognize" it.[35]

Through this brief prolepsis, the reader understands once more that Jesus, though not yet born, will be superior to John the Baptist. Two strands of the thoroughfare motif are introduced here, separate but interconnected. John prepares the way for Jesus by preparing the people for his visitation, and Jesus continues by leading the people into the way of peace. As the narrative progresses, the reader will appreciate more fully the contribution of these passages to the plot as other aspects are introduced, and scenes of reception and rejection are illustrated. Not only does Luke introduce this picture as one of the key figures for transformation through Jesus, he also allows the reader to observe encounters in which thoroughfares are the tangible spaces of reception or rejection of Jesus, or indirectly of his disciples. They are physical portrayals of entering or not entering the way of peace, namely, spiritual transformation accomplished or resisted. In short, it contributes to the initial imagery of the spiritual landscape of Luke-Acts.

This elliptic prolepsis, "the dawn from on high," is a fine example of poetic beauty and subtlety that elicits wonder and curiosity. Pragmatically, its effect depends in part on the reader's repertoire, ability, and memory. Who is this "dawn from on high"? Is it Jesus introduced earlier (1:31)? Furthermore, suspense is added to the story. Who will receive this light and enter the way of peace? What effects will this really bring? How will the hero become a spiritual light and guide for the people? Who will oppose or reject it and stay in the shadow of death? This raises questions and expectations in the reader who will want to hear of their fulfillment by the end of the narrative as Tannehill summarizes, "But Luke's joyful birth story [the *Benedictus*] has a hidden lining of sadness. Great expectations contribute to a sense of tragedy if the expected happiness is lost. Part of the function of the birth story is to awaken a lively sense of great expectations so that readers will feel the tragic loss more vividly."[36] Through this passage, some of the initial state of the people has been clarified for the reader and a transformation anticipated. This will be a threat by spiritual and human forces. As the narrative progresses, darkness symbolically reveals Satan's dominion (Luke 22:53; Acts 26:18). For this reason, Jesus' light for the path to peace will be

---

35. Cf. Tannehill (*Narrative*, 1:37–38) for thematic links such as light imagery, salvation, and peace.

36. Ibid., 1:36–37.

violently opposed.³⁷ Narrative tension becomes more acute as uncertainty of its fulfillment grows.

John the Baptist and "the Way for the Lord" (Luke 3:4–5)

Following the stories of Jesus' birth and childhood, the reader returns to John the Baptist in Luke 3 viewing briefly the beginning of the realization of John's proleptic portrait. John is indeed preparing the people for the hero. He is depicted against the backdrop of the political and religious leadership (3:1–2) as one "preaching a baptism of repentance" whose final objective, "for the forgiveness of sins" (3:3), echoes Zechariah's words (1:77). Again, salvation through "forgiveness of sins" is repeated; thus, it becomes a key expression that qualifies the nature of this projected spiritual transformation (cf. Luke 24:47; Acts 2:38; 5:31; 10:43; 13:38; 26:18). At this point, the reader (re)learns that not only Gabriel and Zechariah had foretold of John's prophetic work, but the prophet Isaiah also had done so (Isa 40:3–5 LXX cited in Luke 3:4–6). In this way, Luke bolsters his narrative strategy since John the Baptist must be seen as part of Jesus' mandate (7:30). As in other key moments of the narrative (e.g., Nazareth and Rome), Isaiah's intertextual voice is integrated into the plot in order to provide coherence for the reader's experience and growing sense of certainty. Similar to the function of the passage in Isaiah (cf. Isa 40:3, 10), Luke overtakes this material in order to illustrate for his reader the grandeur of this moment: God is coming and has sent a messenger to prepare his people. Tannehill sums up well its proleptic value: "This quotation from Isaiah not only interprets John's special mission but reveals the purpose of God which underlies the whole narrative of Luke-Acts."³⁸

The two occurrences of "way" and one occurrence of "path" help the reader to imagine the significance of this preparatory work. John is linked to "the voice of one crying" through the prepositional phrase "in the wilderness" (ἐν τῇ ἐρήμῳ 3:2, 4). It is noteworthy that the voice's exhortation in the assimilated citation is this time addressed to the people ("prepare" and "make") inviting the people to participate in the preparation of the way of the Lord (3:4–6):

---

37. The images in this figure of transformation are echoed later in Jesus' description of Paul's mandate, which illustrates their spiritual unity (Acts 26:18).

38. Tannehill, *Narrative*, 1:47.

⁴ As it is written in the book of the words of Isaiah the prophet: "A voice of one crying in the wilderness: Prepare the way for the Lord, make his paths straight; ⁵ every ravine will be filled and every mountain will be made low, and the crooked will become straight and the rough (ways will become) level ways, ⁶ and all flesh will see the salvation of God.'"

⁴ὡς γέγραπται ἐν βίβλῳ λόγων Ἡσαΐου τοῦ προφήτου· φωνὴ βοῶντος ἐν τῇ ἐρήμῳ· ἑτοιμάσατε τὴν ὁδὸν κυρίου, εὐθείας ποιεῖτε τὰς τρίβους αὐτοῦ· ⁵πᾶσα φάραγξ πληρωθήσεται καὶ πᾶν ὄρος καὶ βουνὸς ταπεινωθήσεται, καὶ ἔσται τὰ σκολιὰ εἰς εὐθείαν καὶ αἱ τραχεῖαι εἰς ὁδοὺς λείας· ⁶καὶ ὄψεται πᾶσα σὰρξ τὸ σωτήριον τοῦ θεοῦ.

The first parallelism with thoroughfare expressions is introduced here: "Prepare the way for the Lord, make his paths straight." As integrated into the narrative, the reader encounters again a picture of preparation for the reception of the divine visitor. The genitival construction "the way of the Lord" (τὴν ὁδὸν κυρίου) is best understood figuratively in light of the imagery and the controlling verb "prepare" (ἑτοιμάζω): "Prepare the way *for the Lord*, that is, the one on which he will travel."[39] Similarly, "Make the paths *that he will travel on* straight!" Given the above images, no semantic difference seems present between the use of the singular form of *hodos* (ὁδός) here and its plural form *hodous* (ὁδούς) in Luke 1:76. This is confirmed through the above parallelism between the singular *hodon* (ὁδόν) and the plural *tribous* (τρίβους). It is an example of stylistic variation. Narratively, as integrated into the story, the difference is that the people are also invited to join in this activity, certainly not to build roads, but to participate in the spiritual preparation for the Messiah's visitation. Similar to Mark 1:3 and Matthew 3:3, it can be argued that the narrator here understands "Lord" in 3:4 as a reference to Jesus via textual evidence in the following phrase "his ways" (τὰς τρίβους αὐτοῦ), which is less explicit than the "for our God" in the MT (מְסִלָּה לֵאלֹהֵינוּ) and "of our God" in the LXX (τὰς τρίβους τοῦ θεοῦ ἡμῶν).[40]

Next, the narrator includes verses 5–6 to depict more vividly this divine intervention for the reader's imagination: ". . . every ravine will be filled and every mountain will be made low, and the crooked will become straight and the rough (ways will become) level ways, and all flesh will see the salvation of God." The natural imagery of ravines, mountains, and paths add to the

---

39. Cf. CPS, 103–4, 234 for thoroughfare expressions qualified by a genitive (κυρίου, αὐτοῦ, σου).

40. Bovon (*Luc 1,1—9,50*, 163, 167) attributes this "correction" to Q.

First Encounters: Portraits of the Hero and the Forerunner

expectation of the whole creation being prepared for the Lord's arrival, so that all obstacles to his approach might be removed. The expression *ta skolia* (τὰ σκολιά n. pl.) refers to that which is crooked (perhaps "crooked places") which needs transformation[41] into a straight road.[42] The reader will meet again the notions of "crooked" and "straight" regarding people's relation to God (Acts 2:40; 8:21; 13:10). Tannehill suggests that these images reflect John's preaching of repentance and the expected effects: ". . . he [John] prepares a repentant people, a people ready to receive the Lord because they have passed through the drastic leveling and straightening that Isaiah described."[43] In short, things need to be made right for the Lord's visit; first with God (1:16; 1:77) but also among themselves (1:17). Part of the narrative tension in Luke-Acts develops around the question whether the people support John in preparing the way for the Lord by preparing themselves.

The last verse of this citation, "and all flesh will see the salvation of God," adds another element to the early development of the theme of salvation. The expression "all flesh will see" hints at God's salvation going beyond the Jewish people, since Luke's use of the expression "all flesh" appears to be a metaphor for "all nations" (or "all humanity").[44] In fact, unlike Mark and Matthew, Luke includes Isa 40:5 to signal to the reader that this manifestation of God has to do with "salvation" and that "all flesh" will see it (Luke 3:6). John's warning of judgment against their false sense of ethnocentric security supports this notion (3:7–9).

Immediately following this citation, the reader receives some confirmation that John's preparation for Jesus has begun to bear fruit toward the above purpose. Positive reactions are indicated by the questions asked by the multitudes (3:10), even among some unlikely responsive groups, such as tax collectors (3:12) and soldiers (3:14).[45] This marks the beginning of a growing

---

41. Expressed via εἰμί accompanied by the preposition εἰς expressing the predicate nominative (BDR §145n3).

42. Here ὁδός is understood via εὐθείαν (feminine, singular) and confirmed by the parallelism with the second occurrence of ὁδός in the expression εἰς ὁδοὺς λείας. Plummer (*Luke*, 87) shows this in his translation: "'The crooked *places* shall become straight *ways*, and the rough *ways* smooth ways': i.e. roads shall be made where there were none before, and bad roads shall be made good roads."

43. Tannehill, *Narrative*, 1:48.

44. Several scholars interpret this as Luke's intention: Robinson, "Way of the Lord," 61; Dupont, "La conclusion des Actes," 509; and Tannehill, *Narrative*, 1:40, 47. See also, Johnson, *Luke*, 67–68; Bovon, *Luc 1,1—9,50*; and, *Luca*, 50. Curiously, the Lukan text does not contain the first part of Isa 40:5 LXX, καὶ ὀφθήσεται ἡ δόξα κυρίου, which in Bovon's words is "inexplicable." Bovon, *Luc 1,1—9,50*, 164.

45. Most commentators understand this substantival participle of στρατεύομαι to

sense that salvation is going to reach the nonreligious, the marginalized, or even the despised, among the Jewish people. All this activity creates suspense in the people ("the people were in a state of expectation," 3:15a) who ask a greater question: ". . . all were wondering in their hearts about John whether he might be the Christ" (3:15b). From this point on, the narrator makes a natural transition from John to Jesus. John points the crowd to another individual, "the one who is mightier than I am" (3:16) and makes a comparison of their baptisms. For this reason, John is described as preaching the good news.[46] Nevertheless, this is contrasted when the reader becomes informed of the opposition to John's ministry through his conflict with Herod, which leads to his imprisonment (3:18–20). The initial orientation thus ends with John in prison and Jesus' identity is confirmed as the Christ and Son of God through the prolepses, his baptism, his father's voice, the presence of the Holy Spirit, and finally his genealogy. The reader has received indications of conflict and opposition, but not yet overtly against the hero on the action level, thus confirming the ending of the initial orientation. The scene has been set for the reader's interpretation and experience of the following narrative sequences.

Summary of the Thoroughfare Motif in the Initial Orientation

In the initial orientation, the narrator has effectively introduced to the reader two interconnected strands of the thoroughfare motif that qualify the proleptic portraits of the hero (Jesus) and his precursor (John the Baptist). The first strand concerns John the Baptist, who is already depicted as accomplishing his mandate (3:4–5). As the forerunner of Jesus, John goes before him and prepares his way by preparing the people to receive him (1:76–77). The second strand awaits its activation in the raveling sequence. Both strands portray a response to the initial state that must be changed: the people are in spiritual darkness. They must turn to the God of Israel and receive forgiveness for their sins. A better state, "the way of peace," is promised for those who receive the hero's light and allow themselves to be led by him as "the dawn from on high" (1:78–79). As is true for the overall portrayals of John and Jesus, the second strand also indicates that the hero is superior to his precursor.

---

refer to Herod's soldiers, not to Roman soldiers, assisting the tax collectors; thus, not warranting an early reception scene among the nations. Cf. Plummer, *Luke*, 92; and Bassin (*Luc*, 170) who refers to Lagrange, *Évangile*, 110.

46. This is the third occurrence of εὐαγγελίζω, first with Gabriel (1:19) and then with an angel of the Lord (2:10).

First Encounters: Portraits of the Hero and the Forerunner

Therefore, the thoroughfare motif, so far in the narrative, has helped Theophilus (and broader audience) to enter the storyworld by preparing his interpretation and experience of characters as they are posited in relation to John the Baptist and, especially, Jesus. The reader's need for certainty will be satisfied since he will progressively observe Jesus providing light so that others might enter into the way of peace. To do this, Luke will highlight the intermingling of the illumination theme and the thoroughfare motif in key moments of the plot. This comprehensive proleptic image of Jesus as "the dawn from on high" helps the reader to anticipate what should take place concerning the hero. It raises expectations and questions requiring further enlightenment.[47] What does it mean that Jesus' light will lead people into the way of peace? Who will recognize his light and be lead into the way of peace? In this sense, the occurrences of *hodos* in Luke 1:78–79, along with other early key prolepses concerning Jesus,[48] can be understood as having symbolic (or programmatic) value for Luke-Acts.[49] This word-picture is like an image at the beginning of a film that passes, quickly but forcefully, across the screen. It prepares the audience for the experience of the transformational thrust of Luke's story. Much focus will be given to this portrayal of Jesus since previous research has not underlined its narrative and theological force. This is further justified by the view that Jesus is the hero not only of Luke, but also of Acts, and that the narrative tension develops around the question of his mandate and reception and rejection among the Jews and the nations. As one of the anticipated images of what should happen through the hero, to various persons and through various means, attention will be given to its realization and opposition in the analysis below.

For the above reasons, the very early appearance of the thoroughfare motif in Luke-Acts is strong evidence that it is a plot-intensive motif because of its objective and pragmatic contribution to the plot centered on Jesus. In the following sequences, it will be noted how the thoroughfare motif enhances the plot that is centered on the hero's mandate. Yet, the strand concerning the relationship between John the Baptist and Jesus still awaits closure. This takes place in the raveling sequence through the next appearance of the thoroughfare motif to which the discussion now turns.

---

47. In Roland Barthes's terms, they are part of the text's *hermeneutic* and *proairetic* codes. Barthes, *S/Z*, 21–24.

48. Here are other early proleptic utterances: Gabriel (Luke 1:31–33, 35), the angels' (Luke 2:11), Simeon (Luke 2:26–35), John the Baptist (Luke 3:15–17), God (Luke 3:22), and finally Jesus (Luke 4:17–21).

49. *Proleptic* refers to the narrative structure and *programmatic* to the author's theological program.

4

Contrasting Encounters: Thoroughfare Imagery for and against the Hero

(Luke 4:1—23:56)

THE RAVELING SEQUENCE CONCERNS various responses to Jesus and spiritual and human opposition to the realization of his proleptic portrait. This chapter elucidates the thoroughfare motif's contribution to the characterization of Jesus, John the Baptist, and Jesus' disciples. The motif enhances the reader's interpretation and experience of the narrative tension that becomes acute in this sequence.

On the Road Transition from John the Baptist to Jesus' Disciples

This section considers how the reader encounters thoroughfare expressions describing the positive evaluation of John the Baptist's mandate and the transition from him to Jesus' disciples. Thus, the two strands of the motif continue to develop and then converge.

Positive Closure between John and Jesus (Luke 7:27)

The first occurrence of thoroughfare imagery in the raveling sequence is *hodos* (7:27). It helps describe the relationship between John the Baptist and Jesus. The narrator has not mentioned John or his disciples on the action level since before Jesus' baptism. From Luke 4 on, the reader experiences the plot's raveling by watching Jesus' implementation of his proleptic portrait in the face of spiritual and human opposition. The reader now knows that Satan is working directly and indirectly against Jesus. Moreover, Jesus' disciples have been woven into the story from Luke 5 on, creating two distinct camps—individuals and groups—portrayed according to their recognition of and response to the hero. This exemplifies the antithetical nature of Luke-Acts.

John comes back into the spotlight through an extended passage (7:18–35), which flows naturally from the preceding one because it concerns the spread of the report of Jesus raising a dead man in Nain. The people's reaction is positive, evidenced by great exclamations about Jesus' identity ("a great prophet") and that God has visited his people (7:16, cf. 1:68, 78). Ironically, this is in stark contrast with John's situation: he is in prison and uncertain about Jesus' identity. In fact, the reader might wonder what had happened to John and what Jesus actually thinks of him since no contact has been mentioned between the two (even at Jesus' baptism, which is presumably a gap that the reader can fill). The reader can assume that John is still in prison per Herod's orders (3:19–20). This adds some degree of curiosity creating in the reader the need for closure.

The reader learns that the report of this miracle spread throughout Judea and the surrounding district, and that John's disciples report these events to him. Being in prison and unable to go see for himself, John sends his disciples with an unexpected question: "Are you the one who is to come, or should we look for another?" It echoes the people's question in Luke 3:15. This, ironically, comes from Jesus' forerunner, about whom one would least expect to have some uncertainty about Jesus' identity.[1] Is it possible that John does not "see" clearly? The reader receives Jesus' point of view to supplement what had already been said about John through the voices of Gabriel, Zechariah, and the narrator (as well as the intertextual voice of Isaiah). Jesus responds affirmatively to John's disciples by showing them his deeds and referring to Scripture about himself and John. After their departure, Jesus uses this occasion to speak to the crowds about John (7:24). The irony of the passage is that the situation has now turned: the Messiah speaks to the crowds about the identity of the precursor and their relationship.[2] Now the thoroughfare motif reappears as Jesus provides an authoritative explanation about John. Again, *hodos* appears in a biblical citation, which introduces another intertextual voice into the narrative, another authoritative link to the Jewish prophetic tradition for the reader.[3] Due to John's relationship to

---

1. Cf. Bovon, *Luc 1,1—9,50*, 365.
2. Meynet (*Luc*, 325, 327) notes well the paradoxes of this ironic situation.
3. This citation is similar to the first part of Mal 3:1 LXX and with the first part of

him, Jesus describes him as "more than a prophet" (7:26) and "greater than all those born of women" (7:28) and then illustrates his importance with the citation:

> This is the one about whom it is written: 'Behold, I am sending my messenger ahead of you; he will prepare your way before you.'
>
> οὗτός ἐστιν περὶ οὗ γέγραπται· ἰδοὺ ἀποστέλλω τὸν ἄγγελόν μου πρὸ προσώπου σου, κατασκευάσει τὴν ὁδόν σου ἔμπροσθέν σου.

The two main actions echoes previous descriptions of John the Baptist's mandate: "to go before" (understood via πρὸ προσώπου σου and ἔμπροσθέν σου) and "to prepare" (κατασκευάσει), whose direct object is again the figurative "way." Gianfranco Nolli makes a suggestive observation that *hodos* is accompanied by the article because it is known from Scripture. The article is absent in the LXX (as is "your" σου). Perhaps then, Luke's addition of the article provides some emphasis: "the way, that is, the one that was spoken about in Scripture."[4] Even so, given the narrator's construction of this familiar pattern, the reader is able to interpret this illustration as a double appropriation—first by Jesus then by the narrator—via a general citation formula (i.e., no explicit prophet is mentioned). In Jesus' appropriation of the passage, the speaker in the citation is God, the messenger is John, and "you" represents Jesus.[5] Again, Luke expresses John's spiritual preparation for Jesus' arrival through thoroughfare imagery.[6] His privileged role in Jesus' mandate explains his qualification as one who is "more than a prophet" (7:26). Jesus' appropriation of Jewish Scriptures, using this *precursor-way-hero* image, now explicitly demonstrates his self-awareness of their relationship and confirms Gabriel's words linking John the Baptist to the prophet Elijah (1:17).[7] Thus, the reader encounters again the narrative strategy linking John to Israel's

---

Ex 23:20. See Plummer, *Luke*, 204; Johnson, *Luke*, 123. Contra the latter connection, see Archer and Chirichigno, *Old Testament*, 165.

4. Nolli, *Luca*, 314.

5. So Fitzmyer, *Luke I–IX*, 671, 674 and Radl, *Lukas 1,1—9,50*, 472–73. Bock understands the referent "you" (σου) for the people and not Jesus, based on the background of Ex 23:20. Bock, *Luke 1:1—9:50*, 672–75.

6. Cf. CPS, 103–4, 234 for the use of thoroughfare expressions a genitive qualifier (κυρίου, αὐτοῦ, σου).

7. Luke has integrated this sending language into his portrayal of Jesus and his messengers (e.g., in 9:52 sending, going before, and preparing). Moreover, the act of sending via ἀποστέλλω (1 person sg.) occurs only in Jesus' voice (10:3 and 24:49 for the disciples; and Acts 26:17 for Paul). Cf. also Ananias's statement to Saul, Σαοὺλ ἀδελφέ, ὁ κύριος ἀπέσταλκέν με (9:17).

prophetic tradition and by positing people based on their reception of John in relation to the hero. This is forcefully illustrated by Luke's authoritative *narrative aside* (Luke 7:29–30).

What is the desired response to the narrator's appropriation of this cited passage? This intertextual support, like the citation of Isaiah 40:3–5 in Luke 3:4–6, buttresses the narrator's argument that John and Jesus are from God and consequently must be received as such. Together they are an indivisible pair, both working toward the realization of God's purposes. This use of redundancy provides assurance for the reader since the citation illustrates once again the correct interpretation of John's relationship to the hero. He is clearly posited on the side of those who receive Jesus. In addition, despite his doubts, John continues to be a positive example for the reader. John has accomplished his mandate: he has prepared the way for the Lord by preparing the people for him. Thus, the thoroughfare motif has played an essential part in depicting Jesus and John's relationship, and it has helped to provide closure to it, for John no longer appears on the action level, nor his reaction to Jesus' response, or his death. His mandate was accomplished; this is Luke's main concern for his audience.

Thus, John the Baptist plays a fundamental role in the earliest part of the narrative confirming the promises said about him, but then gradually fades out of the narrator's focus.[8] Nonetheless, despite the lack of John the Baptist's presence on the level of action in the rest of the narrative, this does not diminish the interpretative value that his figure has for the rest of Luke-Acts, for the reader receives other indications evaluating positively John's role and his disciples' integration into Jesus' movement. Subsequently, the reader's attention will be primarily on Jesus and his disciples' involvement in the mandate.

Excursus: the Seed along the Road (Luke 8:5, 12)

This brief section is an excursus since the occurrences are not directly related to John the Baptist or Jesus' disciples. The two occurrences of *hodos* (8:5, 12) in the Parable of the Sower merit some attention due to their part in creating categories of response to the hero's teaching, the theme of spiritual opposition, and the importance of spiritual understanding (cf. verse 10).[9] Moreover, reading Luke-Acts together requires some commentary on

---

8. Secondary characters in Luke-Acts tend to be phased out when no longer pertinent (Marguerat, "Luc, metteur en scène," 295).

9. The spiritual battle is clear within the first group of scattered seed, but subtle in the

Schuyler Brown's suggestion for an allegorical interpretation of "the way" (τὴν ὁδόν) in Luke 8:5 in relation to the unmodified *hodos* in Acts.

Johnson delineates and entitles appropriately the greater passage (8:1–21) as "Gathering the People of Faith," since the context concerns traveling for the proclamation of the kingdom of God (8:1).[10] The narrator specifically mentions those present with Jesus, "the twelve" and women disciples healed by Jesus. This intimate circle of disciples contrasts with "a great crowd" and "those who were coming to him from every town" (v. 4). The larger passage closes with the visit of Jesus' mother and brothers. His reaction to their visit emphasizes again their relation to him through proper reception of the word of God. The position of the Parable of the Sower before the disciples' missions (Luke 9 and 10) prepares the reader to understand the requirements of discipleship and to anticipate various responses to their teaching.

The parable appears to be addressed to the crowd, but the request for interpretation comes from the disciples. Jesus prefaces his answer by informing them that the kingdom of God is revealed to them without parables, but to the crowds with parables in order to reveal their spiritual state. Jesus then provides, apparently privately, the parable's interpretation.[11] Expressions with *hodos* occur in the following verses:

> 8:5 The sower went out to sow his seed. While he was sowing, some seed fell along the way [παρὰ τὴν ὁδόν]; it was trampled, and the wild birds devoured it.
>
> 8:12 But the ones that fell along the path [παρὰ τὴν ὁδόν] are those who have heard, then the devil comes and removes the word from their hearts, so that they may not believe and be saved.

In Jesus' interpretation (v. 12), the seed fallen along the path represents the situation in which people have heard the word of God (Jesus' teaching), but the devil, as the birds do in the image, remove the word from their hearts, therefore preventing them from believing lest they be saved.[12] This is the only group of seed that represents no apparent progress. Yet, Brown

---

other groups of seed (Bock, *Luke 1:1—9:50*, 734).

10. Johnson, *Luke*, 130–35.

11. Tannehill notes the interaction of the disciples regarding the parable's interpretation and its pertinence to their training as preachers. The family's visit is also "an opportunity for Jesus to make a further comment about those "who hear the word of God and do it." Tannehill, *Narrative*, 1:212.

12. Perhaps not represent a typical sowing, but rather a very generous sowing; thus, it is a parable and not a similitude (Nolland, *Luke 1—9.20*, 372–73).

suggests that this straightforward explanation of *hodos* might have greater significance in Luke-Acts:

> The question arises whether Luke may not have intended τὴν ὁδόν in Lk 8,5.12 to be understood in terms of the absolute usage of "the Way" in Acts. In the interpretation of the parable οἱ παρὰ τὴν ὁδόν are those who do not "believe", i.e. become Christians. Luke could have taken παρὰ τὴν ὁδόν here, as in 18,35 to mean "alongside the Way" and understood the expression allegorically as a designation for those outside the church. This supposition is not weakened by the fact that Palestinian farmers actually sowed on the road (Jeremias, *Gleichnisse*, 6). Our question concerns not the original sense of the parable but Luke's understanding of its allegorical interpretation.[13]

This creative interpretation, however, lacks textual support. For example, the blind beggar near Jericho is described as sitting along the road (παρὰ τὴν ὁδόν 18:35)—the only other construction with "along" and "way" (παρά and ὁδός)—and he receives Jesus. Based on the image above, the blind man should have rejected Jesus. It is difficult to think that the expression could be used allegorically to describe his spiritual state (not a believer) prior to his encounter with Jesus, and only then he received Jesus on the road after he drew near to him. The same could be argued for Zacchaeus who is clearly along the road before he received Jesus. Other scenes of reception will be observed in which thoroughfare terms provide the physical setting for the reception of Jesus. Should one then argue that they were already *on the way* (thus, already "believers") when they encountered Jesus since "along" (παρά) is not used? Brown's suggestion is not convincing; thus, it is reasonable to discard the notion that "along the way" anticipates those people who are not of "the Way" in the second volume.

It may be concluded that the uses of *hodos* in this parable contribute to the overall picture of degrees of spiritual reception, to receive and act on the word of God. The reader is thus encouraged to be a disciple like the fertile ground and dissuaded to be like the other types of ground, especially not like the hard, unreceptive ground *along the way*. The following discussions focus on the uses of *hodos* that express the involvement of Jesus' disciples in his mandate.

---

13. Brown, *Apostasy*, 138n604.

Jesus's Disciples on the Road for Mission (Luke 9:3)

The thoroughfare motif contributes to closure on John's ministry of spiritual preparation of the people. The focus is now on Jesus and his disciples, and the reader learns in Luke 9 and 10 that the disciples begin to have a greater role in the realization of Jesus' mandate. This provides continuity between John the Baptist and Jesus' disciples. In this context, the reader encounters three occurrences of thoroughfare when Jesus prepares his disciples to go before him in two different journeys (9:3, 57; 10:10). In between the two trips, there is also a thoroughfare rejection scene (9:57), which illustrates the difference between those who follow Jesus and three "would-be disciples."

Due to the similarities between the two journey scenes, some common elements are mentioned here. Both scenes have three parts: commission, mission, and debriefing. In both scenes, *hodos* occurs in the commission sections, namely, as part of Jesus' instructions to his disciples. Both recall John the Baptist's ministry of preparation for Jesus.

In the first scene (9:1–10), Jesus uses *hodos* in his command, "Do not take anything for the road" (μηδὲν αἴρετε εἰς τὴν ὁδόν 9:3), which is explicitly described by the complements that follow introduced by the conjunction "nor" (μήτε), "neither a staff, nor a bag, nor bread, nor money, nor to have two tunics [each]." For this expression with *hodos* (εἰς τὴν ὁδόν), one could render it literally, "for the road,"[14] or, figuratively, by extension, "for the journey."[15] In any case, narratively, the imagery of *hodos* helps portray Jesus' disciples in their greater involvement in his mandate, namely, movement toward the people in preparation for Jesus' reception. The object then is to give instructions how they are to accomplish their mandate *as they take to the road*. Some similarities between John's role and the disciples' role begin to emerge. Similar to John, they have people as the focus of their mission. As such, they are collaborators in Jesus' mandate, because they prepare the people for him. They also perform their assignment with minimal mate-

---

14. Marshall (*Luke*, 352) comments on the article in εἰς τὴν ὁδόν: "Luke's addition of the article with ὁδός may be due to Q, 10:4, or perhaps to indicate that one particular journey is in mind." No particular emphasis is present here.

15. Various values for *hodos* reflect the expressions available in the target language: "Take nothing on the road . . . ." (Johnson, *Luke*, 144); "Ne prenez rien pour la route . . ." (Meynet, *Luc*, 394); "Nehmt nichts mit auf den Weg . . ." (Radl, *Lukas 1,1—9,50*, 579; so Schürmann, *LkEv*, vol. 2, 499). Also, by extension, "journey": "Non prendete nulla per il viaggio . . ." Nolli (*Luca*, 401); "Take no provisions for the journey . . ." (Fitzmyer, *Luke I–IX*, 753). *Hodos* has a stronger sense of journey in *ex hodou* (ἐξ ὁδοῦ Luke 11:6): literally "from (a) road", or, better in English, "from a journey."

rial possessions (cf. 7:25). There is also the aspect of conflict and the task to pronounce judgment on those who do not receive their message (9:5). This element continues in the second mission passage in connection with a thoroughfare setting (10:10). Some differences, however, exist with respect to John's ministry. Their mission includes three tasks: to set people free from evil spirits, heal the sick, and preach the kingdom of God (9:1-2). Thus, they are to imitate their master, which fulfills Jesus' promise to Peter ("from now on you will be catching men" 5:10). The twelve are now a part of the hero's mandate, which began with John, and is on the move for the people's transformation. The more extensive mission in 10:1-24 and Jesus' command to them in 24:46-49 for an even greater mission leads Tannehill to describe these links as examples of "climactic parallelism."[16] These connections with John the Baptist are further supported by the mention of Herod's reaction to this activity, who is "very perplexed" and wishes to see Jesus (9:7-9). As this type of activity increases, opposition to it grows as well. This prepares the reader for the moment when Herod's name is mentioned as a threat (13:31). All of these elements—sending, preaching, conflict, and judgment—echo past events early in the story and foreshadow later developments in the plot.

In between the above occurrence of *hodos* and two others related to the disciples in Luke 10 is an occurrence depicting another category of persons, "the would-be disciples."

Would-be Disciples on the Road (Luke 9:57)

The next occurrence of *hodos* appears in the description of three individuals who reject Jesus' invitation to follow him: "And as they were going on the road, someone said to him: "I will follow you wherever you go" (Καὶ πορευομένων αὐτῶν ἐν τῇ ὁδῷ εἶπέν τις πρὸς αὐτόν· ἀκολουθήσω σοι ὅπου ἐὰν ἀπέρχῃ 9:57). At this point in the narrative, the reader comes to the borders of Samaritan territory, which provides a key indication of Jesus' intention to go to Jerusalem (9:51). Following this major shift in the story, Luke indicates that this stage will not be without difficulty. Jesus sends messengers before him to seek passage through a Samaritan village. They refuse his request because he was travelling to Jerusalem. After his disciples' reaction to this rejection, Jesus rebukes them by reminding them that divine destruction of that village would not be in line with his mandate "to save" (9:56). It is not clear from the text whether he tried to enter another Samaritan village.

16. Tannehill, *Narrative*, 1:216.

The use of the verb "go" (πορεύομαι) here and in the ending of the rejection story in Nazareth (4:30) provides a suggestive narrative link.[17] Luke underlines that the hero will not stop in the face of opposition. Johnson thinks the second mission takes place in Samaritan territory and is supported by Jesus' command to not greet anyone on the road (due to danger) and by the placement of the parable of the Good Samaritan (10:30–37).[18]

Other rejection episodes follow this conflict with the Samaritans. The first has the physical setting "on the road" (ἐν τῇ ὁδῷ), which is actually the first occurrence in which thoroughfare terms depict an encounter with Jesus (9:57). The precise location of the passage, as in much of the central travel section, is quite vague (9:57–62). What is essential to the narrator is that Jesus is still on the move toward Jerusalem, accomplishing his mandate. Three other thoroughfare reception scenes will follow in the raveling sequence before Jesus enters Jerusalem. The narrator highlights here three individuals, who seem to have good intentions, but do not follow Jesus after their encounter with him. The scene takes place just before the mission of the seventy disciples (10:1–24). The implicit evaluation is clear for the reader: they are not worthy to take part in this mission.

The first and third individuals express initiative to follow Jesus and the second one is actually invited by Jesus to follow him. Therefore, the scene is similar to the very personal interaction that Jesus had with his disciples at the beginning (5:8–11; 27–28). This invitation implies following him, which, in the execution of his mandate, meant going to people, journeying on roads, and not having fixed places to stay (9:58). Marshall sums it up well: "The thought is of belonging to the close group of disciples who accompanied Jesus on his travels rather than to the wider group who were not called to be with him in this way."[19] This may be the reason why the narrator portrays Jesus and his disciples "on the road." The reader can imagine that this excited person might have already followed Jesus for at least a short stretch for his enthusiastic interjection implies some fascination with the hero: "I will follow you wherever you go." Here, as in other episodes, the narrator highlights exuberant exclamations from observers whom Jesus must correct (cf. Luke 11:27–28; 14:15–24; but not in 19:38).

Likewise, in the portrayal of the other two would-be disciples, the key verb "follow" (ἀκολουθέω) is repeated and provides parallelism. They understand Jesus' requirements: to walk with Jesus on the way to Jerusalem,

---

17. Fitzmyer, *Luke I–IX*, 830.
18. Johnson, *Luke*, 167.
19. Marshall, *Luke*, 410.

and not have a place to lay their heads. For this reason, they make excuses. Nevertheless, regarding the intended impact of the passage, Bock is right: "The individuals who converse with Jesus are not a focal point in the account, for there is no indication of their response. The point resides solely in Jesus' responses, which are given for the reader's reflection."[20] Once again, categories are created so that the reader clearly knows what is expected. A parallel, through one's relation with the kingdom of God, is present: ". . . but as for you, go and proclaim the kingdom of God" (9:60) and "No one who has put his hand to the plow and keeps looking back is useful for the kingdom of God" (9:62). Thus, these three would-be disciples were not worthy to enter the inner circle of disciples and be sent as "apostles." This language provides a natural link with the next passage, the second mission of Jesus' disciples (10:1–24).

Jesus' True Disciples and the Second Mission (10:4, 10)

In the following passage, Jesus laments, "the harvest is great, but the workers are few" (10:2). Consequently, he prepares and sends seventy disciples.[21] In this context, the narrator employs two words for thoroughfare, *hodos* and *plateia*. Again, Jesus provides instructions for his apostles in the commissioning section of the passage, which is much longer (10:1–16) than the previous one (9:1–5). Jesus warns them that they are going into a hostile situation, "as lambs in the midst of wolves." As stated, Johnson asserts that the context is an unreceptive Samaria: "There is a good narrative reason for this new element which is new to Luke. In contrast to the mission of the Twelve in a Galilee receptive to Jesus, the present mission is in dangerous Samaria, which has already been shown in the narrative (9:53) to be hostile."[22]

In Luke 10:3–4, the disciples are prepared for conflict, which explains Jesus' apparently odd command at the end of verse 4, ". . . do not greet anyone along the road" (καὶ μηδένα κατὰ τὴν ὁδὸν ἀσπάσησθε). Once more, *hodos* plays a part in the physical imagery in which Jesus and his disciples

---

20. Bock, *Luke: 9:51—24:53*, 974.

21. "Seventy" is favored over "seventy-two" despite a balance of external evidence and inconclusive internal questions (e.g., If the number has symbolic value, what is its referent?). Thus, *two* (δύο) is placed within square brackets. Metzger, *Textual*, 126.

22. Johnson, *Luke*, 167. Fitzmyer translates, "do not exchange greetings with anyone on the way," mentioning possible interpretations: (1) not wasting time due to the urgent mission; (2) dedication to the task over worldly matters; and (3) the hostility that awaits them. Fitzmyer, *Luke (X-XXIV)*, 847.

are going toward people in view of spiritual transformation. The narrator explicitly describes this action as preparatory for his ensuing visits: "and he sent them two by two ahead of him in every town and place where he was going to go" (10:1). This echoes the relationship between John the Baptist and Jesus (e.g., key expressions ἀποστέλλω and πρὸ προσώπου αὐτοῦ). The notion of spiritual preparation is implicit since Jesus is described as coming after them. Moreover, an interesting link is "the way of peace" (1:79) and "a man of peace" (10:6) that the disciples should seek during their mission.[23] In both contexts, "peace" indicates harmony and not enmity with God's plan.

Additional evidence for the parallels between John the Baptist and the disciples is Jesus' command to his disciples to pronounce judgment on those cities that reject their message (10:16). This is the first use of *plateia*, which, as seen above, indicates a type of urban thoroughfare, wide streets.[24] There are specific instructions in cases of reception (10:8-9) or rejection (10:10-11). In the latter situation, Jesus instructs them how to perform a public rebuke "in their streets" (εἰς τὰς πλατείας αὐτῆς 10:10): "In whatever city you enter that does not receive you, go out into their streets and say: 'Even the dust from your city that clings to our feet we brush off against you. However, know this: the kingdom of God has drawn near.'"

Jesus' disciples not only preach the kingdom of God but also pronounce judgment on those who reject Jesus, directly or indirectly. A fundamental difference is that this takes place in public spaces, no longer outside in the rural Jordan valley with John the Baptist, but in the urban thoroughfares where the people congregate. This is a more insistent program that will place the apostles "in the midst of wolves." The wide streets (or squares) are the hub of human activity and an ideal setting to expose God's message to the local population.[25] The cities that reject them will have rejected the kingdom of God which has drawn near, because, "... the one who rejects you rejects me; and he who rejects me rejects the one who has sent me" (Luke 10:16). The wording "however know this" (πλὴν τοῦτο γινώσκετε 10:11) is another parallel that prepares the reader for later reproaches to the Jewish people

---

23. Fitzmyer explains the latter expression thus: "a person open to and receptive of the prime quality of Christian salvation brought by Jesus." Ibid., 848.

24. This word is the feminine form of πλατύς with ὁδός understood, hence "wide road" or "street." Cf. Plummer, *Luke*, 275 and Nolli, *Luca*, 471.

25. Nolli captures this notion by using "piazza" (*town square*): "go out in the (town) square," for these are points in the roads large enough for groups of people to form. Ibid., 471. Similar expressions are suggested in other languages: "les places" (Meynet, *Luc*, 488); "marketplace" or "city square" (Bock, *Luke: 9:51—24:53*, 1001); and "die (Haupt-) Strassen *in* der Stadt" (Schürmann *LkEv*, vol. 2, 76).

(e.g., Acts 13:38–51; 28:28). The reader encounters *plateia* three other times that portray interaction between Jesus' movement and city dwellers (Luke 13:26; 14:21; Acts 5:15). The focus of the discussion below is on the first two occurrences.

Pictures of the Plot: Thoroughfare Imagery and Responses to the Hero

Indicative of the central travel narrative in which there is a wealth of Jesus' teaching, the next eight occurrences of thoroughfare expressions occur in Jesus' illustrations in embedded narrative. The first three occurrences (all *hodos*) provide the physical setting for actions in three different illustrations pronounced by Jesus (10:31; 11:6; 12:58), yet they do not merit particular attention concerning the plot's development.[26] The subsequent five occurrences of thoroughfare are in Jesus' illustrations. They merit some attention because of their link with previous occurrences in contexts of rejection of the hero and sentences of judgment. The first one occurs alone (13:26) while the other four appear in two parallelisms to form a cluster (14:21–23). In both cases, they contribute to the reader's interpretation of Jesus' ministry especially toward the Jewish people. Each one adds to the narrative progression of Jesus' mandate and has proleptic value since Jesus presents himself as the authoritative figure in each parable, the "head of the house" (οἰκοδεσπότης) in 13:25 and 14:21.

Superficial Familiarity: You Taught in Our Streets! (Luke 13:26)

The word *plateia* in 13:26 occurs in a passage that recounts how Jesus, while proceeding toward Jerusalem passing through cities and villages, reacts to two interjections (13:22–35). The first question concerns salvation and the second refers to the news of Herod's threat to kill him. Again, the question comes from "someone" among the travelers: "Lord, are those (being) saved a few people?" (13:23b). Jesus responds by exhorting them to enter through the "narrow door" and ensues with a grave announcement: "for many, I tell you, will seek to enter and will not be able" (13:24b). It is a severe warning

---

26. In the Parable of the Good Samaritan, "on that road" (ἐν τῇ ὁδῷ ἐκείνῃ) illustrates in story form the danger for travelers. In his teaching on prayer, Jesus tells the story of a traveler who comes from (the) road (ἐξ ὁδοῦ) in need of food (11:6). Finally, *hodos* occurs in Jesus' instructions on conflicts, ". . . on the way [ἐν τῇ ὁδῷ] make an effort to come to a settlement with him . . ." (12:58a).

that is immediately applied to his listeners, since he switches to the second person plural and reinforces the impact through an illustration of a household. The reader can perceive that the head of the house (οἰκοδεσπότης) represents Jesus (13:25).[27] It depicts in story form the real interaction between Jesus and the Jewish people. First, the people speak directly to him, "We have eaten and drunk before you and you have taught in our streets (13:26)." Luke has shown specific examples of Jesus at mealtimes and teaching situations among the people in homes and in public spaces. Evidence for this is the summary sentence in 13:22, which describes Jesus as teaching in villages and towns.[28] Bock writes, "Though we are still in parabolic material, the reference is very clear: before the door to the banquet was shut they had sat at other tables with the householder and had heard his teaching."[29] Jesus thus reveals to his listeners that he has the authority to let people in the door and to keep them out. The people in the parable speak collectively as "we" and to him as "you," attempting to persuade him based on the personal contact they had had with him.

Yet, since Jesus assumes the role of the head of the house, familiarity with Jesus does not satisfy the requirements for entering the "narrow door" and to recline at the table in the kingdom of God (13:39). The notion is clear: some of the Jewish people will not be permitted to take part in the banquet. This is again intrinsic evidence that, although via an illustration, thoroughfare expressions occur as a part of the description of public spaces where people encounter Jesus and are called to make a choice to receive or reject him. The nature of conflict in this passage is enhanced by moving immediately to the Pharisees' sudden interruption signaled by "in that same hour" (13:31). They warn him to go away because Herod wanted to kill him. Yet, the context is clear that they understood the force of his illustration and wanted Jesus to stay away from Jerusalem. Again, Luke underscores their collaboration with spiritual and human forces to thwart the hero's mandate. Jesus, however, is not deterred because of his compassion for the people of Jerusalem (13:32–35).

Pragmatically, this illustration poignantly depicts the relationship between Jesus and the people. Consequently, it exhorts Luke's audience to evaluate themselves whether they have truly entered through the narrow

---

27. "At the moment it is not clear who the master is, God or Jesus; v. 26 will clarify that." Fitzmyer, *Luke X-XXIV*, 1025.

28. It is a major transition opening the second part of the central travel narrative. Ibid., 1020.

29. Bock, *Luke: 9:51—24:53*, 1237.

door in order take part in the master's banquet with the patriarchs and prophets. A superficial encounter with Jesus, so clearly illustrated by this scene and that of the would-be disciples, does not suffice. Finally, it prepares him for the next passage that shares several common features. There is a master of the household; he is also called Lord. Judgment is announced; yet, there is opening to others to enter the kingdom. This shift to the second person plural alerts the reader that Jesus, as the embedded narrator, assumes the voice of the master and announces judgment on his listeners. Finally, thoroughfare imagery helps the reader visualize the picture of the parable and its pragmatic force.

The Marginalized on Urban and Rural Thoroughfares (Luke 14:21, 23)

The following occurrences represent a cluster of four different thoroughfare expressions in pairs: *plateia* (wide street) and *rumē* (narrow street) in 14:21, and *hodos* (road) and *phragmos* (hedgerow path) in 14:23. The reader encounters them in an illustration that is part of a larger passage (14:1–24) in which Jesus is a guest in a Pharisee's home on the Sabbath (v. 1). The presence of a man with dropsy provides an occasion for Jesus to heal, but also to ask questions (vv. 3, 5) and to teach about dinner etiquette (how to behave when invited, vv. 8–11; and how to invite others, vv. 12–14). The second parable in the passage, the Parable of the Great Supper, is prompted by an interjection from one of the guests: "Blessed is everyone who will eat bread in the kingdom of God!" (v. 15b). As in other occasions, Jesus qualifies this exclamation by telling the guests about a "great supper" (vv. 16–24). Thus, the narrative segues quite naturally from instructions about manners and invitations related to banquets to the great supper offered in the kingdom of God (cf. vv. 15, 24). This is also a picture in story form of the relationship between Jesus and "the people." Similar to other illustrations, an explicit comparison describes those who receive and reject him (e.g., the Parable of the Sower). Those who reject are represented by three individuals who present their excuses for not accepting the invitation to the supper offered by "a certain man" (vv. 18–20). Their excuses also reflect a lack of priority, similar to the three would-be disciples (9:57–62). Those who receive the invitation are surprisingly represented by another group of persons: the poor, crippled, blind and lame (v. 21, cf. v. 13).

Upon the first group's rejection of the invitation, the servant reports this news to his master (κύριος v. 21), that is, the master of the house (οἰκοδεσπότης v. 21).³⁰ The master is furious and sends his servant to invite others (v. 21). The objective of this action appears at the end of the parable: "so that my house may be full" (v. 23). These two invitations contain the four terms of thoroughfare. They provide the physical setting of two actions stimulating the reader's imagination of the scene and appreciation of its pragmatic value. The master sends his servant to the poor who are found in the wide streets and even to those in the narrow ones, the alleys ("of the city," made explicit via τῆς πόλεως). Nevertheless, those invited are not just a new group of the same kind of guests. Rather, they are "the poor and crippled and blind and lame" (v. 21). They are the marginalized weak of society, and the search for them is rigorous, including even the back streets (14:21):

> Go out quickly into the streets and alleys of the city and bring in here the poor, crippled, blind and lame.
>
> ἔξελθε ταχέως εἰς τὰς πλατείας καὶ ῥύμας τῆς πόλεως καὶ τοὺς πτωχοὺς καὶ ἀναπείρους καὶ τυφλοὺς καὶ χωλοὺς εἰσάγαγε ὧδε.

Furthermore, given that there is still more room in the house, the master sends the servant outside the city to seek those people on the roads, even those on the paths along the hedgerows (14:23):

> Go out into the roads and hedgerow paths and compel them to come in, so that my house may be full.
>
> ἔξελθε εἰς τὰς ὁδοὺς καὶ φραγμοὺς³¹ καὶ ἀνάγκασον εἰσελθεῖν, ἵνα γεμισθῇ μου ὁ οἶκος·

The parallels between the master's two commands are evident. Two imperatives occur in both verses; the first is the same ("go out") and the second has similar meaning, "to bring in" paralleled by "compel to enter." In both expressions a sense of urgency is felt: "quickly" (ταχέως) and "compel them to enter." Also, these doublets as a rhetorical feature express a comprehensive search, moving from city to countryside, and from greater thoroughfares to smaller ones (πλατείας to ῥύμας paralleled by ὁδούς to φραγμούς).

Could there be a difference between the two groups since a specific group of beneficiaries occurs in the first command and none in the second? The reader fills in this gap inferring that it is the same type of people, the outcasts. Yet, Lagrange finds an implicit comparison in the story going from

---

30. Cf. 13:25; these two titles and language are similar to 13:24–30.

31. The article used with both substantives emphasizes that both places are outside the city. Nolli, *Luca*, 674.

poor to poorer: "It is necessary to go further and from there go down a degree on the scale of misery, since the poor that one will find along the roads and hedges, who were not even able to drag themselves into town, are even more miserable."[32] This would enhance the parable's aspect of compassion. The main point, however, is that the master wants his house full of guests, and he knows there are more outcasts along the roads and hedgerow paths. The second command ends with a final clause ("so that my house might be full" 14:23), which is also the objective for the first group of commands. This is the thrust of the entire parable, for the three groups of explicit invitations indicate an expanding list of invitees because of the master's wish. Some exegetes view the second group as a symbol for "the Gentiles." This will be discussed further below.

Finally, judgment is pronounced in verse 24 on those who rejected the master's invitation: none of the previously invited will take part in the supper. It is suggestive that Jesus, who is outside the parable, takes over the voice of the "head of the house" in verse 24 speaking directly of "my supper" to those present in the Pharisee's home. This is supported by the second person plural "you" (λέγω γὰρ ὑμῖν ὅτι οὐδεὶς τῶν ἀνδρῶν ἐκείνων τῶν κεκλημένων γεύσεταί μου τοῦ δείπνου). If "you" singular (σοι) were in the place of "you" plural (ὑμῖν), then the reader would understand that the voice is still that of the master speaking to his servant. Furthermore, given that this is a common manner to conclude a parable in Lukan material[33] as well as the presence of "my supper," it is plausible to understand Jesus' voice providing the pronouncement of judgment.[34] Therefore, the illustration in the context of the supper in the Pharisee's home serves to communicate that some people will not be present in the kingdom of God, because they have not received Jesus according to his divine mandate. More specifically, Jesus addresses the warning directly to his host Pharisee and the other guests, alluding that they are "those men" (λέγω γὰρ ὑμῖν ὅτι οὐδεὶς τῶν ἀνδρῶν ἐκείνων τῶν κεκλημένων γεύσεταί μου τοῦ δείπνου.).

In the narrator's portrayal, if Jesus is indeed to be identified as the master of the house, then a picture in story form is present with analeptic and proleptic value for the reader in two ways. First, the overall picture illustrates for the reader what Jesus had said he would accomplish (e.g., his interest in the needy in the Nazareth episode, 4:18) and has already accomplished (e.g.,

---

32. Lagrange, *Luc*, 405.

33. See Luke 11:8; 15:7, 10; 16:9; 18:8, 14; 19:26. Narratively, this ending "takes on a further connotation." Fitzmyer, *Luke X–XXIV*, 1057.

34. See Wolter, *LkEv*, 514.

various healings, 4:38–41; 5:13, 24; 6:10, etc.). The image also has proleptic value in that Jesus—and later his disciples (Acts 3:1–10)—will continue to show concern for people from among the marginalized and despised (e.g., the blind beggar and Zacchaeus). As his disciples begin to fade from the spotlight in the climactic movement to Jerusalem, Jesus performs what the servant in the parable was sent to do, namely, to bring people into the kingdom of God regardless of their social status. In fact, this illustration, as appropriated by Jesus, will be tangibly demonstrated through certain reception scenes that take place on thoroughfares, among other spaces, in which Jesus or his disciples bring physical and spiritual healing for Jews and non-Jews. Although Jesus identifies himself as the "head of the house," Luke will demonstrate to his audience that Jesus goes out to the outcasts and sinners inside the city and outside just as the servant does in the parable. In effect, he is inviting people to join him at his table in the kingdom of God (cf. 13:29–30; 22:29–30). This image, like the "dawn from heaven... into the way of peace," symbolizes salvation, a return to God.

Second, the illustration functions also as an external prolepsis: those who reject Jesus will be excluded from the kingdom of God, since Jesus' interpretation in verse 24 relates the kingdom to himself via the expression "my supper." This link between Jesus and judgment builds on previous allusions to judgment by John the Baptist (Luke 3:9, 17) and in various statements by Jesus.[35] Marshall notes that the use of "Lord" (κύριος) to describe the servant's master supports this interpretation: "It may be significant, however, that by this point in the story the host has become ὁ κύριος, with an obvious allegorical indication. There is no way to the messianic feast except by responding to the invitation once given."[36]

Given the narrator's interest (and presumably also the reader's) in the Jews and non-Jews, it is legitimate to ask whether this picture via thoroughfares, inside and outside the city, represents respectively the Jews and the nations. Commentators disagree on the allegorical value of the locations.[37]

---

35. Cf. the Parable of the Rich Fool, 12:15–21; the Parable of Lazarus, 16:19–31; Jesus' encounter with the rich ruler, 18:18–30; Jesus' lament over Jerusalem, 19:41–44; and the Parable of the Wicked Tenants, 20:9–18.

36. Marshall, *Luke*, 591.

37. In favor of this interpretation are Plummer, *Luke*, 363; Godet, *Luc*, 201; Geldenhuys, *Luke*, 394. Marshall, *Luke*, 590. Bock (*Luke: 9:51—24:53*, 1277) opines that it is probably an allusion to Gentile mission. Johnson (*Luke*, 232) links it to 13:28–20. Talbert (*Reading Luke*, 174), like Johnson, argues that this story follows the outline of salvation history in Luke-Acts (similar to the story in Luke 20:9–16). Contra Lagrange, *Luc*, 405–6; Wolter, *LkEv*, 513; and Klein, *LkEv*, 509.

Reading retrospectively, Johnson interprets the "threefold invitation ... [as the element which] makes the parable a fairly transparent allegory of Luke's narrative as a whole."[38] The first group would be for the "self-righteous," the second for the "outcasts," and the third for "the Gentiles," relating it to the promise that people from every corner of the earth would be present at the banquet in the kingdom of God (13:29).[39] Marshall, redacting synoptic material, thinks that it is not impossible that Jesus could have been the origin of this invitation to those in the country, "a wider circle of people, who can most plausibly be identified with the gentiles....Hence it is far from certain that Luke has expanded the original parable here." Lagrange, however, suggests that the explicit expression "outside" (*en dehors*) would be needed to justify this interpretation.[40] Yet, one could argue that the reader could fill this gap quite easily.

Nevertheless, in the context of the embedded narrator (Jesus), it is not a picture about Jews and non-Jews, rather an illustration of those who have received an invitation from God and have rejected it, and those who still need to be invited and receive it (some being unlikely guests). Tannehill is right about the polyvalence of the story: a reproach to the religious leaders who are mostly rejecting Jesus and an encouragement to the poor and outcasts who are responding positively to Jesus. Thus, the parable illustrates "God's rule of exalting and humbling (14:11)."[41] It echoes the narrator's early mention that Jesus is concerned about the poor and their part in the kingdom (6:20).

Narratively speaking, however, the parable has proleptic value in that it helps prepare the reader for the moment when the nations are *specifically* included (Luke 24:47; Acts 9:15).[42] The picture illustrates again Jesus' care for those who are in physical or spiritual need (e.g., the poor, the tax collectors, and "sinners"), whose logic defies that of Jewish religious leadership that opposes his contact with the outcasts and sinners (e.g., 7:37–39; 19:5–7). The reader sees Jesus performing good actions to the Jews and the nations, even among the marginalized. Jesus also clearly explained to the Jews in Nazareth that God had intervened in the past in favor of certain non-Jews although

---

38. Johnson, *Luke*, 232.
39. Marshall, *Luke*, 590.
40. Lagrange, *Luc*, 405.
41. Tannehill, *Narrative*, 1:185.
42. This is similar to the allusion by the other "head of the house" (οἰκοδεσπότης) regarding a flux of persons from all directions into the kingdom, an unexpected reversal of positions (Luke 13:29–30).

there were needs among the Jewish people (Luke 4:25–27). Therefore, why should the reader expect it to be any different in Jesus' mandate?

In summary, this cluster of thoroughfare imagery via parallelism helps the reader to appreciate the pragmatic force of the parable because of its emphasis on the extent of the search and the level of compassion demonstrated. Jesus' identification with the voice of the "head of the house" emphasizes his authority as one sent from God, which is enhanced when he assumes the role of the servant going to the outcasts. This prepares the reader to interpret and experience highlighted thoroughfare reception scenes, which provide tangible illustrations of the parable and of the implementation of Jesus' mandate. The discussion now turns to those scenes that take place during the climactic movement from Jericho to Jerusalem.

Thoroughfare Reception Scenes from Jericho to Jerusalem

The reader now follows the spotlight on three episodes in the climactic movement from Jericho to Jerusalem in which Jesus is received in a thoroughfare setting. Those who receive Jesus are the blind beggar outside Jericho, Zacchaeus in Jericho, and the crowd of disciples during Jesus' entry into Jerusalem. Similar to Baban's nomenclature ("post-Easter on the road encounters"), these episodes will be referred to as *thoroughfare reception scenes* as an integral part of the plot's reception-rejection pattern. In addition to providing illustrations for the Parable of the Great Supper on the action level, certain characteristics of these three episodes recall the intermingling of the thoroughfare motif and illumination theme introduced in Zechariah's proleptic portrait of Jesus (Luke 1:78–79). This suggestion is plausible when compared to other highlighted thoroughfare scenes in the pivot (the disciples of Emmaus) and unraveling sequence (the Ethiopian eunuch and Saul of Tarsus). Since I will discuss each of these six reception scenes, an overview justifying this literary connection is constructive.

Introduction to the Thoroughfare Reception Scenes in Luke-Acts

First, the statistics show that when Luke uses thoroughfare terms for circumstantial description on the action level, he does so in order to highlight encounters, in particular with Jesus. Eight different episodes occur in a thoroughfare setting (using twelve occurrences in circumstantial description). Second, six of the eight episodes describe encounters of two or more

Contrasting Encounters: Thoroughfare Imagery for and against the Hero

parties except the two episodes related to Peter.[43] Third, five encounters involve Jesus, one with Philip, and two concern other actions and types of scenes in relation to Peter. Consequently, focusing on the hero, all five episodes that involve Jesus may be considered encounters. Two others may be added to these based on the criteria of a thoroughfare setting and the reception of Jesus: (1) the encounter between Philip and the Ethiopian eunuch, which is completely centered on Jesus, and (2) Jesus' encounter with Zacchaeus through the implicit use of *hodos* via "by that road" (the local genitive ἐκείνης) and additional circumstantial evidence. In summary, there is only one encounter scene where Jesus is not received (the would-be disciples), and five reception episodes where Jesus is present (three before the resurrection, and two after), and one reception episode in which Jesus is not physically present but the scene is undeniably centered upon his reception (Philip and the Ethiopian). Thus, the narrator specifically highlights six thoroughfare reception scenes. The significance of this point is enhanced when one considers that despite the abundance of actual physical movement in Luke-Acts, thoroughfare terms have a small part in providing circumstantial information.[44]

Another point concerns the placement of these thoroughfare reception scenes in relation to the plot. From the beginning of the central travel narrative in 9:51 until the first thoroughfare reception scene (18:35), terms for thoroughfare have been used only once to describe the physical setting of a completed action (9:57). That occurrence describes the rejection scene with the three would-be disciples. The position of this rejection scene is suggestive. Placed at the very beginning of the central travel narrative (9:51—19:44), it calls to the reader's attention the question: who will receive or reject Jesus on his way to Jerusalem? Only toward the end of the long travel narrative does the narrator once again use thoroughfare imagery on the action level, namely, for the three thoroughfare reception scenes (18:35; 19:4, 36).[45] These highlighted scenes respond in part to the question above and to the explicit

---

43. Jesus meets the would-be followers (Luke 9:57), the blind man (Luke 18:35), the crowd (Luke 19:36), the Emmaus disciples (Luke 24:32, 35), and Paul (9:17, 27; 26:13). Other encounters are Peter and the sick (Acts 5:15) and an angel of the Lord (12:10), and Philip and the Ethiopian (Acts 8:26, 36, 39).

44. In addition, there is even one case where Luke has substituted Mark's ἐν τῇ ὁδῷ (10:52) with δοξάζων in Luke 18:43. Matthew has also omitted ἐν τῇ ὁδῷ in 20:34.

45. This gap lacking thoroughfare imagery shows the narrator's lack of interest in a detailed travel itinerary with localities and physical settings. The central travel narrative is a framework for highlighting Jesus' interactions with people and teaching situations, as the multitudes continue to grow leading to Jerusalem, the pivot city.

question "Then who can be saved?" in 18:26. The reader is perhaps somewhat surprised to observe who actually recognizes and receives Jesus. They take place when the narrator accentuates Jesus' final movement to Jerusalem. Luke builds the climactic movement toward Jerusalem by providing more *travel notices*, and he highlights these three specific thoroughfare reception scenes. Each one is chosen for a specific purpose for the reader's experience. These examples of reception contribute to heighten the reader's encounter with Jesus' rejection in Jerusalem. Next, the fourth thoroughfare episode takes place in the pivot: the encounter between Jesus and the disciples from Emmaus. This is *the* highlighted episode in the pivot since several motifs and themes converge to heighten the reader's passionate involvement in the pivot. The beginning of the transformation of Jesus' disciples is highlighted for this reason.[46] Finally, the fifth and sixth thoroughfare reception scenes are recounted, as Baban has rightly shown, as a part of the narrator's transition from the evangelization of the Jewish people to the nations. The conversions of the Ethiopian eunuch and Saul of Tarsus both illustrate this important transitional movement. Moreover, Saul's thoroughfare reception of Jesus is so important for the plot that it is recalled in four other occasions through the voices of Ananias, Barnabas and Paul (twice).

The third point of evidence concerns the parallels that these thoroughfare scenes have in common.[47] Further details will be indicated in the course of the discussion. Jacques Dupont and Coert Lindijer commented on the parallels between the Emmaus account and Philip and the Ethiopian, and Baban included Paul's conversion with the previous two.[48] Intrinsic evidence warrants the claim that the narrator appears to treat them, not as isolated scenes, but as interconnected, based on content and style. For the above reasons, the three thoroughfare reception scenes between Jericho and Jerusalem can be linked with the other three scenes. The list below summarizes the elements that these six scenes in a thoroughfare setting have in common:

1. All are reception episodes in which Jesus is recognized according to an aspect of his proleptic portrait.[49] The scenes are a part of the

---

46. Fitzmyer, *Luke X–XXIV*, 1557–58.

47. Benoît Standaert has provided a useful, more general description of the types of encounters present in Luke-Acts. He covers many examples and proposes a pattern, which is, A: a person (group or point of view); B: another person (group); C: the moment of the encounter; D: the results from the encounter. Standaert, "Luc," 282–95.

48. Cf. Dupont, "Meal," 105–21; Lindijer, "Two creative encounters," 77–85; and Baban, *On the Road*, 227–71.

49. (1) Blind beggar: heir of David's throne (18:38–39, "Son of David"); but also "Lord" (perhaps as a title of respect (18:41); (2) Zacchaeus: as *savior* via Jesus' words

greater reception and rejection pattern in Luke-Acts. They are also in direct contrast to the first specific thoroughfare episode with the would-be disciples in Luke 9:57 ("Lord" occurs in vv. 59, 61, but they do not follow him).

2. The actions of recognition and reception are confirmed by an indication that those who encountered Jesus performed an additional action that demonstrates their positive response to Jesus.[50] This is in contrast to the episodes in which a divine intervention occurs (and perhaps recognized) but no further action is provided to indicate reception of Jesus.

3. All of the passages also include the illumination theme, helping to see physically or spiritually. This is evidence for the interrelationship between the illumination theme and the thoroughfare motif introduced in Luke 1:78–79. Light is brought to people experiencing some form of darkness in a thoroughfare setting, and this action is almost always divinely initiated (cf. point 1 below). The scene with the crowd of disciples is less obvious than the other scenes, but it can be plausibly included in this parallel.

4. All of the scenes are narrated in significant moments of the plot's development (cf. "the second point of evidence" above).

Additional parallels are listed here that are not present in all the scenes in descending order (e.g., 5/6 for "five out of six times"). In addition, some of these parallels are present in other types of encounters with Jesus but are not specifically unique to them:

1. All represent direct encounters with Jesus except the encounter between Philip and the Ethiopian, which is centered on Jesus, three before the resurrection and two after (5/6). This provides continuity in the narrative and is significant for the question whether Jesus can

---

(19:9–10); and "Lord" in the narrator's portrayal of Jesus (19:8a), but also by Zacchaeus in 19:8b (perhaps also only to show respect); (3) the crowd: "king" as heir of David's throne (19:36–38); (4) the Emmaus disciples: "the Christ" via Jesus' voice (24:26) and "Lord" (24:34); (5) the Ethiopian eunuch: savior (8:32–35); and (6) Saul: "Lord" by Saul in 9:4 (perhaps for respect), but then also by Ananias to Saul (9:17); yet, in the following episode, "the Son of God" (9:20) and "the Christ" (9:22).

50. The blind beggar follows Jesus (Luke 18:43). Zacchaeus vows to give to the poor and return money (Luke 19:8). The crowd of disciples welcomes him with gesture and praise (Luke 19:36–38, 48). The Emmaus disciples express joy and return to Jerusalem (Luke 24:33–35). Ethiopian submits to baptism and rejoices (Acts 8:38–39). Saul obeys Jesus' command (Acts 9:8), submits to baptism (9:18) and preaches (9:20, 22).

be plausibly considered the hero of Luke-Acts.

2. All the encounters are specifically portrayed as divinely initiated except the blind beggar (5/6). God or Jesus takes the initiative to bring illumination to those who need it.

3. All of the persons are unlikely or unexpected beneficiaries of Jesus' mandate except the crowd of disciples and the Emmaus disciples, thus enhancing Luke's overall strategy to show how those who should receive him often do not, and those who are not expected to receive him, actually do receive him (4/6).

4. All the encounters experience some form of opposition except with the Emmaus disciples and Ethiopian eunuch (4/6), which is clearly a part of the greater pattern of opposition to the hero (alluded to in Luke 2:34 and demonstrated already in Luke 4:1–30).

Is it not artificial to exclude certain scenes because the narrator has not specifically indicated that they took place in the setting of a thoroughfare?[51] One might argue that the reader can fill in the gaps where there is a lack of specific circumstantial information.[52] This is true. Yet, when Luke uses thoroughfare imagery in circumstantial description on the action level, he mainly illustrates encounters centered on the hero (six out of the eight episodes) appearing in significant moments in the plot's development. This is one of the narrator's techniques to put the spotlight on particular encounters with or about the hero. Given the powerful image spoken by Zechariah (Luke 1:78–79) uniting the illumination theme and thoroughfare motif so early in the narrative, it is profitable to explore this link with these six specific thoroughfare reception scenes sharing certain parallels.[53]

---

51. Certain passages resemble the thoroughfare episodes but do not contain thoroughfare imagery: the healing of the widow's son in Nain (Luke 7:11–17); the healing of Jairus's daughter and the woman with the hemorrhage (Luke 8:40–56); the healing of the ten lepers and the Samaritan's recognition of Jesus (Luke 17:11–19). On the other hand, rhetorical theory in Antiquity also encouraged orators to use omissions in order that their audience might use their imagination to *see* the narrative. Cf. Quintilian, *Institutio Oratoria*, 8.3.64–65. For a brief, useful discussion, see Maxwell, *Hearing*, 53. Luke might have expected his audience to imagine certain scenes that implied literal thoroughfares or expressions involving figurative uses.

52. The list does not include verses that indicate: introductory or summary verses (8:1; 9:51–53; 10:1; 10:38; 13:22; 17:11); final verses indicating someone beginning to follow him or moving on to the next destination (5:11, 28; 9:56; 23:26); or a crowd already following him or gathering (8:4; 9:11; 11:29 or in another public space; 12:1; 14:25; 22:39; 23:27).

53. The healing of the ten lepers (17:11–19) has much in common with the Parable of

Contrasting Encounters: Thoroughfare Imagery for and against the Hero

What pragmatic response might the narrator seek from the reader through these thoroughfare reception scenes? First, these scenes prepare the reader for an enhanced experience of later developments: Jesus' ironic rejection in Jerusalem, the disciples' transformation toward the fulfillment of their mandate, and mission expansion toward the nations. Second, these tangible reception scenes are sources of pleasure for Theophilus, who, as if he were there, observes Jesus bringing illumination, directly or indirectly, to people for a greater understanding of his identity and devotion to him. Third, these reception scenes are also sources of certainty and encouragement. The reader, as one of "the Way," can identify with these individuals, perhaps some more than others, and experience the force of these highlighted thoroughfare reception scenes. It helps him to appreciate what has happened to himself. In fact, these scenes are a part of a larger pattern in Luke's strategy to provide examples of persons or groups who experience a type of transformation from lesser to greater certainty about Jesus' identity, for example, John the Baptist (Luke 7:18), Apollos (Acts 18:25–26), and the "disciples" in Ephesus (Acts 19:2). Assurance or certainty comes through the narrator's enlightenment. Theophilus may be encouraged by discovering that he is not the only one with this need, since others were susceptible to moments of doubt or in need of enlightenment regarding Jesus. We now turn to discussion concerning episodes in climactic movement from Jericho to Jerusalem.

Background to the Climactic Movement from Jericho to Jerusalem

Since the climactic movement to Jerusalem is in the raveling sequence, the question that guides the following discussion is whether these thoroughfare reception scenes actually participate in the raveling of the plot. To answer this question adequately, it is necessary to understand how they fit in the overall climactic movement from Jericho to Jerusalem. The transition from the preceding section to the climactic movement toward Jerusalem is signaled after the rich ruler's rejection of Jesus (18:18–26), which closes with the question, "Then who can be saved?" Here Luke shifts his focus to the

---

the Great Supper and the thoroughfare reception scenes. It is the only highlighted healing in this section (14:25–18:35) and it illustrates two aforementioned elements: Jesus' compassion for the outcast and his reception by an unlikely character (a Samaritan). This scene is not included in the discussion due to the lack of specific thoroughfare imagery. As stated, ironically, the central travel narrative frequently omits localities or physical settings.

imminent level of action via foreshadowing in Jesus' voice (18:31–33). Jesus' words are the first of two transitional passages of the literary frame for the climactic movement, which emphasize a lack of understanding of Jesus' identity and mandate (18:31–34 and 19:41–44). In the first transitional passage, Jesus privately reminds his disciples where they are going (Jerusalem), what is going to happen to him there (handed over to the nations, tortured and killed), and what will happen after that (his resurrection). Even so, the narrator inserts a significant interpretative aside to alert the reader that Jesus' disciples understood none of this (18:34). This enhances the reader's experience of the transformations that will take place in Jesus' closest disciples, who "have begun the journey of discipleship (cf. 18:28), but remain oblivious to the nature of God's plan."[54] In the second outer transitional passage (19:41–44), Jesus weeps over Jerusalem because of the blindness of its inhabitants, announces judgment upon them, then enters the temple. Both transitional passages are descriptions of spiritual blindness in need of illumination and evoke the initial state of the people depicted by Zechariah (1:78–79). In this sense, the reader becomes aware that Jesus' disciples, to recall a familiar image, have not yet completely entered the way of peace, since they have not been fully enlightened. They too are still in need of clarity about Jesus' identity and mandate. Thus, the reader is invited to learn from their experiences as Green summarizes, "The need for self-evaluation and appropriate response is rendered urgent, too, by Luke's portrait of the disciples. The last we hear of them in this narrative segment concerns their lack of understanding (18:31–34), after which they fade temporarily into the background. The general lack of distinction between these followers and others who witness Jesus' ministry is disconcerting."[55]

In this context of gradual progression to Jerusalem, Luke finally gives Theophilus a travel notice, a specific location (Jericho) for his orientation (18:35). This is actually the first city (other than Jerusalem) mentioned in the central travel narrative. Knowing the proximity of the two cities (from 10:30 in the Parable of the Good Samaritan), the reader perceives that Jesus' journey to Jerusalem is going to end soon. From this point on, the momentum moves with no apparent break from Jericho to Jerusalem. The mention of localities becomes more frequent and precise, an indicator of climactic development.[56] They are finally getting close to Jerusalem as illustrated by

54. Green, *Luke*, 661.
55. Ibid., 643.
56. Cf. approaching Jericho (18:35); in Jericho (19:1); near Jerusalem (19:11); going up to Jerusalem (19:28); approaching Bethphage and Bethany (19:29); the descent of

key terms: "close" (ἐγγύς 19:11) and "draw near" (ἐγγίζω 18:35, 40; 19:29, 37, 41). Furthermore, expectation among the characters is clearly brought to the reader's attention, "... they supposed that the kingdom of God was going to appear immediately" (19:11b). This situation elicits the Parable of the Pounds, which adds to the narrative tension, as the consequences of reception and rejection are again reiterated (19:26–27).[57] Hence, this emotionally charged context enhances the narrative tension, in which the reader encounters three thoroughfare reception episodes before Jesus enters Jerusalem. Moreover, these scenes are in direct contrast to the cluster of three rejection episodes among the religious leaders that take place after Jesus had cast out those who were selling in the temple (Luke 20:1–8, 19–26, 27–40). The reader is again in a privileged position to understand what the disciples do not comprehend: Jesus is going to face intense violence and suffering to the point of death. We now turn to specific commentary on three thoroughfare reception episodes.

Reception of Jesus on a Road outside Jericho (Luke 18:35)

The first reception scene takes place on a road outside Jericho (18:35–43). The narrator describes the initial state of the story in verses 35–36. Jesus is in movement toward Jericho, toward the place of encounter, which will be a road outside the city. That is where "a certain blind man" was sitting and begging "by the road" (παρὰ τὴν ὁδόν 18:35). The physical context recalls the second group of persons and places in the Parable of the Great Supper to whom the servant was sent. Jesus is portrayed as coming to meet the needs of a man like them. This man's curiosity is aroused by the sound of a crowd passing by and he seeks information. Now the complication begins to take form (vv. 37–39): Jesus of Nazareth, the healer, is passing by, and the blind man risks losing this chance with no help from those around him.[58] The reception of this story is enhanced since the reader, from his perspective, already knows that Jesus heals the blind (7:21–22). Yet, the blind man has no other means to meet him except by crying out with insistence that Jesus might have mercy on him. In fact, this is the only thoroughfare scene that is

---

the Mount of Olives (19:37); viewing Jerusalem (19:41); and finally in the temple area (19:45).

57. "With this repeated rejection of Jesus by the people, the theme of Jesus' rejection reappears here in this emphatic final position, which could already be observed in 9:52–56 (v. 53a: οὐκ ἐδέξαντο αὐτόν)." Baum, *Lukas*, 364.

58. Nolland, *Luke 18:35—24:53*, 901.

not explicitly depicted as divinely initiated. Ironically, the blind beggar, who *sees* Jesus' identity, shows great tenacity to make this direct encounter with Jesus happen.

Again, irony is present when those leading the crowd command the blind man to be silent. Perhaps these are Jesus' closest disciples. They are followers of Jesus, but they do not see the needs of the blind man, for they also do not clearly *see* Jesus' identity. This ironic opposition is similar to the occasion when his disciples' were preventing the children from being presented to Jesus for blessing (18:15). In several micro-narratives, a need arises, and then an obstacle to it, even opposition, and Jesus' intervention to resolve it.[59] Again, the disciples in Jesus' mandate at this point are portrayed as distant.[60] Ironically, the blind man actually appears to *see* quite well, perhaps better than some of those following Jesus, when he calls out, "Jesus, son of David," a clear allusion to Jesus as heir of David's throne (vv. 38–39, cf. Luke 1:32–33).

The direction of the story is going against fulfillment of the needs of the blind beggar until Jesus takes notice of him (i.e., the turning point in vv. 40–42). He stops and gives orders for the blind man to be brought to him. Yet, the blind man remains active in the entire story, since he draws near for the encounter (ἐγγίσαντος δὲ αὐτοῦ), and he is asked to express a request to Jesus.[61] Perceiving the man's faith, Jesus performs the transforming action, and adds, "your faith has healed you" (v. 42).[62]

The immediate effects of the transforming action appear in verse 43: the blind man is instantly healed (καὶ παραχρῆμα ἀνέβλεψεν). Not only is physical transformation immediately apparent, the now "seeing man" is so moved that he begins to follow Jesus and gives glory to God for the miracle (18:42). This response confirms his reception of Jesus and recalls episodes where gratitude follows healing (the Gerasene demoniac, 8:38–39; the Samaritan leper, 17:16). Interestingly, also a part of the resolution is the positive effect that the encounter has had on the crowd (v. 36). They too experience a type of transformation, which is nuanced in the narrator's portrayal for they

---

59. See the discussion on this narrative technique in Tannehill, *Narrative*, 1:92–93.

60. Bock's assessment is right: "Luke employs literary tension in the first half of the account when the populace attempts and fails to quiet the blind man." Bock, *Luke: 9:51—24:53*, 1504. However, "populace" misses the irony since Jesus' disciples could be the obstacle to this man's healing.

61. Green (*Luke*, 662) describes this story as an exemplary narrative since it epitomizes (1) the soteriological significance through the healing for the poor, (2) the proper attitude of those desiring benefits of the kingdom, and (3) the "continuing resistance" of some toward God's work for the good of the least privileged.

62. See Meynet (*Luc*, 711) for the beggar's active role in this episode.

are now called the "people" (in "all the people" πᾶς ὁ λαός v. 43). The narrator appears to be making a shift here in the characterization of the people especially concerning their position vis-à-vis Jesus.[63]

This thoroughfare reception scene is a practical demonstration that recalls the picture of the "dawn" bringing light to lead people out of darkness into the way of peace (Luke 1:78-79). This is the most concrete example in the raveling section where an individual is shown to receive physical and spiritual sight, leaving darkness and the shadow of death and entering the way of peace through Jesus. The whole scene remains within the setting of thoroughfare imagery, illustrated well by the antithetic parallels: blind and sitting (v. 35) and seeing again and following (v. 43). In fact, what accentuates the importance of this scene for the narrative is that it is the only specific account of the healing of a blind person in the first volume. This healing and the cry for "Jesus of Nazareth" evoke Jesus' words in the synagogue of Nazareth via the passage in Isaiah (4:18). In addition, the only other healing in the first volume after this is Jesus' healing of the servant's ear (Luke 22:51). Moreover, the force of this passage is enhanced when compared to the encounters that surround it, that is, the rich ruler (rejection) and Zacchaeus (reception). Both men have an encounter with Jesus: one leaves sad (18:23) and the other glorifies God (18:43).

This scene recalls the image of the "head of the house," who commands his servant to go out on the roads and hedgerow paths outside the city to bring people to the master's feast. The reader has witnessed once more how an unlikely person, like one of those in the Parable of the Supper, has been transformed through Jesus' mandate in contrast to the theme of blindness framed by the two transitional passages. The reader can imagine that the now doubly "seeing man" accompanied Jesus to Jericho to meet Zacchaeus, and then on to Jerusalem as a part of the crowd that welcomed him on the road.[64] In fact, the appellation, "Son of David," foreshadows for the reader the great reception of Jesus entering Jerusalem as their king.

---

63. "People" (λαός) does not occur between 9:13 and this use in 18:43; yet, later it occurs eighteen times, all in Jerusalem. The people are very favorable to Jesus in contrast to the religious leaders, and it is difficult to distinguish the crowd of disciples from the people. Cf. Kodell, "Laos, 'People,'" 327-43.

64. For the placement of this episode in relation to Mark's Gospel, see Fitzmyer, *Luke X-XXIV*, 1213 and Marshall, *Luke*, 692.

Encountering Images of Spiritual Transformation

Reception of Jesus on a Road in Jericho (19:4)

The next reception episode segues naturally into the city of Jericho, on one of its roads, because Jesus was passing through it. This is the physical setting of the encounter between Jesus and Zacchaeus, a wealthy, Jewish chief tax collector. This episode is clearly the highlighted reception scene from the category *tax collectors* in whom Luke has particular interest.[65] In addition, being directly preceded by the apostles' inability to understand God's plan and the blind beggar's encounter with Jesus (i.e., *blindness* theme), the reader is prepared to interpret this picture of illumination in Jericho.

As stated in the introduction on thoroughfare expressions, no specific occurrences of these terms are in the text, but the thoroughfare setting can be established on three observations. First, the introductory sentence—"and having entered, he was going through Jericho" (19:1)—assumes the same setting from the previous passage (cf. 18:35, 43).[66] Second, *hodos* in verse 4 is understood through the ellipsis "that one" (ἐκείνης) in place of "by that way" (ἐκείνης τῆς ὁδοῦ) in the phrase "because he was going to pass by that way" (ὅτι ἐκείνης ἤμελλεν διέρχεσθαι).[67] Therefore, Luke, using the imperfect tense (διήρχετο τὴν Ἰεριχώ), prepares the reader for another event that takes place in the course of this action. Movement to Jerusalem is still the focus, since Jesus is only "passing through." Third, the presence of the crowd in verse 3 is an indicator of continuity with the preceding passage (cf. 18:43b). The crowd has followed him into the city. The same multitude and others who have joined them are blocking Zacchaeus from seeing Jesus. The reader then can imagine the scene that takes place on one of Jericho's thoroughfares where the same crowd has followed him, and others from the city have joined them, so much that Zacchaeus was not able to find a position among the crowd.

Despite the difference in their economic status, several parallels are evident between the blind beggar and Zacchaeus. The themes of "not seeing"

---

65. Cf. Aletti's narrative-critical reading of the Zacchaeus pericope in which he illustrates this example of the theme of recognition in the Gospel of Luke ("Lc 19,1–10: voir et être vu. L'enjeu d'une rencontre"). Aletti, *L'art de raconter*, 17–38.

66. Cf. Fitzmyer, *Luke X–XXIV*, 1222.

67. Justification for including this passage as a thoroughfare reception scene is based on the above observations and its close parallels to the others explained in Chapter 1. For the value of ἐκείνης as a genitive of place, see BDR §186.1 and Wallace, *Greek*, 124 and the corresponding interpretations ("by that way") in Marshall, *Luke*, 213, 696; Wolter, *LkEv*, 612; Klein, *LkEv*, 597; Robertson, 709 (who points to a similar expression ποίας in Luke 5:19 [p. 1202]); and Plummer, *Luke*, 433–34. CPS (p. 588) suggest the translation "there" following BDAG (p. 301).

and "seeing" are present, as well as the resulting irony. Similar to the blind beggar, Zacchaeus is also on the side of the road, and his vision of Jesus is hindered by two factors (19:3): the presence of a crowd (καὶ οὐκ ἠδύνατο ἀπὸ τοῦ ὄχλου) and a restrictive and marginalizing physical feature, his shortness (ὅτι τῇ ἡλικίᾳ μικρὸς ἦν). Thus, Zacchaeus, like the blind beggar, is also a marginalized character, but for different reasons: "Zacchaeus, a short, rich tax collector, was on all three counts despicable."[68] He also shows great enthusiasm about Jesus' presence by the effort he makes to get in the right position to see Jesus as he passes by (v. 4). Zacchaeus could have run forward and placed himself in front of Jesus. Yet, his only goal was to see him.[69] Ironically, Jesus too sees him, and the encounter is made possible. By attracting Jesus' attention, Zacchaeus becomes a protagonist in the thoroughfare encounter. The narrator, however, depicts this as a divinely planned encounter, for Zacchaeus had only wanted to see Jesus, not for the goal of being healed or obtaining something. Jesus, however, has plans for an encounter through which Zacchaeus will be transformed. He knows Zacchaeus's name, and Luke uses a recurring construction *dei* ("it must" δεῖ) suggesting that Jesus *must stay* there according to his divine mandate.[70] Also, the temporal adverb "today" (σήμερον) has been used prior to this to indicate salvation through Jesus (2:11; 4:21; 13:32–33; then also in 19:9). Similar to the previous encounter, Jesus perceives a need in Zacchaeus and is willing to fulfill it (vv. 5–6), even interrupting his journey.[71] The pivot is in verses 5–6 where the narrator describes Jesus' invitation to Zacchaeus to receive him, and Zacchaeus's positive response is illustrated by his joyful disposition (v. 6b). Here the reader assumes that the scene has moved from the road to Zacchaeus's home.

In verse 7, Luke reveals that, similar to the blind beggar's experience, a form of opposition appears in this encounter. Zacchaeus, being a tax collector, is a marginal character, associated with another broad, disliked group, "the sinners" (5:30). For this reason, opposition is expressed verbally,

---

68. Talbert, *Reading Luke*, 205. For the pragmatic aim of this depiction, see Parsons, "'Short in Stature,'" 50–57.

69. Wolter, *LkEv*, 612.

70. Fitzmyer (*Luke X–XXIV*, 1224) interprets this as "It is destined that I do this." Likewise, Wolter (*LkEv*, 612) notices σήμερον from a salvation history perspective and the δεῖ clause: "Jesus identifies his self-invitation to Zacchaeus as an integral component of his mission mandate:"

71. Bock (*Luke: 9:51—24:53*, 1516) thinks that Jesus had already planned to stay the night in Jericho and had a specific host in mind. It appears that Jesus' stay in Jericho is quite brief, perhaps only the day.

a grumbling against Jesus from "all that were watching" (v. 7; a gap which the reader can easily fill with "Pharisees"). Though they do not hinder him from receiving Jesus into his home, they are against this encounter between prophet and "sinner." Yet, the reader has been prepared to interpret this clash of points of view, since the narrator has thus far shown tax collectors in a positive light in relation to Jesus (3:12; 5:27; 7:29, 34; 15:1; 18:9–14) as well as the Pharisees' negative opinion of them (5:29–30). Ironically, the tax collectors are depicted as more responsive than the religious leaders (cf. Luke 7:29); this scene provides further evidence.

Verse 8 reveals the effects of the encounter: Zacchaeus's reception of Jesus is also confirmed also by his vow to give to the poor and pay back what he had illicitly taken from others. Similar to the blind beggar but unlike the rich ruler (18:22–23), Zacchaeus—perhaps portrayed as a lost sheep of Israel—has been changed by the encounter, benefiting from Jesus' mandate, which is "to seek and save the lost" (19:10).[72] Thus, this thoroughfare encounter is a tangible illustration of salvation coming through Jesus, which recalls the image of Jesus' mandate of illumination and guidance (Luke 1:78–79). The wealthy Zacchaeus has received light through Jesus, which has brought him into a new state, salvation (cf. "the way of peace" in 1:79). The narrator confirms for the reader the spiritual transformation that has taken place in Zacchaeus by allowing Jesus' words to function as a literary *evaluation* of the passage: "Today salvation has come to this house, because he also is a son of Abraham. For the Son of Man has come to seek and save that which is lost" (19:9b–10).[73]

Thus, taking into account the two transitional frames highlighting the blindness of Jesus' disciples and the people of Jerusalem, Luke places the spotlight on another unlikely person (from the Pharisees' perspective) who actually *sees* Jesus. Here again the juncture of the themes of salvation and seeing is evident.[74]

Unlike the previous story, this episode does not explicitly conclude in the setting of a thoroughfare. It is not easy to understand the location of the various actions.[75] If Bovon is right, the expression in verse 6 "and he received

---

72. As suggested in NA27, an interesting link is the use of the neuter (ζητῆσαι καὶ σῶσαι τὸ ἀπολωλός) in 19:10 that might be an allusion to the lost sheep in 15:3 expressed also as τὸ ἀπολωλός in 15:4.

73. Cf. σωτηρία in Luke 1:69, 71, 77 and σωτήριον in 2:30; 3:6.

74. Cf. Green, *Luke*, 667.

75. This depends in part on the rendering of σταθείς (v. 8) and when it took place: "stopped" (Johnson, *Luke*, 285) rather than "stood up" (Geldenhuys, *Luke*, 470), or perhaps a description of "a set attitude," reflecting the formality of Zacchaeus's announcement

him rejoicing" (καὶ ὑπεδέξατο αὐτὸν χαίρων) indicates effective reception in Zacchaeus's home.[76] Thus, there would be a gap between Zacchaeus's two actions "he came down" and "he received." It is possible that the context for the telling of the Parable of the Ten Pounds (vv. 11–27) takes place back on the road to Jerusalem, which might lend support to the notion that Zacchaeus had joined Jesus in his journey.[77] This would contribute to the episode's final orientation concerning the transformation of Zacchaeus, who, along with the seeing beggar, might also have joined the crowd to welcome Jesus as heir to David's throne. Again, the audience encounters highlighted reception scenes in this climactic movement from Jericho to Jerusalem, preparing them for the great contrast of rejection that will take place in the city of destiny.

Reception of Jesus on a Road into Jerusalem (19:36)

The next thoroughfare reception scene takes place on a road just outside Jerusalem, as Jesus prepares to enter the city. The occurrence of *hodos* (19:36) describes the physical setting where a crowd of disciples has gathered to welcome him. The full passage is 19:28–44, which covers the ascension toward Jerusalem until his lament over it. For the reader's pleasure, the narrator describes a remarkable *mise en scène*[78] performed by Jesus (19:30–31), which consists of his sending two disciples to bring a colt so that he might ride upon it into Jerusalem. No explanation is given for this action, but the reader understands it as the story progresses. The redundancy of the wording slows down the story and builds expectation (vv. 32–34). As in Jericho, everything is divinely prepared: the colt is where it is supposed to be (v. 32), the owners ask the predicted question (v. 33), and the disciples' response is sufficient to take the animal (v. 34). The reader understands that Jesus ("the Lord" ὁ κύριος v. 34) has prepared the scene for a purpose, which is understood later. By doing this, Jesus helps them to recognize him as the heir to David's throne. He is the king of Israel established by God. Thus, he is helping them

---

(Plummer, *Luke*, 434).

76. He translates the expression, "and he received him in his home with joy," adding that the verb ὑποδέχομαι implies hospitality. Bovon, *Luc (15,1—19,27)*, 232, 241.

77. This is supported by the participial phrase in v. 11 that links the two passages ('Ακουόντων δὲ αὐτῶν ταῦτα) and the causal phrase (διὰ τὸ ἐγγὺς εἶναι Ἰερουσαλὴμ αὐτόν).

78. A *mise en scène* serves "to signify a director's overall conception, staging, and directing of a theatrical performance." Abrams, *Glossary*, 285.

to see a part of his identity (and, for the reader, a part of his proleptic portrait). Some will recognize and receive it; others, like the Pharisees, should be able to see it but do not. This leads to opposition in the episode, which escalates in Jerusalem.

Jesus' disciples take part in embellishing the scene by recognizing and responding positively to Jesus' intentions. They place their cloaks on the colt (v. 34). Then similar to the scenes of Jericho, the narrator describes the presence of a great gathering, "the whole plenitude of the disciples," who welcomes Jesus on the road (v. 37) by performing two actions: (1) they spread their garments on the road and (2) they joyfully sing praises to God. The actions of his going (singular form) and their casting of garments are simultaneous and continued (πορευομένου δὲ αὐτοῦ ὑπεστρώννυον τὰ ἱμάτια αὐτῶν ἐν τῇ ὁδῷ.). This procession accompanied by joyful singing. Jesus allows them to do this, and, as mentioned, he has actually prepared the scene for such a reception.

The narrated gestures might cause the reader to make associations with similar instances in Israel's history, adding intertextual force to the scene as a symbolic act. This red-carpet welcome is worthy of a king, which is possibly an allusion to the honoring of Jehu as the new king in 2 Kgs 9:13.[79] Yet, as Green suggests, perhaps Zechariah 9:9 is the closest image that Jesus (and the narrator) wishes to evoke:

> Thus far, Jesus has been making pilgrimage to Jerusalem on foot. That he now rides a colt, for only the last mile of the journey, intimates the symbolic character of this act. The most obvious interpretation is provided by Zech 9:9: as the triumphant, victorious, yet humble king, Jesus comes riding on a colt ... This means that, in setting Jesus on the colt, etc., they are taking their own initiative in acclaiming him as the Davidic Messiah.[80]

Moreover, the wording of their praise echoes various pronouncements of Jesus' identity that the reader has already encountered (2:14; 3:22; 9:35). It also echoes Jesus' words: "Behold, forsaken to you is your house. I say to you, you will certainly not see me until you say, 'Blessed is the one who comes in the name of the Lord'" (13:35). The crowd of disciples welcomes Jesus, but Jerusalem will not. This kindles in Jesus another moving lament for the city's inhabitants (19:41–44) echoing the previous one (13:34–35).

---

79. Cf. e.g., Nolland, *Luke 18:35—24:53*, 926; Johnson, *Luke*, 297; Fitzmyer, *Luke X-XXIV*, 1250; Bock, *Luke: 9:51—24:53*, 1557; and Green, *Luke*, 685. For Jehu's honor, cf. Josephus, *Antiquities* 9.6.2 §111; and *Antiquities* 18.6.7 §204 for Agrippa's bed in prison.

80. Green, *Luke*, 685.

Contrasting Encounters: Thoroughfare Imagery for and against the Hero

Opposition to this reception of Jesus is also present. The words of welcome are spoken by Jesus' disciples, and the reader is again informed that not all of the bystanders in the crowd agree. The Pharisees request Jesus—whom they address as "teacher"—to command his disciples to stop their loud, joyful praise in which Jesus is recognized as king (v. 39).[81] Jesus' response that even the rocks would cry out for this occasion adds dramatic value to the scene (v. 40). Consequently, the central travel narrative ends with the Pharisees' rejection of Jesus as he enters into Jerusalem similar to the Samaritans' rejection of him at the beginning (9:52–53).[82] Thus, there is a great contrast between the joyous welcome and Jesus' solemn lament viewing Jerusalem, most of whose inhabitants will not recognize the time of God's visitation through Jesus (19:44).[83]

In summary, how do these thoroughfare reception scenes help ravel the story for the reader's experience? The audience is guided to interpret previous statements and actions that prepare them for the next step, Jesus' rejection in Jerusalem. Looking back to Jesus' proleptic portrait, various encounters on thoroughfares have illustrated Jesus' mandate to bring light to those in darkness in order to bring them out of the shadow of death and guide them into the way of peace. Different aspects of Jesus' proleptic portrait have been highlighted, especially as savior and heir to David's throne. They also serve to illustrate the Parable of the Supper, since Jesus not only sent his disciples to them, he also has come to them in person in public spaces to reach those inside and outside the cities. Jesus allowed himself to be met and recognized by those who ironically *see* (recognize) Jesus' identity better than the religious leaders. These scenes also help answer the question posed just before the transition to Jericho: "how can one be saved" (18:26). The answer is clearly explained through these illustrations: even the outcasts (the blind beggar), the despised (Zacchaeus), and "the people" (ὁ λαός). No social barriers prevent Jesus from seeking and saving the lost (19:10).

In this way, the reader is prepared for future developments, for example, the ironic rejection that Jesus will face, especially by those who should be able to see better. It raises the question: Who is in the darkness and needs to be enlightened by Jesus' light? Jesus' disciples are not immune to this spiritual

---

81. Part of the accusation brought against Jesus concerned his claim to be "king" (23:2), which later becomes a part of the soldiers' mockery and is publically exposed on the cross (23:37, 38).

82. Fitzmyer, *Luke X–XXIV*, 1246.

83. The notion of visitation was introduced very early in 1:78 regarding the hero ἐπισκέψεται. John the Baptist prepared the way for the Messiah by preparing the people for his visitation.

myopia illustrated by the two scenes in Luke 24. In addition, some have not completely entered "the way of peace" as illustrated by Judas Iscariot's betrayal. Finally, the reader is better prepared to interpret and experience the three other thoroughfare reception scenes (with the Emmaus disciples, the Ethiopian eunuch, and Saul of Tarsus), each one illustrating how Jesus dissipates various types of blindness. Before reaching those scenes, a nuance of *hodos* will be now examined that the reader has not yet encountered.

Jesus: the Teacher of the Way of God (Luke 20:21)

The last occurrence of *hodos* in the raveling sequence (Luke 20:21) is a figurative use that presents the reader with another nuance of thoroughfare imagery. It can be linked to earlier and later images involving *hodos*. The narrator uses the expression figuratively with a brilliant use of irony in the context of Jesus' rivals attempting to trap him through flattery. From the last occurrence of *hodos* in Jesus' entry into Jerusalem, the reader has entered directly into the temple where Jesus began to drive out the merchants. Due to this scene and Jesus' daily teaching in the courts, the tension grows so much between him and Jerusalem's leadership that the narrator informs, "And the chief priests, the scribes, and the leading men of the people were seeking to destroy him" (19:47b). Thus, Theophilus returns to Jerusalem where he had viewed Jesus among the teachers. There the reader learned first of Jesus' early self-awareness about his relationship with God and his mandate (Luke 2:49). The focus is now Jesus' superiority over the religious leaders, his identity as heir to David's throne, and judgment on the people and the temple (cf. 19:41–44). Moreover, Jesus is portrayed as superior to David (20:41–44). It is noteworthy that no miracles are reported from Jesus' entry until his death.

In three episodes, the religious leaders ask questions to trap Jesus. Each episode depicts Jesus as superior to the religious leaders and results in his rejection.[84] The narrator's portrayal of the people, however, is the opposite; they receive him.[85] They actively seek his teaching in the temple: they

---

84. The chief priests, scribes, elders (20:1); the scribes and the chief priests send spies (20:19–20); and the Sadducees (20:27). The objective of these encounters is finally frustrated, "For they no longer dared to question him about anything" (20:40). Thus, they seek other means to condemn Jesus.

85. The descriptions are remarkable: "for all the people were hanging on to him (i.e., *his words*) while listening" (19:48), as well as "And all the people came early in the morning to him in the temple courts to listen to him" (21:38). Moreover, Jesus' arrest is delayed because the leaders feared the people's reaction (20:19; 22:2). Nevertheless, a shift is noticeable when "the people" are summoned with the "chief priests" and "rulers"

see him better than the religious leaders. In the first episode, Jesus reveals to the leaders the fundamental link about authority with John the Baptist (20:1–8). One cannot have Jesus without John. The Parable of the Vineyard follows this, illustrating his rejection. The people understand it (20:16) as do the leaders (20:19); this motivates them again to seize him. However, they must do this more subtly, because "they feared the people" (v. 19). For this reason, according to the narrator's sketch, they send "spies" who "pretend to be righteous" in order to "catch him in a word" and hand him over to the governor (i.e., Pilate). No specific setting is given for this episode, but the reader may assume from 20:1 (ἐν τῷ ἱερῷ) that it takes place either in or near the temple. The reader is well prepared to interpret their scheming and is further guided by the narrator's aside: "but having perceived their trickery" (v. 23). The focus here is not on their question about the tribute to Caesar, but on their use of the expression containing *hodos* as a part of their deceit and the resulting irony. Verse 21 reveals a parallel thought, which is helpful for understanding the expression "the way of God":

> And they questioned him saying: "Teacher, we know that you speak and teach correctly, and that you are not partial. Rather, you teach the way of God according to the truth."
>
> καὶ ἐπηρώτησαν αὐτὸν λέγοντες· διδάσκαλε, οἴδαμεν ὅτι ὀρθῶς λέγεις καὶ διδάσκεις καὶ οὐ λαμβάνεις πρόσωπον, ἀλλ᾽ ἐπ᾽ ἀληθείας τὴν ὁδὸν τοῦ θεοῦ διδάσκεις·

The episode is full of irony. Those who address Jesus are in fact not righteous. Jesus is exalted, but implicitly compared with "those whose authority to interpret the ways of God is generally without question, whose status vis-à-vis the temple has practically provided them a magisterium-like function."[86] They describe Jesus as one who is not deceived by appearances, and yet that is their very scheme. In this sense, another type of group is presented: not as true disciples, nor would-be disciples, but scheming, false disciples. This places them in the category of those who trust in themselves as righteous (Luke 18:9). They are trying to flatter him in order to win their game. They hypocritically address him as "teacher," when it is clear that they do not accept his teaching. They have a question, but it is not sincere; it is only a guise to trap him.

---

by Pilate (23:13), and verbs in the third person plural indicate participation in Jesus' condemnation (23:18, 20, 23).

86. Green, *Luke*, 714.

The spies begin their flattery with a preamble, "Teacher, we know," which is followed by three statements indicating their understanding of what a true teacher should be, of which one and three are parallel: (1) "that you speak and teach correctly"; (2) "you do not show partiality,"[87] and (3) "you teach the way of God according to the truth."

The import of the spies' flattery and the ensuing irony can be appreciated through some examples of *hodos* with verbs of instruction and knowledge follow (all references are to LXX). Various formulations of "the way(s) of Lord/God" were significant in Jewish literature, which Luke and Theophilus probably knew.[88] For example, psalmists pray to be taught (in) the way of the Lord (Ps 24:8; 27:11 with νομοθετέω; and διδάσκω 50:15; and ὁδηγέω 86:11). *Hodos* is also the object of verbs of knowledge, for example, when the psalmist prays that God's way ("your way") might be known on earth (γινώσκω Ps 67:2). Consequently, the Jewish people and leadership are reproached for not knowing "the way of the Lord" (Jer 5:4–5 γινώσκω and ἐπιγινώσκω; Wis 5:7 ἐπιγινώσκω). Moreover, the author and reader might have been familiar with Abraham's charge to his family to keep "the ways of the Lord" (καὶ φυλάξουσιν τὰς ὁδοὺς κυρίου Gen 18:19) and the reproach to priests for having turned away from "the way" (ὑμεῖς δὲ ἐξεκλίνατε ἐκ τῆς ὁδοῦ Mal 2:8).

What then is the meaning of *hodos* in statement 3? This is the first use of *hodos* as the object of a verb of transmission of knowledge (here, διδάσκω and other verbs will follow).[89] Although the expression "prepare the way of (for) the Lord" (ἑτοιμάσατε τὴν ὁδὸν κυρίου) in Luke 3:4 contains a genitival construction with "Lord" as the qualifier, it is not helpful for this discussion because it illustrates with thoroughfare imagery the preparation for Messiah's coming. Here the reader comes across a different nuance of *hodos*. Based on the parallel with the first statement (ὀρθῶς λέγεις καὶ διδάσκεις ‖ ἐπ' ἀληθείας τὴν ὁδὸν τοῦ θεοῦ διδάσκεις)[90] and other intrinsic information (earlier and later), it could mean, "that which is in conformity with what God has revealed." Jesus' teaching is correct, because it is "of God"; it is *his*

---

87. Peter uses a similar expression regarding God's dealings with Cornelius (Acts 10:34).

88. Cf. Wolter, *LkEv*, 651–52 and Morgan, *derek YHWH*, 75–76; 95–96; 98–100.

89. With verbs of instruction: γνωρίζω (Acts 2:28); κατηχέω (18:25); ἐκτίθεμαι (18:26); and communication: καταγγέλλω (16:17); κακολογέω (19:9).

90. In both sentences the verb διδάσκω is repeated and qualified by an adverbial expression ὀρθῶς ("correctly"; cf. Luke 7:43; 10:28) and ἐπ' ἀληθείας ("truly" or "in truth"; cf. Luke 4:25; 22:59; Acts 4:27; 10:34).

instruction.⁹¹ Two other nuances of the genitival construction are possible and do not exclude each other, "the way (that leads to) God" (destination, cf. Luke 1:79) and "the way (that comes from) God" (its origin). In general, it is difficult, nor perhaps always necessary, to restrict a metaphor to one nuance. The context must determine whether the expression has a primary nuance among other values. Here the expression enhances Jesus' identity as one who is able to express God's teaching for his people. Likewise, it is not constructive to impose a dichotomy on the expression by restricting it to things ethical (what God requires of humanity) or doctrinal (what God has revealed about himself). The narrator's portrayal of Jesus' teaching reveals both aspects.⁹² He knows the *divine way*: "the way of God."

Narratively, the imagery that sheds most light on Jesus as a religious teacher is again the early image depicted by Zechariah (Luke 1:78–79). This image initiates the thoroughfare motif in relation to the hero, and the reader finds a confirmation of it in this and other passages. If Jesus is "the dawn" that brings light to those sitting in darkness (i.e., spiritually blind), and guides them into the way of peace, then it is possible to link it with Jesus as the teacher of the way of God. Through his light (Jesus' knowledge of God's instruction), he is able to guide others to God. This image also corresponds with the description of Jesus' identity and the spiritual state of the people in this passage. Moreover, it also confirms the foreshadowing of Jesus as the teacher among the teachers described in the initial orientation (Luke 2:46–47).

Jesus' luminous response (20:25) and their reaction ("and being astonished by his answer, they became silent" 20:26b) confirm their statement about him as teacher of the way of God. Here is the great irony: instead of Jesus being caught by them, he has caught them, and he is once again portrayed as *the* teacher of Israel.⁹³ The narrator's mention of the spies' failure in

---

91. The positive portrayal of the people's appreciation of Jesus' teaching comes very early in the narrative, thus preparing the reader to consider Jesus as an authoritative teacher (cf. Luke 4:15, 32).

92. Most scholars use extrinsic data to shed light on this expression. Godet (*Luc*, 381) links it to previous revelation: "the way of God, the holy line drawn by God himself in his law." Similarly, but with an emphasis on divine ethics, i.e., what God requires (Fitzmyer, *Luke X–XXIV*, 1295; Marshall (*Luke*, 734); or how one is supposed to walk (i.e., live) before God (Nolland, *Luke 18:35—24:53*, 958; Bock, *Luke: 9:51—24:53*, 1610). Similarly, CPS (p. 630) suggest "the way God wants people to live." Klein (*LkEv*, 630) brings in the aspect of salvation (*Weg des Heils*), but also the "way of life" according to God.

93. It is noteworthy how Jesus is portrayed via his own voice before and after entering Jerusalem through the instructions of preparation he gives to his disciples (ὁ κύριος Luke 19:31; ὁ διδάσκαλος Luke 22:11).

the presence of the people (v. 26) serves again to emphasize the superiority of Jesus in their eyes. Pragmatically, the main point of this passage is probably not to instruct the reader about the tribute to Caesar, but to demonstrate once more Jesus' realization of his mandate in the face of unrighteous opposition. All of the reader's confidence depends on the reality of the spies' statement.[94] They meant it falsely, but the narrator shows that the statement turns against them by actually being verified in this incident and in his entire portrayal of Jesus as a faithful teacher of God's instruction. Nolli sums up well the force of the spies' description: "[It is] Praise that, false or sincere, suits Jesus wonderfully."[95] He indeed is the teacher of the way of God, a spiritual leader, and for this reason is worthy to be followed. The reader is inspired to follow Jesus as a true disciple. Thus, the narrator depicts Jesus as the teacher of "the way of God" in Jerusalem, now superior to those from whom he received instruction in his childhood (Luke 2:41–52). The passage contributes to the thread that compares Jesus to the teachers of Israel, foreshadowed very early in the narrative and continually developed in the various scenes where he shows his superiority. Luke continue this comparison in the second volume when Jesus' followers show their superior understanding of God's purposes (e.g., Peter and John, Acts 4:13; Stephen, 6:10; Paul, 9:22; Apollos, 18:28). This recalls the prolepsis in Jesus' voice: "for I will give you speech and wisdom that none of your opponents will be able to withstand or refute" (Luke 21:15; cf. Luke 12:11). Consequently, "the way of God" here provides a narrative link to the unmodified *hodos* in Acts (e.g., in Acts 9:2, "so that if he found some belong to the Way). This will be explored below in the unraveling sequence.

This is the final occurrence of thoroughfare terminology in the raveling sequence. From this point to the end of the sequence, the narrator leads the reader to experience further clashes with the religious and political parties, his betrayal through Judas Iscariot, the (apparently) final instructions to his disciples, his arrest, trials and crucifixion and burial. Much physical movement appears while in Jerusalem, but literal and figurative occurrences for thoroughfares are absent.[96] No other reception scenes are recounted. His disciples seem also increasingly distant. From all appearances, the story

---

94. "For the Christian reader the spies speak the truth, about which they themselves are not convinced." Eckey, *LkEv II*, 829.

95. Nolli, *Luca*, 878.

96. For example, Jesus is led (ἄγω, 22:54; 23:1, 32 (two criminals as object) and led away (ἀπάγω, 22:66; 23:26. Nonetheless, on the way to the place of crucifixion ("the skull" in 23:33), he is still followed (23:27) and he turns (23:28) to speak to those following him. Cf. the use of στραφείς when Jesus is leading people (7:9; 14:25).

about Jesus seems over. Consequently, the thoroughfare motif that is centered on him appears to end.

Summary of the Thoroughfare Motif in the Raveling Sequence

In the raveling sequence, the thoroughfare motif participates in the plot by helping the reader to interpret and experience the story through two interrelated strands depicting Jesus, John the Baptist, and Jesus disciples. The motif continues to be very positive—from the narrator and reader's point of view—for it describes the protagonists' forward movement in the face of opposition. First, the motif reappears when the narrator brings positive closure for John the Baptist's role as the hero's precursor through Jesus' own voice (7:27 a citation of Mal 3:1). This adds to the voices that have already described the precursor-hero relationship: Gabriel (1:17), Zechariah (1:76), and the narrator citing Isaiah (3:4–5). Then, there is a transition between John the Baptist and Jesus' disciples, since Jesus sends his disciples on the road to preach in the towns where he is going to pass through. He gives them instructions to announce divine judgment in their streets in case of rejection, which also recalls John the Baptist's prophetic role.

Second, thoroughfare imagery depicts Jesus fulfilling his mandate in illustrations, highlighted reception scenes, and an ironic confirmation of Jesus as the teacher of "the way of God" in Jerusalem. In the contexts of the Parables of the Narrow Door and of the Great Supper, Jesus assumes the role of the "head of the house" as the rejected teacher in their streets and as the master who sends his servant to invite the outcasts scattered on the thoroughfares inside and outside the city. Then, in the climactic movement from Jericho to Jerusalem, the reader encounters tangible illustrations of how people receive Jesus in thoroughfare settings, which exemplify Jesus as "the dawn from on high" coming to those in darkness (Luke 1:78–79) and the image of the servant going to the outcasts. This cluster of three thoroughfare reception episodes prepare the reader for later reception scenes in the pivot and unraveling sequences (the Emmaus disciples; the Ethiopian eunuch; and Saul of Tarsus).

Finally, the reader admires Jesus as the teacher of Israel, confirmed by the spies that Jesus teaches "the way of God." Thus, the early image of Jesus being "the dawn from on high" (a spiritual guide or teacher) is also confirmed with great irony. The people realize this, but the leaders do not, because they are spiritually blind. Up to this point in the narrative, the very positive portraiture of Jesus and his co-protagonists through the thoroughfare motif has contributed to the reader's certainty as a follower of Jesus. At the same time, however, narrative tension increases since what the reader knows is strongly contrasted with the hero's rejection on the action level. This leads the reader to have a heightened experience of Jesus' ironic and tragic rejection in Jerusalem.

5

Pivotal Encounter: An About-face on Emmaus Road

(Luke 24:1—Acts 2:13)

THE PIVOT SEQUENCE IS short but crucial for the narrative. It spans the two volumes and highlights the transforming actions accomplished by Jesus and their effects. Thus, the reader encounters the resumption of the hero's mandate following his execution and death, but also the significant results produced in Jesus' disciples, that is, the overcoming of their own blindness and their preparation for greater involvement in the hero's mandate. The reader learns that Jesus is no longer in the tomb and overhears the angels' explanation of it to the women disciples at the tomb (24:4, 23). These followers leave in order to report this "to the eleven and to all the others" (24:10). Yet, the first scene of an encounter with Jesus takes place on a road from Jerusalem to Emmaus. In the pivot sequence, three thoroughfare expressions appear, and all are *hodos*. Two occur in the Emmaus passage (Luke 24:32, 35). The third occurs as an adverbial modifier in a description of the distance between Jerusalem and the Mount of Olives (Acts 1:12).[1] Similar to the aforementioned use of *hodos* in Luke 2:44, this occurrence also does not contribute to the plot's development. For this reason, the discussion below will focus entirely on the encounter with Jesus on the road to Emmaus.

---

1. The syntactical function of *hodos* in the accusative in Luke 2:4 and Acts 1:12 responds to questions like how far? and how long? Cf. BDR, §161:1:

Jesus and Disciples on Emmaus Road (24:32, 35)

This is the fourth of six thoroughfare reception scenes. This scene stands out compared to the previous three in that it occurs after Jesus' resurrection. This is the first *appearance scene* mentioned in Luke-Acts, and it takes place in a thoroughfare setting. The verbs of movement in verses 13 and 15 provide further details about the setting. The disciples are moving away from Jerusalem for a reason that the narrator will reveal. The reader learns via flashbacks later in the passage that the event took place on a road (from the two occurrences of *hodos* in verses 32 and 35). Therefore, the entire passage (24:13–35) begins with the description of the two disciples' dejected state and ends with their joyful return to Jerusalem to report their encounter with Jesus. The passage then segues naturally into Jesus' appearance to all the disciples (24:36–49).

It is noteworthy that the reader discovers later that "the Lord" had also appeared to Peter (24:34), but this encounter is not described. This demonstrates that the narrator has placed the Emmaus road encounter as a showcase in the pivot of Luke-Acts. This scene is particularly engaging in that it is not just a snapshot of an event, but also a depiction of the process of transformation that the reader witnesses. Divine initiative is evident since Jesus joins them in their walk from Jerusalem to Emmaus. These disciples are in that location, because for them the story has ended: "it has been three days since these things happened" (v. 21). They have lost all hope. Movement away from Jerusalem reveals their state of mind, since they are symbolically moving in the opposite direction than that of the entire narrative and the previous thoroughfare reception scenes. The disciples are not described as marginalized persons, but as hopeful Jews in Jesus' liberating intervention ("But we were hoping that he was the one was going to deliver Israel" 24: 21; cf. 1:68; 2:38). Unlike the first two thoroughfare reception scenes, Jesus sets out to recover two wayward disciples, not outcast or despised persons. The focus is on the transformation of those who were already following Jesus.[2] During this walk together, Jesus rebukes them for their lack of faith and understanding (v. 25); they are in effect still partially blind. As the "dawn from on high" portrayed in Luke 1:78–79, Jesus figuratively brings light to them on the road by showing what "Moses and the prophets" had said about him (v. 27). The narrator thus includes another example of irony: some of the disciples went to the tomb and found things as described by the women,

---

2. For example, they recognize the action of the breaking of the bread (24:30) and know "the eleven" (24:33).

"but him they did not see" (v. 24).³ Now Jesus is standing in front of them and they still cannot recognize him. They need Jesus' help to see his identity.

It is significant that there are other hints of illumination in the actions of explanation of the Scriptures (διερμηνεύω, v. 27; echoed in the analepsis διανοίγω, v. 32) "opened to us the scriptures," and its effects: "our hearts burned" (v. 32), and "got up . . . and returned" (v. 33). It consists of a very concrete example of Jesus accomplishing his mandate according to the proleptic image in Luke 1:78-79. A spiritual enlightenment takes place to take away their inability to recognize him due to their lack of understanding of what had happened in Jerusalem. This lack of recognition requires two complementary revelatory actions, mental (24:16 → 31, 35) and spiritual (24:25 → 27, 32).⁴

Both occurrences of *hodos* occur after the encounter with Jesus in two analepses, which relate the disciples' interpretation of the event. The first occurrence (v. 32) is in the voice of the two disciples (direct speech) as they discuss with one another their encounter with Jesus. The second (v. 35) is in the narrator's voice (indirect speech) for the two disciples' report to "the eleven and those who were with them" (v. 33):

> 24:32 —And they said to one another: "Were not our hearts burning [within us] while he was talking to us on the road and explaining the Scriptures to us?"
>
> καὶ εἶπαν πρὸς ἀλλήλους· οὐχὶ ἡ καρδία ἡμῶν καιομένη ἦν [ἐν ἡμῖν] ὡς ἐλάλει ἡμῖν ἐν τῇ ὁδῷ, ὡς διήνοιγεν ἡμῖν τὰς γραφάς;
>
> 24:35 —And they were explaining the things (that had happened) on the road and how he had been made known to them through the breaking of the bread.
>
> καὶ αὐτοὶ ἐξηγοῦντο τὰ ἐν τῇ ὁδῷ καὶ ὡς ἐγνώσθη αὐτοῖς ἐν τῇ κλάσει τοῦ ἄρτου.

By the end of the story, a clear pattern of transformation has emerged.⁵ The explanation of the Scriptures takes place "on the road," since movement

---

3. Narrative irony has already emerged with Jesus' question and his disciples' response compared to the reversed roles in verses 19-26. Wolter, *LkEv*, 779.

4. This procedure is echoed in Jerusalem with the other disciples; first mental in verses 36-43, then spiritual in verse 45: "Then he opened their mind(s) so that they could understand the Scriptures."

5. The inverted parallelism of the passage is convincing, which serves to sketch "the import of disclosure and perception to the Lucan agenda:" Green, *Luke*, 842.

can be inferred form v. 28 since they reached their destination (Emmaus). Fitzmyer is right: "The prepositional phrase *en tē hodō* again strikes the chord of the geographical motif."[6] The transformation occurs through verbs of communication ("explain" διερμηνεύω, v. 27, "speak" λαλέω and "explain" διανοίγω (v. 32), and through a familiar act, the breaking of bread (vv. 30–31, 35).[7]

The same verb "open" (διανοίγω, v. 31) confirms spiritual illumination: "their eyes were opened" (διηνοίχθησαν, passive voice). This figurative use envisages "the eyes of their mind" and the need for corrected vision (i.e., understanding) leading to their recognition and reception of Jesus according to his proleptic portrait (i.e., as "the Christ," v. 26). They come to the understanding that Jesus is greater than their previous idea of him as a "mighty prophet" (v. 19). Their decision to return to Jerusalem confirms their illumination.[8] They have been transformed through Jesus' illumination on the road, and, figuratively, have been brought into "the way of peace" (Luke 1:79). The event could have turned out differently; it could have been a rejection scene without the ensuing transformation.

Hence, pragmatically, the narrator has provided once again a concrete example of how a type of blindness was overcome through Jesus' illumination in a thoroughfare setting. Fitzmyer summarizes the importance of this scene in a decisive moment of the plot's development:

> It is precisely the geographical setting in which Christ instructs them about the sense of the Scriptures. Thus at the end of the Lucan Gospel the appearance-story par excellence takes place, not only in the vicinity of the city of destiny, toward which Jesus' entire movement in the Gospel has been directed, but his final and supreme instruction about the relation of his destiny to that which Moses and the prophets of old had announced is given "on the road." The subtle, yet highly deliberate, use of this Lucan motif is not to be missed.[9]

---

6. Fitzmyer, *Luke X–XXIV*, 1568. For Nolli (*Luca*, 1061) the expression ἐν τῇ ὁδῷ in both verses is a temporal modifier that indicates the duration of the event. Yet, it is more likely a prepositional phrase of location, responding to the question "Where?"

7. The two clauses with "as" (ὡς) joined closely asyndetically indicate complementary actions that help their understanding in verse 32. Klein, *LkEv*, 733.

8. The phrase in verse 33 ("... the eleven and those who were with them gathered together") indicates that the story has come full circle as it echoes the phrase "to the eleven and to all the others" in 24:9 (cf. also vv. 22–23).

9. Fitzmyer, *Luke X–XXIV*, 1557–58.

Nolland suggests that the expression "on the way" might evoke Jesus' teaching activity on the way to Jerusalem (cf. 9:57) rather than the path of discipleship as a *way*.[10] More certainly, it represents a tangible example of Jesus pursuing people for their spiritual transformation, again, a showcased thoroughfare reception scene that gives confidence to the reader. Yet, this scene is perhaps more meaningful to the reader than the previous thoroughfare reception scenes due to the higher degree of identification with the Emmaus disciples. Although they were already following Jesus, they could not clearly see his identity. According to Jesus' point of view, they should not have been going away from Jerusalem in a dejected state and should have recognized him on the road. He helps them overcome this state caused by darkness. For this reason, this scene is another example of a *mise en abyme*[11] strategically highlighted so that Theophilus and others see something of their experience with Jesus within the narrative. The narrator had already related this figuratively through images (e.g., Zechariah's prophecy and the Parable of the Great Supper), namely, not only do people go before Jesus (John the Baptist and Jesus' disciples), he also goes toward those who need him, even after the resurrection. Although he is in a resurrected state, Jesus is still able to perform this revelatory action, which will be further confirmed in the encounters with Saul and Ananias. This episode prepares the reader for the two other thoroughfare reception scenes in the unraveling sequence involving encounters with Jesus.[12]

Summary of the Thoroughfare Motif in the Pivot Sequence

The pivot reopens the fulfillment of Jesus' mandate by highlighting Jesus on the road encountering those who are spiritually blind. The thoroughfare motif reappears in another crucial moment of the narration: the turning point from defeat and desperation to victory and joy. The Emmaus road encounter is a showcase for the opening image of Jesus as the dawn leading people into the way of peace (Luke 1:78–19). Jesus is back and appears on the road for the purpose of spiritual transformation of his two disillusioned disciples.

---

10. Nolland, *Luke 18:35—24:53*, 1206.

11. *Mise en abyme* may be defined as "A miniature replica of a text embedded within that text; a textual part reduplicating, reflecting, or mirroring (one or more than one aspect of) the textual whole." Prince, *Narratology*, 53.

12. A similar scene is described with similar language in Acts 9:27 where Barnabas recounts (διηγέομαι) to the leaders in Jerusalem how Jesus had spoken (λαλέω) to Saul on the way (ἐν τῇ ὁδῷ).

Through his illumination, they understand that he is the Christ, one of the aspects of his proleptic portrait. This reception scene provides a link with the previous thoroughfare reception episodes in the raveling sequence. It also prepares the reader for two others in the unraveling sequence. Thus, narrative tension begins to decrease as the reader observes with pleasure the transformation in Jesus' disciples. The reader's questions and expectations are being met in part through the thoroughfare motif's appearance in this crucial moment of the plot as it contributes significantly to the plot's unity and cumulative effect on the reader through his identification with the Emmaus disciples. We now turn to the thoroughfare motif's performance in the unraveling sequence.

6

Expanding Encounters: From Roads to "the Way"

(Acts 2:14—28:15)

THE THOROUGHFARE MOTIF CONTRIBUTES to the unraveling of the plot by enhancing the reader's interpretation and experience of the responses to and effects of Jesus' *transforming actions*. The thoroughfare motif has already illustrated the transformation in the Emmaus disciples. Therefore, there is a degree of overlapping between the pivot and the unraveling sequences as regards the transformation of Jesus' disciples. Yet, the story is far from being complete since the narrator has made no mention of the effects on Jewish people outside the circle of Jesus' disciples or on the nations. Consequently, does the thoroughfare motif have any part in responding to the reader's questions or expectations?

Spotlight on Peter's Extension of Jesus' Mandate in Jerusalem

The distribution of the occurrences would lead one to think that it is initially not so important, since twenty of the twenty-two occurrences of the thoroughfare motif occur starting with Philip and the Ethiopian's encounter (8:26 ff.). Therefore, from the beginning of the unraveling sequence (2:14) until the above encounter (8:26), there are only two occurrences (Acts 2:28; 5:15). The motif begins slowly in the unraveling sequence, but then accelerates as the narrative progresses. What factors are involved in this development? Does the motif appear in important moments of the unraveling sequence? The first two occurrences are a part of the description of Peter's role in extending Jesus' mission.

Proclaiming "the Ways to Life" (Acts 2:28)

A thoroughfare expression occurs immediately after the third transforming action in the context of Peter's speech in Jerusalem. It is an intertextual expression "ways of life" (ὁδοὺς ζωῆς) in Acts 2:28 from Ps 15:11. The reader views various reactions to Jesus' sending of the Holy Spirit on the day of Pentecost, including mockery (2:13), which gave rise to Peter's public explanation. The narrator recounts Peter's speech (2:14–36) and his appropriation of Psalm 15:8–11 (LXX) as a part of a longer passage (2:14–42). Peter's preaching is supported by several citations from the Jewish prophetic tradition.[1]

Concerning specifically Ps 15:11, Peter uses David's praise to God to express his hope in the resurrection as support for his teaching on the Christ's resurrection (περὶ τῆς ἀναστάσεως τοῦ Χριστοῦ 2:31). In Peter's speech, it appears in the context of contrasts, death and life, burial and resurrection, signifying questions of physical life and the Christ's power over it (2:24). The essential point is that what David had hoped for, knowledge of life in God's presence after death, the Christ has made known fully.[2] In fact, though historically David is speaking of himself, Peter claims that David was speaking prophetically of the Christ's death and resurrection.[3]

The reading from NA27 of Acts 2:28 is identical to Ps 15:11 (LXX) except the omission of the final phrase in LXX (τερπνότητες ἐν τῇ δεξιᾷ σου εἰς τέλος).[4] It reads "you have made known to me the ways of life, you will fill me with joy through your presence" (ἐγνώρισάς μοι ὁδοὺς ζωῆς, πληρώσεις με εὐφροσύνης μετὰ τοῦ προσώπου σου). Some syntactical elements and lexical links help appreciate its contribution to the passage in question and to the larger discussion. As in other genitive constructions in Luke-Acts when *hodos* is joined to another substantive, the idiom "ways of life" may be functioning as a genitive of destination (= "that leads to"), thus "the ways that lead to life."[5] This is supported by its intrinsic relation to the notion of

---

1. All are citations from LXX: 2:17–21 (Joel 3:1–5); 2:25–28 (Ps 15:8–11); and 2:34–35 (Ps 109:1).

2. MT Ps 16:11: תּוֹדִיעֵנִי אֹרַח חַיִּים; LXX ἐγνώρισάς μοι ὁδοὺς ζωῆς.

3. Cf. Moessner, "*Two Lords*," 227 and Moyise, *Old Testament*, 53.

4. Which renders the Hebrew, נְעִמוֹת בִּימִינְךָ נֶצַח (Ps 16:11). No textual problems are indicated in NA27 for Acts 2:28. Conjectures can be proposed as to its absence. Perhaps the manuscript that Luke had did not have this phrase. Alternatively, he was citing from memory. Perhaps he omitted it to focus on the first part that illustrates the resurrection.

5. As a genitive of destination, see CP, 40 and Wallace, *Greek*, 101. Cf. "the way of peace" (Luke 1:79), "the way of God/the Lord" (Luke 20:21; Acts 18:25, 26), and "the way of salvation" (Acts 16:17).

movement from one place to another, or, figuratively, from one realm to another. The expression contrasts with preceding images such as "death" (v. 24), "Hades" and "decay" (v. 27). The connection between *hodos* and "life" (ζωή) is noteworthy since "life" takes on a significant nuance in Acts after Jesus' resurrection. For example, he is described as the "originator/author of life" (in τὸν δὲ ἀρχηγὸν τῆς ζωῆς ἀπεκτείνατε, 3:15). The angel of the Lord commands the apostles, "speak to the people in the temple all the words of this life" (5:20), that is, the life that one can obtain through Jesus' resurrection (cf. also 11:18; 13:46, 48).

Moreover, the expression "ways of life" is the object of the verb "make known," which indicates communication of knowledge. In Luke 20:21 it was observed that "the way of God" is the object of "teach" (διδάσκω). As the narrative progresses, other verbs of communication occur with *hodos* in a figurative meaning: "proclaim" with "way of salvation" (16:17); "instruct" with "the way of the Lord" (18:25) and "expound" with "the way of God" (18:26).[6] Thus, in the context of preaching, Peter, having understood the meaning of Jesus' death and resurrection, now proclaims God's instruction concerning death and resurrection.[7] He now knows the "ways that lead to life" through Jesus and makes them known to the crowd that has gathered. This meaningful expression has its purpose in Peter's speech and, as it is recontextualiazed by the narrator, contributing to the reader's understanding and experience of the story.[8]

Narratively, it contributes to the interpretation of the events that have just transpired, the sending of the Holy Spirit and its effects among the

---

6. Here one finds the plural form, qualified by ζωή, both without article. The plural form is found qualified by an adjective and a substantive in a later occurrence, "the straight ways of the Lord" (13:10, τὰς ὁδοὺς [τοῦ] κυρίου τὰς εὐθείας). No significant difference is apparent between plural and singular forms.

7. In the MT (Ps 16:11), only one verb occurs, a Hiphil imperfect תּוֹדִיעֵנִי, which may be rendered with verbal expression "cause to know," possibly with the nuance of "to teach" (BDB, 395.) either in the future tense ("you will make known to me") or in the present ("you make known to me"). The LXX (as well as the NA27), however, contains two verbs, an aorist indicative ἐγνώρισας, followed by another indicative in the future πληρώσεις, which renders the construct chain שֹׂבַע שְׂמָחוֹת. Consequently, the sense of ἐγνώρισας is usually understood as a cognitive action already realized ("you have made known to me"), then completed by the more experiential verb that follows (πληρώσεις), which for the psalmist was to be realized ("you will fill me with gladness").

8. Not all exegetes, however, find value in verse 28 for Peter's sermon. For example, Barrett (*Acts*, 1:146) writes, "This verse does not add substantially to the argument and does not appear when the Psalm is used in the *Acts of Philip* 78 (15) (L.-B. 2.2.31)." Similarly, Bruce (*Acts*, 125) opines, "The remainder of the quotation from LXX presents no marked deviations from MT and plays no part in Peter's exposition."

Jewish public. By anchoring the resurrection in the Jewish prophetic tradition, Peter thus gives credibility to this central event. He cites David, who is buried in Jerusalem, as speaking of his heir (the Christ) who would not experience the decay of the grave.[9]

Pragmatically, as appropriated by the narrator in the flow of the account, the expression further buttresses for the reader the hero's resurrection through the sending of the Holy Spirit, and in so doing, increases his confidence in the transformation that Jesus is able to bring. The now familiar thoroughfare imagery, especially *hodos*, adds to his certainty in the teachings regarding what leads away from death to life through the resurrection. Again, thoroughfare imagery—even in its figurative uses—has the intrinsic force to describe movement and transformation, leaving one domain and entering another; from darkness to light, from the shadow of death into the way of peace (Luke 1:79) and from death to life (Acts 2:28). Jesus' *transforming actions* lead to life. The prophet David had foreseen it, and Peter (and the narrator) claims this. This message motivates the disciples' proclamation to the gathered crowd: "Therefore, with certainty (ἀσφαλῶς) let all the house of Israel know" (γινωσκέτω, 2:36a). The certainty of the psalmist and Peter should also become the certainty of the people and through the narration also that of the reader. Similar to the two citations from Isaiah and Malachi concerning John the Baptist, the use of *hodos* here from an intertextual voice adds to the spiritual landscape of Luke-Acts, thus adding to its cumulative objective and pragmatic force. In addition, as an object of a verb of communication, it prepares the reader for the increase of figurative uses of *hodos*, specifically those concerning Jesus' disciples and their message.

Healings through Peter in the Streets of Jerusalem (Acts 5:15)

The next occurrence of thoroughfare imagery is a literal use in Acts 5:15. Following the dramatic deaths of Ananias and Sapphira, the reader considers Peter's successful ministry (5:12–16). Narratively, this passage functions as the initial orientation of the larger passage (vv. 12–42), preceding the ensuing sequences, which depict the opposition from the religious authorities, Gamaliel's intervention, and the resumption of apostolic preaching (v. 42). A familiar picture appears with the apostles among the people in the temple area (v. 26). Teaching is not specifically mentioned in vv. 12–16, but it may be assumed (cf. vv. 20–21, 25, 28, 40, 42). What is emphasized in

---

9. See Marguerat, *Actes (1–12)*, 91.

verses 12–16 are the miraculous works performed publicly by the apostles. More people are joining their ranks, but now "the people" are afraid (v. 13a; perhaps due to the news about Ananias and Sapphira) and, ironically, so are the leaders (v. 26).

Luke summarizes this successful moment with a result clause (using ὥστε) in verse 15:

> so much that they brought the ill even in the streets and placed them on stretchers and beds, so that while Peter came by his shadow might fall upon any of them.
>
> ὥστε καὶ εἰς τὰς πλατείας ἐκφέρειν τοὺς ἀσθενεῖς καὶ τιθέναι ἐπὶ κλιναρίων καὶ κραβάττων, ἵνα ἐρχομένου Πέτρου κἂν ἡ σκιὰ ἐπισκιάσῃ τινὶ αὐτῶν.

The physical setting (εἰς τὰς πλατείας) is the wide streets of Jerusalem where Peter passes. These thoroughfares, as observed above, are the streets that allow people to gather.[10] This specific use of πλατείας helps the reader to imagine that the people are not hiding in the narrow back streets or alleys, but are openly seeking God's favor through the apostles. Moreover, their expectations for healing are extraordinary.[11] Great miracles are taking place, thus Peter and the other apostles are accomplishing what Jesus was doing (previous scenes are evoked, Luke 4:40; 5:19; 6:18–19). This is enhanced by the explicit mention of the people's expectation.[12] The apostles are also fulfilling Jesus' teaching in the Parable of the Great Supper in that they are going to the people, even the marginalized, in the streets. Yet, a reverse movement is also visible, people are coming from outside to inside, as Jervell notes, ". . . now even the masses are coming from towns around Jerusalem, and it happens exactly that which the Sanhedrin feared (4:17)."[13]

Consequently, this summary passage using thoroughfare imagery contributes to the unraveling of the plot by showing that the apostles bring transformation in the streets of Jerusalem, thus extending Jesus' mandate into public spaces. The unraveling sequence is moving in the direction of victory in Jerusalem where the narrator had brought the reader into the

---

10. Bruce (*Acts*, 168) suggests renderings and etymological development: "'broadways', 'main streets', 'squares', whence (via Lat. *platea*) Ital. *piazza*, Fr. *place*, Ger. *Platz*, in this sense."

11. A similar situation appears in relation to Paul (19:12). A precedent is Luke 6:19, which describes power coming out of Jesus. Touching him appears necessary for healing, even if only his garment, cf. 8:44.

12. Johnson, *Acts*, 95.

13. Jervell, *Apg.*, 202.

story. The apostles are struggling against Satan and other opposing forces (here, the "high priest" and his associates, the "sect of the Sadducees," 5:17).[14]

This section concludes the contribution of the thoroughfare motif in the spotlight of Peter. A later literal use of *rumē* (12:10) is a part of the narrator's detailed description of Peter's escape from prison being led by an angel of the Lord (12:7). It does not merit particular attention. The discussion now turns to the next seven occurrences of *hodos* used to highlight the final two thoroughfare reception episodes with the Ethiopian eunuch and Saul of Tarsus.

Highlighted Thoroughfare Reception Scenes for the Jews and the Nations

Gentile Reception on the Road to Gaza: Philip and the Ethiopian (Acts 8:26, 36, 39)

Following the focus on Peter and Stephen's witness in Jerusalem and on the witnesses who have gone beyond Jerusalem and Judea toward Jews in other regions, and even to the Samaritans (8:4–25), the thoroughfare motif reappears in the spotlight on Philip (from 8:4ff). Philip is sent to meet an Ethiopian eunuch who is on his way to his homeland but also in search of meaning for a passage in Isaiah. Immediately after this, the reader witnesses the rise of a new witness, Saul of Tarsus, who is in search of "those of the Way." In fact, the next seven occurrences of *hodos* occur in this cluster of two thoroughfare reception scenes to highlight the reception of Jesus among the nations and the Jews. Together they serve to prepare the reader to experience the missionary thrust to the nations. The discussion below builds on the results of Baban's contribution on the "post-Easter on the road encounters." Indeed, the passage on the Ethiopian eunuch has literary affinities with the accounts of Emmaus and Saul.[15] Baban and other scholars, however, do not make the connections in Luke-Acts that are specifically related to the

---

14. The disciples' authority over spiritual antagonists was described by Jesus as seeing Satan fall "from heaven like lightning" (Luke 10:18). Now Satan is back on the scene (Acts 5:3). Furthermore, the disciples' mandate could have been truncated by human adversaries if Gamaliel had not intervened. Yet, shortly thereafter, the apostles were back in the temple (5:42), again another parallel with Jesus (*syncrisis*) in the temple (Luke 19:47; 21:37).

15. Cf. Spencer, *Philip*, 141–45.

Expanding Encounters: From Roads to "the Way"

strand of the thoroughfare motif centered on Jesus' identity and mandate (e.g., Zechariah's "dawn from on high"; the Parable of the Great Supper; the first three thoroughfare reception scenes; and Jesus as the teacher of "the way of God").

The discussion turns to specific commentary on the passage concerning Philip and the Ethiopian (8:26–40) in which *hodos* appears three times (Acts 8:26, 36, 39). The vocabulary provides continuity of movement and setting in the passage: the verb "go" (πορεύομαι) occurs with each of the three occurrences of *hodos*. They appear before, during, and after the encounter. All three are literal uses, providing the physical setting for various sequences of the micro-narrative. The entire act of reception takes place on the same road, which descends from Jerusalem to Gaza. The narrator's use of the imperfect (ἐπορεύοντο, v. 36) provides continuous movement and action on the same road. The first occurrence of *hodos* describes the command to Philip, the second helps illustrate the encounter with both characters, and the third the Ethiopian's final action. This suggests a literary frame that highlights the transformation of the Ethiopian, the object of the divinely led encounter.[16] The two outer occurrences describe the Ethiopian's state before and after the transformational encounter.

The first occurrence in 8:26 indicates the location of the command that, when performed, will place Philip on the road upon which the Ethiopian is traveling:

> An angel of the Lord spoke to Philip saying, "Arise and go toward south on the road that goes down from Jerusalem to Gaza. This is a desert road[17]."
>
> Ἄγγελος δὲ κυρίου ἐλάλησεν πρὸς Φίλιππον λέγων· ἀνάστηθι καὶ πορεύου κατὰ μεσημβρίαν ἐπὶ τὴν ὁδὸν τὴν καταβαίνουσαν ἀπὸ Ἰερουσαλὴμ εἰς Γάζαν, αὕτη ἐστὶν ἔρημος.

Likewise, the third occurrence in 8:39 indicates that the Ethiopian went "his way" (τὴν ὁδὸν αὐτοῦ), continuing his journey on the same road whence he came. The final state of the Ethiopian is qualified by "rejoicing"

---

16. Cf. Marguerat's suggestion of a chiastic structure, based on Dionisio Minguez's article ("Hechos 8,24–40," 168–191), which emphasizes the importance of the scripture by placing verses 32–33 at the center, the citation of Isaiah 53,7b–8c. Marguerat, *Actes (1–12)*, 303.

17. "This is a desert road" (αὕτη ἐστὶν ἔρημος) could be the author's parenthetical note. It qualifies ἡ ὁδός, which is the center of activity, and not ἡ Γάζα. BDR (§290.1n2); Bruce, *Acts*, 225; Jervell, *Apg.*, 270; and Schneider, *Apg.*, 1:501.

(χαίρων), which evokes the reactions of the blind beggar (δοξάζων τὸν θεόν Luke 18:43) and of Zacchaeus (χαίρων Luke 19:6):

> When they came up from the water, the Spirit of the Lord seized Philip, and the Eunuch did not see him anymore, for he went on his way rejoicing.[18]
>
> ὅτε δὲ ἀνέβησαν ἐκ τοῦ ὕδατος, πνεῦμα κυρίου ἥρπασεν τὸν Φίλιππον καὶ οὐκ εἶδεν αὐτὸν οὐκέτι ὁ εὐνοῦχος, ἐπορεύετο γὰρ τὴν ὁδὸν αὐτοῦ χαίρων.

Similar to the sudden movement towards one another (vv. 26-27), a brusque movement away from one another follows (v. 39, cf. ἁρπάζω), both due to divine instructions.

In the middle of the passage, the second occurrence in 8:36 provides the setting of the Ethiopian's baptism, the result of the transforming action:

> While they were going down the road, they came to some water, and the Eunuch said, "Here is water, what keeps me from getting baptized?"
>
> ὡς δὲ ἐπορεύοντο κατὰ τὴν ὁδόν, ἦλθον ἐπί τι ὕδωρ, καί φησιν ὁ εὐνοῦχος· ἰδοὺ ὕδωρ, τί κωλύει με βαπτισθῆναι;

This thoroughfare encounter is enhanced when linked to previous reception scenes on thoroughfares, in particular with the Emmaus passage, since the Ethiopian's experience evokes some striking parallels with Jesus' illuminating journey with the disciples from Emmaus. The similar portrayal recalls what Theophilus has already read in the first volume. Philip is now accomplishing Jesus' mandate through divine direction.[19] These parallelisms between characters—examples of an ancient literary technique called *syncrisis*—provide further evidence for the narrative unity of Luke-Acts.[20] Below, the parallels with the Emmaus passage are specified in parentheses. The first reference represents elements from the Ethiopian passage and the second from the Emmaus passage:

---

18. It is possible to understand τὴν ὁδὸν αὐτου as figurative, that is, by extension *road* for *journey*. BDR (§198.5n6) however opts for the literal sense due to the accusative.

19. Although Jesus is not physically present, it is clearly portrayed as a divinely organized encounter, as the "angel of the Lord" (8:26) and the "Spirit" (v. 29; and "spirit of the Lord," v. 39) also intervene with brusque movements (e.g., ἁρπάζω).

20. Marguerat, *Actes (1-12)*, 304. According to Aletti, parallelisms represent the dominant narrative technique in Luke-Acts. Aletti, *Racconto*, 72-79ff. Cf. also Johnson, *Acts*, 160.

Expanding Encounters: From Roads to "the Way"

1. The itinerary is clearly indicated moving away from Jerusalem (Gaza; Emmaus).[21]

2. One party is already traveling on the road, and another party joins them (Ethiopian and Philip; disciples and Jesus).

3. A *complication* (spiritual blindness) becomes apparent on the road: lack of understanding of God's plan in Jesus revealed in the Jewish Scriptures (Acts 8:31–34; Luke 24:26). The Ethiopian pericope includes a specific passage (Isa 53:7f LXX), but the Emmaus pericope does not (only general references to "Moses and all the prophets" and "all the Scriptures" 24:27). Of note is the Ethiopian's figurative use of the verb "guide" (ὁδηγέω v. 31). This subtle connection between the verb and the physical context suggests a "spiritual quest."[22] They are on a road, but the guidance he needs is not geographical but spiritual. He needs "light" for entering "the way of peace" (cf. Luke 1:78–79). This explains the reason for the divinely led encounter.

4. The transforming action is presented as the exposition of the Scriptures by the party that has joined the other on the road (Acts 8:35; Luke 24:27, 32; echoed again in the Apollos passage). Both tangibly illustrate Jesus as "the dawn from on high." This thoroughfare reception scene is the only one where Jesus is not explicitly present. Yet, in various ways, the narrator has already established spiritual union between Jesus and his disciples; hence, this passage provides a concrete example of how a disciple accomplishes Jesus' role to bring light to someone in darkness. Transformation takes place only through Philip's action, "he preached Jesus to him" (v. 35). The Christocentric interpretation of the passage in Isaiah is significant.[23] Here Philip's teaching parallels Jesus' teaching in the first volume regarding his sufferings, humiliation, and death.[24] Yet, Jesus' teaching is not only paralleled, he is also portrayed as being present in the Scriptures. Moreover, the phrase "the Spirit of the Lord" (v. 39) suggests Jesus'

---

21. Marguerat, *Actes (1–12)*, 304.

22. Ibid., 308.

23. Talbert demonstrates seven parallels of salvation history in which Luke shows that the church's interpretation of Scripture is the same as Jesus' interpretation. Talbert, *Reading Acts*, 77–78.

24. Cf. Luke 9:22, 44; 13:33; 17:25; 18:31–34; 22:37; 24:7, 25–27, 46. Furthermore, Jesus' use of Isaiah in Nazareth to illustrate his mandate is an intriguing link.

presence through the Holy Spirit.[25]

5. Illumination leading to recognition of Jesus is achieved while on the road. The Ethiopian sees Jesus in Philip's Christocentric interpretation of Isaiah. The Emmaus disciples see him in person via the breaking of the bread and the explanation of the Scriptures.

6. Upon recognition, action is reported to confirm reception of Jesus (baptism; return to Jerusalem and report to disciples), and they are "deeply affected emotionally by their 'recognitions' of Jesus" (Acts 8:39; Luke 24:32).[26]

7. A liturgical act is present (baptism; breaking of bread).[27]

8. After reception, an abrupt separation takes place between the two parties, when the one bringing illumination leaves suddenly (Philip; Jesus).

Given this evidence, Luke's interest in linking these two thoroughfare reception scenes exemplifies Luke-Acts as a narrative constructed on motifs and other literary techniques.

How does this thoroughfare reception scene prepare the reader for further plot developments? Although there are greater parallels between the passages of the Emmaus disciples and the Ethiopian, the latter certainly prepares the reader to experience the intriguing encounter between Jesus and Saul. Tannehill states the passage's value: "The scene is important for what it anticipates and symbolizes rather than for its consequences. It is prophetic of the gospel's reach."[28] In fact, the extent of reception of Jesus' mandate is supported by the narrator's choice of the Ethiopian episode, which may be due to his acquaintance with the promise in Isa 56:4 for eunuchs to have a place in God's house. Foreigners are also given this privilege in the same passage (56:6). This man then fits both descriptions. It recalls the integration of the blind beggar and Zacchaeus since they were both marginalized characters.[29]

Pragmatically, perhaps the reader can identify more closely with the Ethiopian as a "God-fearer" than with previous marginalized Jewish

25. The expression πνεῦμα κυρίου occurs twice elsewhere in Luke-Acts: Luke 4:18 and Acts 5:19 (with article).

26. Spencer, *Philip*, 142.

27. Cf. Lindijer's reference to "sacred acts" in his "Two creative encounters," 79.

28. Tannehill, *Narrative*, 2:108.

29. See Spencer (*Philip*, 173) for the eunuch's status and conversion, and the pericope's value for Philip's portrayal and narrative development.

personages.³⁰ The reader observes again how an individual passes from uncertainty to certainty, then acts upon it, thus confirming the transformation. This episode is the first narrative of an individual conversion in Acts, the others being all reports of groups turning to God.³¹ The eunuch represents a marginal character to Jewish faith who is guided into "the way of peace" through one of Jesus' messengers. The repetition of *hodos* in connection with "lead" (*hodēgeō* ὁδηγέω)—in light of the thoroughfare motif's strand centered on Jesus—prepares the reader for the encounter that will take place between Jesus and Saul. Looking ahead, this Ethiopian represents an outsider to ethnic Israel who has become a part of those of "the Way," the target of Saul's murderous threats. This sets up the great ironic twist in Luke-Acts: a persecuting Pharisee becomes a part of the persecuted, "those of the Way."

What is the purpose of this cluster of two thoroughfare reception scenes in the macro-narrative? The narrator's choice of placing these two scenes together recalls the previous cluster of three between Jericho to Jerusalem in an important moment of the plot's development. Baban is right in identifying their transitional function from evangelism of the Jews to the nations.³² It is indeed a decisive moment in the plot, but the emphasis on the nations should not be overstated. Both scenes serve also to illustrate Jewish reception, and not only movement toward the nations. In the first, a God-fearer (of the Jewish God) becomes a disciple of Jesus through Jewish Scriptures, which support the story about Jesus, the Jewish Messiah. In the second, a murderous Pharisee is won over by Jesus himself. Both, however, illustrate an advance toward the nations, the Ethiopian being a foreigner, and Saul being inextricably linked to Luke's report about the evangelization of the nations. In effect, this is the beginning of the pattern of placing the spotlight on the Jews and the nations during Paul's missionary journeys outside Judea. The presence of only two specific thoroughfare reception scenes in the unraveling section supports this pattern: one concerning a proselyte from the

---

30. On the Ethiopian as a "God-fearer," see Marguerat (*Actes [1–12]*, 307), who finds in the centurion of Capernaum (Luke 7:5) a valid comparison with the Ethiopian.

31. Ibid., 302.

32. Witherington (*Acts*, 290) demonstrates that Luke's presentation is according to geographical region and ethnic groups (κατα γενος). Ethiopia and Ethiopians were considered "the ends of the earth" in Greek historiography and mythological geography; thus, a fulfillment of Jesus' command (Acts 1:8). Cf. Snowden, *Blacks in Antiquity*, 206. Schneider (*Apg.*, 1:498) finds a closer connection with the Samaritans based on Isa 56:3–5 (LXX), while Johnson (*Acts*, 159) argues for "the ingathering of the scattered people of Israel."

nations and one a Jewish Pharisee. The analysis now continues to the next thoroughfare reception scene between Jesus and Saul of Tarsus.

Jewish Reception on Damascus Road: Saul, Jesus and "Those of the Way" (Acts 9:2, 11, 17, 27)

This section discusses thoroughfare expressions in the depiction of Saul's encounter with Jesus and his followers in three subsections according to the main characters present: (a) Saul and Jesus; (b) Saul and Ananias; and (c) Saul and Barnabas.

Saul, Antagonist of "Those of the Way," and Jesus on Damascus Road

The reader's attention is now drawn from Philip's ministry to the conversion of Saul of Tarsus and the beginning of his ministry (9:1–31).[33] This is the sixth thoroughfare reception scene. Thoroughfare expressions occur four times: *hodos* three times (9:2, 17, 27) and ῥύμη once (9:11). The occurrences of *hodos* are specifically related to Saul's encounter with Jesus, and ῥύμη may have some symbolic significance in the narrator's characterization of Saul. All have literal meanings except the first one (9:2) and merit some discussion. This indicates a shift in the use of thoroughfares since all seventeen remaining occurrences in Luke-Acts, except the one in relation to Peter in 12:10, describe Paul and his missionary entourage.

In the passage Acts 9:1–9, the reader encounters the first of six occurrences of the unmodified *hodos*, which, as discussed in Chapter 1, have been the focus of scholarly research.[34] Saul of Tarsus had already been presented to the reader as one of the great antagonists against the church in Jerusalem (Acts 7:58 ff.). He had an active role in the stoning of Stephen and in the following violent persecution of Jesus' followers. The reader understands that Paul's aim is to continue this persecution in Damascus (Acts 9:1–2). The stark contrast between Paul's persecution and calling has a significant effect

---

33. Then the spotlight returns to Peter among the nations in Lydda, Joppa and Caesarea (10:1—11:18), then to Saul, Barnabas and the Antiochian church (11:19–30), and briefly back to Peter and Herod (12:1–25) before focusing completely on Saul's (Paul's) mandate.

34. Cf. 19:2, 23; 22:4; 24:14, 22. The occurrence in 22:4 is qualified by οὗτος (ταύτην τὴν ὁδὸν), which does not appear to affect its meaning. Cf. similar uses with "word" (Acts 8:21) and "name" (Acts 9:21).

on the reading experience.³⁵ The reader, therefore, is prepared for this ironic twist in the story: a murderous Pharisee will become the great protagonist in bringing the gospel to the nations, that is, from being persecutor to being persecuted by the end of the passage (cf. 9:30).

The reader encounters for the first time an enigmatic nuance of *hodos* (9:2). It concerns the unmodified *hodos* (ἡ ὁδός) and its perplexing referent. Has the narrator prepared the reader for this peculiar use of *hodos*? Should the reader know the referent and fill in the gap? Since the context is a journey from Jerusalem to Damascus, one expects that the first occurrence of *hodos* would be a literal use, indicating the physical setting. Instead, the first occurrence is figurative while the other occurrences refer to the physical setting, as recounted by Ananias and then Barnabas. I explain the first occurrence on intrinsic data without suggesting, however, that the other five unmodified *hodos* occurrences must have the same meaning. On the contrary, there appears to be a shift in nuance between this first use and the other five. Each of the occurrences will be discussed as they appear in the narration.

Since the few textual variants do not affect the interpretation of the unmodified *hodos* in Acts 9:2, its form is discussed first then its syntactical function.³⁶ Here *hodos* qualifies the disciples in a partitive construction ("of the Way") within a participial conditional clause ("if") and a purpose clause ("so that").³⁷ Literally, it reads, "so that, if he found any being of the Way, men and women, he might bring them bound to Jerusalem."³⁸ Here is the full sentence:

> While Saul was still breathing threat and murder on the disciples of the Lord, having gone to the chief priest, he asked from him letters for the synagogues in Damascus, so that if he should find any belonging to the Way, men or women, he might lead them bound to Jerusalem.

35. Cf. Eisen, *Poetik*, 190.

36. A well-attested variant changes the order to *3 1 2* (P74 ℵ A 81. 323. 453. 945. 1739 *pc*). A minor variant contains only *1* and *2*, excluding ὄντας (33. 1175. 1891 *pc*). Metzger mentions six variant readings (three including ταύτης not listed in NA27). The insertion of ταύτης served "to relieve the peculiarity of the term ἡ ὁδός used here for the first time in reference to Christianity" (*Textual*, 316). The more difficult reading (*txt*) between the two primary attested variants is to be preferred, because the easier sequence *3 1 2* places ὄντας closer to τινάς in order to avoid its connection with ἄνδρας τε καὶ γυναῖκας. Ibid., 317.

37. Cf. BDR, §478n2.

38. The word τινάς may have emphatic value, "any at all" (CP, 170). Likewise, Talbert (*Reading Acts*, 85) writes, "The conditional sentence in Greek allows the possibility that there may be Messianists in Damascus, although the narrative of Acts has given no hint of such to this point."

¹ Ὁ δὲ Σαῦλος ἔτι ἐμπνέων ἀπειλῆς καὶ φόνου εἰς τοὺς μαθητὰς τοῦ κυρίου, προσελθὼν τῷ ἀρχιερεῖ ² ἠτήσατο παρ' αὐτοῦ ἐπιστολὰς εἰς Δαμασκὸν πρὸς τὰς συναγωγάς, ὅπως ἐάν τινας εὕρῃ τῆς ὁδοῦ ὄντας, ἄνδρας τε καὶ γυναῖκας, δεδεμένους ἀγάγῃ εἰς Ἰερουσαλήμ.

The reader can interpret the expression "some belonging" (τινας ... ὄντας) by referring to the expression "the disciples of the Lord" in v. 1 and "men and women" in v. 2. It concerns Jesus' disciples, who are characterized also as adherents to (in the sense of, "belonging to") "the Way."[39] This is supported by the word "disciple" that provides continuity to the passage in various key moments (vv. 1, 10, 19, 25, and twice in v. 26). Thus, the entire passage not only relates Saul's encounter with Jesus, but also his encounters with Jesus' disciples. The spiritual unity between Jesus and his disciples is dramatically depicted in Jesus' haunting question: "Saul, Saul, why are you persecuting me?" (9:4).

Yet, what is the referent of *hodos*? What does it mean to be "disciples" and "men and women" of "the Way"? The narrator uses "of the Way" (τῆς ὁδοῦ) as an ellipsis (an omitted element) which the reader is expected to fill in, either by his prior knowledge of the story or through what the narrator has told him thus far, or possibly, what he is going to tell him later. It is an ellipsis because a qualifier is omitted in the expression: to whom or to what does the Way belong? Three points of internal evidence suggest that the reader is prepared to interpret the expression and to experience its rhetorical force: (1) other elliptical expressions in Luke-Acts which assume "God" or "Lord" in the genitive case, (2) previously encountered uses of *hodos* (also supported by later uses), and (3) the parallelism with "the disciples of the Lord" in verse 1.[40] Additionally, based on external evidence—assuming the audience's acquaintance with Jewish Scriptures—they probably recognize this figurative expression

---

39. The closest construction in Luke-Acts to this one is τοὺς ὄντας τῶν Ἰουδαίων πρώτους in Acts 28:17, which expresses the idea of "from among the Jews." Acts 12:1 demonstrates the idea of belonging, but with ἀπό, κακῶσαί τινας τῶν ἀπὸ τῆς ἐκκλησίας. Several commentators translate the expression using verbs or substantives that render the sense of belonging or adherence. See, for example, Delebecque, *Les actes des apôtres*, 44n2; Boismard and Lamouille, *Les actes*, 96; Eck, *Handelingen*, 216; Pesch, *Apg.*, 1:216; Eckey, *Apg.*, 1:208; Weiser, *Apg. Kapitel 1–12*, 214; Barrett, *Acts*, 1:437; Fitzmyer, *Luke I–IX*, 418; and Talbert, *Reading Acts*, 85. Pervo (*Acts*, 230) translates every occurrence of the unmodified ὁδός with "Movement," thus in 9:2, "... any adherents of the Movement." Johnson (*Acts*, 161), however, uses the verb "to follow," "so that if he found anyone following the Way."

40. Marguerat (*Actes [1–12]*, 326–27) adapts another approach. He does not link this expression with previous occurrences in Luke-Acts, only with later ones, of which it is an abridgment, "the way of salvation" (16:17) and "the way of the Lord/God" (18:25, 26). Cf. also Giles, "Church," 196.

associating Jesus' disciples' with divine "ways" or "paths" (cf. Gen 18:19; Exod 33:13; Pss 25:4; 27:11; Prov 10:29; Isa 35:8; Mal 2:8).

Up to this point, the reader has already encountered other elliptical constructions that assume "God" and "Lord" in the genitive case (i.e., "of God" or "of the Lord"). They are objects or persons pertaining to God (i.e., of Israel) or Lord, such as "word," "law," "Spirit," and "kingdom."[41] This is the first instance in which *hodos* occurs in an elliptical construction, which the reader could probably recognize. Moreover, having already encountered a very close expression, "the way of God" concerning Jesus (Luke 20:21), it is plausible that the reader might associate that ellipsis with the one in Acts 9:2. This question is clarified by later expressions "the way of the Lord" and "the way of God" (Acts 18:25, 26), which also refer to instruction from God as in Luke 20:21. In addition, the expression "the way of peace" in the image of Luke 1:78-79 has contributed to the reader's expectation that Jesus would lead a group of people into a better spiritual state, reconciliation with God. Consequently, the narrator confirms here this reality through thoroughfare imagery.

Given the parallelism with "the disciples of the Lord" in verse 1 and the narrator's focus of the passage, the fuller expression would include either "Lord" or "God" as in, "if he should find any of the way of God/the Lord" (ἐάν εὕρῃ τινας τῆς ὁδοῦ [θεοῦ/τοῦ κυρίου] ὄντας). In light of the immediate context and the movement of the plot, the fuller expression is either "the way of the Lord" or "the way of God," whose meaning includes the idea of the teaching of and about Jesus, since Saul is seeking to find any man or woman who adheres to the way (teaching) of or concerning Jesus. If the omitted element is τοῦ κυρίου, then some ambiguity is possible whether it refers to "the way of Jesus" or to "the way of God." The expression "way of life" (*Lebensart*) is too general, and does not zero in on the real problem for which Saul requests the authorization of the high priests, namely, the teaching of the disciples of and about Jesus.[42] In fact, the Jewish authorities had not prohibited the disciples from healing, but from teaching (4:18; 5:28, 40). Thus, the unmodified *hodos* represents here Jesus' teaching of the way

---

41. Cf. absolute constructions with λόγος (Luke 1:2; 8:12, 13, 15; Acts 4:4; 6:4; 8:4; 10:44; 11:19; 14:25; 17:11; 18:5); νόμος, but some ambiguity exists when Moses is implied (Luke 2:22; 24:44; Acts 13:38; 15:5) and to Lord/God "law of the Lord" (Luke 2:23, 27; 10:26; 16:16, 17; Acts 6:13; 7:53; 13:15; 18:13; 21:10, 24, 28; 22:12; 23:3; 24:14); πνεῦμα (Luke 2:27; 4:14; Acts 2:4; 6:3, 10; 8:18, 29; 10:19; 11:12; 20:22; 21:4); βασιλεία (Luke 12:32; Acts 20:25). Similarly, ὄνομα occurs in the absolute only in Acts 5:41 for the name of Jesus.

42. Schneider, *Apg.*, 2:25; 25n2. More comprehensive is Eckey's formula: "'The Way' (ἡ ὁδός) designates their overall faith-, teaching-, and life orientation" (*Apg.*, 1:213).

of God, but also, after his death and resurrection, the teaching about Jesus, which has created conflict in the Jewish community. Therefore, the expression "any belonging to the Way" expresses the attachment of the disciples to Jesus and his teaching.

Anticipating discussion on other uses of "the Way," the expression is *not*—at this point in the narrative—the full metonymic expression that the reader will encounter later (19:9, 23; 22:4; 24:14, 22) when the narrator presents the group more forcefully as "the Way" through association, not only belonging to it but representing it. Additionally, before encountering this metonym, in between this expression in 9:2 and 19:9, he will come across several expressions involving *hodos* with other genitival expressions (13:10; 16:17; 18:25, 26).[43] Consequently, the expression should not be connected, as primary referent, to the occurrences of *hodos* that describe the relationship between John the Baptist and Jesus, that is, to illustrate John's mandate of preparation for the Messiah's coming, especially "the way for the Lord" in Luke 3:4.[44]

Narratively, when read in light of the various images, illustrations and expressions using thoroughfare imagery, the primary referent is Jesus.[45] The narrator enhances the difference in spiritual orientation between those who are already enlightened (those "of the way of the Lord") and Saul who is on a road and in spiritual darkness when he meets Jesus who brings light and guides him into a new state of spiritual existence. Therefore, this expression's immediate function is the characterization of Jesus' disciples over against the characterization of Saul. The passage exemplifies the play of literal and figurative meanings of *hodos* to describe the physical and spiritual crossroads where Jesus, his disciples, and Saul clash, resulting in the persecutor being leveled to the ground. To illustrate this further, the illumination theme reappears powerfully, but in a different way than on the Emmaus road. It illustrates not accompaniment leading to illumination, but physical shock leading to spiritual illumination, since it comes as a blazing physical light which temporarily blinds Saul until he has experienced spiritual illumination and his physical blindness is symbolically removed to demonstrate this

---

43. If, however, it can be demonstrated that the reader already knew this metonym prior to the reading, it is possible that the expression τῆς ὁδοῦ in 9:2 already signifies "group" and not "teaching" (without metonymy). Yet, in this case, Luke could have been more direct: "so that if he found the Way" (ὅπως ἐάν εὕρῃ τὴν ὁδόν).

44. Cf. e.g., the interpretations of S.V. McCasland and David Pao in Chapter 1.

45. For example, especially through the proleptic image of Jesus' mandate in Luke 1:78-79, the Parable of the Great Supper, the preceding thoroughfare reception scenes, Jesus as the teacher of "the way of God" (Luke 20:21), and the "ways of life" (Acts 2:28).

(cf. 9:18).[46] As the thoroughfare motif contributes to the characterization of Jesus' disciples, the sympathetic reader can identify himself with "those of the Way." This gives him further certainty knowing that his faith in Jesus is "the way of God," which also provides a sense of belonging. He too belongs to the way that Jesus taught and continues to provide through his disciples. Consequently, he is also a part of those who have received Jesus who has guided them by his light into "the way of peace."

Moreover, as mentioned in Chapter 1, this identification with Jesus' disciples is strengthened through this expression's nuance of distinctiveness or even exclusiveness. Cadbury observed this, noting that this type of nuance is signaled in English with quotes ("the way") or capitalization (the Way).[47] Hence, the expression as an ellipsis illustrates the narrator's point of view of the special nature of this *hodos*. In addition, Daniel Wallace finds in this expression an example of the article's "par excellence" function, when the article emphasizes this *hodos* as the only one deserving that name, *the way*, though there may be other "ways" (*hodoi*).[48] In fact, the reader will read later that this *hodos* connected to Jesus is superior to other Jewish groups and other "ways" among the nations (14:16).[49] Finally, the use of omissions was encouraged in ancient rhetorical theory for motivating the audience's participation. Listeners were expected to fill in omitted elements through a common source of knowledge with the orator. Similarly, Luke may have employed "the Way" and other ellipses as a way to engage his audience. In fact, the first occurrence of this type of omission, "the word," in Luke 1:1 is subtle but forceful in what it affirms, that is, none other than "the word of God."[50] It participates in Luke's narrative strategy to present claims about knowledge of the God of Israel.

---

46. Cf. Marguerat, *Actes (1–12)*, 328.

47. Cadbury, "Names," 392. Eck moves forward to the other references of the unmodified *hodos* expressing the emphatic force of the expression through the article, which indicates exclusiveness, *the* way. Others indicate emphasis through capitalization, e.g., Eck, *Handelingen*, 218 and Boismard and Lamouille, *Les actes*, 96.

48. Wallace (*Greek*, 224) compares this use of the article with *hodos* with the expression in Acts 18:26 (ἡ ὁδὸς τοῦ θεοῦ) that illustrates the "monadic" function of the article, indicating the "one of a kind" or unique nature of an object. He clarifies this: "When the articular substantive has an adjunct (such as an adjective or gen. phrase), the entire expression often suggests a monadic notion. If no modifier is used, the article is typically *par excellence*." Thus, "the way of the Lord" conveys a monadic notion and the "the Way" is *par excellence*.

49. Cf. the comparisons via "sect" αἵρεσις in 5:17; 15:5; 24:14; 26:5; 28:22.

50. See the discussion in Maxwell, *Hearing*, 51–58.

The discussion now turns to the occurrences of *rumē* and *hodos* in the scene with Saul and Ananias, which further qualify Saul's transformation.

A Visit to Saul on "Straight Street" (Acts 9:11)

The next thoroughfare expression appears in the passage concerning Saul's encounter with Ananias, one of Jesus' followers (9:10-19a). The word *rumē* (street) appears in Jesus' command to Ananias to go to Saul. The narrator provides directions to find the house where Saul is staying. He is in the house of a certain Judas, located "on a street called straight" (or, "Straight Street" ἐπὶ τὴν ῥύμην τὴν καλουμένην Εὐθεῖαν). This additional detail adds to the reliability of the account, since it was a well-known street, and suggests a touch of irony.

This scene evokes powerfully the sending theme that has been developed from the very beginning (e.g., John the Baptist; Jesus' disciples; the Parable of the Great Supper; and Philip). In Luke-Acts, God's initiative to reach those in spiritual and physical darkness involves also sending messengers in order to bring them out through spiritual illumination. Tension develops through resistance since Ananias must go to someone who seems very unlikely to receive Jesus. This represents yet another divinely organized encounter, which the audience may experience with pleasure, since they already know what Ananias must discover.[51] This time, the resurrected Jesus organizes the encounter through a sort of simultaneous, double vision.[52]

Ananias clearly has reservations about this divine appointment, called as it were "by vision to save his torturer."[53] Ananias's fear is echoed later by the reaction of the disciples in Jerusalem who do not think Saul is a disciple (9:26). As in the three reception scenes between Jericho and Jerusalem, thoughts of opposition contrary to the divine will are apparent. Luke takes pleasure in showing that Jesus thinks differently. A divinely organized visit is

---

51. Narratively, Ananias is behind the narrative's flow of information. Marguerat, *Actes (1-12)*, 334.

52. Talbert finds a pattern of comparison between two sets of two panels, which would indicate thematic unity between Saul's experiences with Ananias and Barnabas. Panel One (9:1-9) compares Paul's vision to Ananias's vision in Panel Two (9:10-19). Next, Panel One (9:13-25) concerning Ananias's hesitation corresponds to the fear of the disciples in Jerusalem in Panel Two (9:26-30). The effect on the reading is that "The very pattern that makes the narrative repetitious indicates that the issue is whether or not Saul's experience is genuine" (*Reading Acts*, 87-88).

53. Marguerat, *Actes (1-12)*, 333.

being planned between one who was against those of the Way and one who is already of the Way.⁵⁴

Now Luke describes what happened when Ananias met with Saul. Through Ananias's visit on "Straight Street," Saul's thoroughfare encounter is confirmed to the reader. The reader must fill in the gap that Ananias had been informed by Jesus himself in the same vision or in another.⁵⁵ Ananias provides this information to confirm to Saul (now a "blind man"), who had already seen him, the person (Jesus) who sends him. He says in verse 17:

> Brother Saul, the Lord, Jesus who appeared to you on the road by which you were coming, has sent me so that you might see again and be filled with the Holy Spirit.
>
> Σαοὺλ ἀδελφέ, ὁ κύριος ἀπέσταλκέν με, Ἰησοῦς ὁ ὀφθείς σοι ἐν τῇ ὁδῷ ᾗ ἤρχου, ὅπως ἀναβλέψῃς καὶ πλησθῇς πνεύματος ἁγίου.

The occurrence appears in a prepositional phrase "on the road" connected to a relative phrase "by which you were coming." It adds physical imagery to the first analepsis of Saul's conversion. Jesus' appearance is highlighted here, whereas the focus in 9:27 is Saul's visual and audible experience of Jesus.⁵⁶ This brief scene depicts the first intersection with those of the Way in Damascus.⁵⁷ Jesus is again portrayed as the initiator of this meeting. Ananias, against his initial wishes, becomes thus a witness of the transformation that is taking place in Saul's life through his thoroughfare encounter with Jesus. No teaching of Scripture appears as in the two preceding thoroughfare reception scenes, but the illumination comes through Jesus' revelation of himself on the road and in the following double vision to Saul and Ananias. Later the reader discovers, through the analepsis in Paul's voice, the other words that Jesus spoke to him in their first encounter (26:14–18). His reception of Jesus is gradually revealed, beginning with his obedience to Jesus' command to enter the city (v. 8) and culminating in his baptism (v. 18).⁵⁸

---

54. This simultaneous vision prepares the reader for the double vision experienced by Peter and Cornelius. Ibid.

55. Cf. Fitzmyer, *Acts*, 429.

56. Perhaps the active role of Saul's experience was necessary to convince the skeptical disciples in Jerusalem.

57. The narrator reveals nothing about Judas in whose house he was staying. He might have already been a disciple. Ananias calls Saul "brother," which might have meant "fellow Jew," at least proleptically (Fitzmyer, *Acts*, 429), and confirms him as a fellow disciple of Jesus (Barrett, *Acts*, 1:457).

58. Talbert (*Reading Acts*, 87) notes that in 9:19b and 26–28, "Saul participates in the community of the Way . . . Christ has changed an opponent into an ally. When the

More enlightenment comes to him through the later vision and through Ananias's visit. The reader is led to interpret the scales that fell from his eyes as a symbol of Saul's spiritual egression from darkness into Jesus' light (v. 18). Formerly a violent, zealous Pharisee, Saul has now entered the way of peace. Having encountered various nuances of thoroughfare imagery, one notices here a touch of irony, namely, that Saul is further characterized by the fact that he really is on the *right path* now. He resides on "Straight Street" and receives a visit from one of "the Way"; a subtle symbol that stimulates the reader's imagination and illustrates Luke's humor.[59]

Barnabas's Account of Saul's Thoroughfare Reception in Jerusalem (9:27)

To highlight further the importance of Saul's transformation, the narrator includes Barnabas's description of Saul's encounter with Jesus (9:27). The passage (9:26–31) describes Saul's introduction to the "disciples" in Jerusalem, who are fearful of him and skeptical that he had actually become a disciple. Barnabas, who was introduced to the reader in Acts 5, intervenes on Saul's behalf and recounts Saul's encounter with Jesus:

> Barnabas took him and led him to the apostles. He related to them how he [Paul] had seen the Lord on the road and that he had spoken to him and had spoken boldly in Damascus in the name of Jesus.
>
> Βαρναβᾶς δὲ ἐπιλαβόμενος αὐτὸν ἤγαγεν πρὸς τοὺς ἀποστόλους καὶ διηγήσατο αὐτοῖς πῶς ἐν τῇ ὁδῷ εἶδεν τὸν κύριον καὶ ὅτι[60] ἐλάλησεν αὐτῷ καὶ πῶς ἐν Δαμασκῷ ἐπαρρησιάσατο ἐν τῷ ὀνόματι τοῦ Ἰησοῦ.

The occurrence of *hodos* appears in indirect discourse through the voice of Barnabas.[61] His use of physical imagery serves to convince the apostles

---

risen Jesus encounters a person, he produces radical transformation." Ananias's gesture of laying his hands on Saul confirms his acceptance as a member of the community. Johnson, *Acts*, 165.

59. Another link between thoroughfares and the notion of straightness is found in Luke 3:4–5 and Acts 13:10.

60. Based on stylistic questions (the proper flow between the two πῶς clauses), Bruce (*Acts*, 243) prefers the variant ὅ τι (945. 1704 *al*), "what he had said to him," rather than "that he had spoken to him."

61. Barrett (*Acts*, 1:469) rightly observes that the subject of διηγήσατο is Barnabas and not Saul. So Schneider, *Apg.*, 2:38–39; Fitzmyer, *Acts*, 439; Eck, *Handelingen*, 228. Jervell (*Apg.*, 287), however, argues that Saul is probably the subject. So Pesch, *Apg.*, 1:313.

Expanding Encounters: From Roads to "the Way"

that Saul's experience took place in a physical context, not just a vision in the spiritual realm, but an encounter on an actual road to Damascus. The reader can imagine that Barnabas and Saul needed to provide more details to convince the leaders in Jerusalem. The three essential points are summarized through two clauses introduced by "how" (πῶς): (1) Saul saw the Lord, (2) the Lord spoke to him, and (3) Saul began to preach about Jesus in Damascus. Jervell identifies a validating function in Barnabas's intervention, which emphasizes that Paul saw Jesus "on the way" and not in a vision.[62] Barnabas thus functions as a valid mediator to corroborate this evidence.

This episode also has a validating function for the reader. Johnson describes this passage as, "A remarkable example of Luke's technique of building a shared story. Barnabas validates Paul's experience for the Jerusalem leadership (and also for the reader) by reciting it in a straightforward and unequivocal fashion."[63] The two occurrences of *hodos* by Ananias and Barnabas help describe Saul's experience thoroughfare to different characters in different places. They take part in the "postconversion evidence of the genuineness of Saul's conversion."[64] Thus, by now it has become clear to the reader how important this event was. In fact, this is the last thoroughfare reception scene in Luke-Acts. Moreover, this conversion narrative (on a thoroughfare) appears in Paul's defense speeches twice more in 21:40–22:22 (*hodos* in 22:4) and 26:12–18 (*hodos* in 26:13). Table 6.1 below summarizes the various aspects of the thoroughfare motif and voices that depict Paul's thoroughfare reception of Jesus (similar to the various voices recounting John the Baptist's mandate). Nonetheless, these do not cover all of the thoroughfare occurrences that are related to Paul and his entourage.

---

62. Jervell, *Apg.*, 287.
63. Johnson, *Acts*, 172.
64. Talbert, *Reading Acts*, 87.

Table 6.1: Thoroughfare imagery concerning Paul's thoroughfare reception of Jesus

Reference	Discourse, voice, audience, and location	Literal or Figurative	Expression
9:2	Indirect discourse: the narrator to reader (action takes place outside of Damascus)	Figurative	τινας τῆς ὁδοῦ ὄντας "any being of the way"; ἐν τῇ ὁδῷ "on the road" not mentioned but inferred from 9:3.
No reference	Via a "gap" in the narration: Jesus to Ananias in Damascus	Literal	Omission may be filled in by reader: ἐν τῇ ὁδῷ "on the road"
9:11	Direct discourse: Jesus to Ananias in Damascus	Literal	ἐπὶ τὴν ῥύμην τὴν καλουμένην Εὐθεῖαν "on the street called Straight"
9:17	Direct discourse: Ananias to Paul in Damascus	Literal	ἐν τῇ ὁδῷ ᾗ ἤρχου "on the road by which you were coming"
9:27	Indirect discourse: Barnabas to leaders in Jerusalem	Literal	ἐν τῇ ὁδῷ "on the road"
22:4	Direct discourse: Paul before a mob in Jerusalem	Figurative	ταύτην τὴν ὁδὸν "this Way"
26:13	Direct discourse: Paul before Festus, Agrippa and Bernice in Caesarea	Literal	κατὰ τὴν ὁδὸν "according to the Way"

The pattern of thoroughfare reception scenes has become familiar to the reader. The cumulative force of their repetition evokes previous episodes and helps the reader to appreciate Saul's unique transformational encounter with Jesus. This, in turn, prepares the reader for Luke's intentional focus on Saul as the primary human protagonist from Acts 13 on. In fact, all of the remaining occurrences, except *rumē* in 12:10 concerning Peter's escape from jail, depict something about Paul or his missionary entourage. This provides further evidence for the narrator's shift in focus, that is, Paul as main human protagonist in the plot's unraveling. The narrator has provided several transformational encounters that illustrate the picture of Jesus' mandate in Luke

1:78–79, but Saul's encounter clearly has a greater function in the plot than the other encounters. As Marguerat explains, "Our narrative [9:1–9] plays a programmatic role since it abruptly reorients the activity of the persecutor of Christians to make him the vector of universal mission. It explains the accession of Paul to the mission of which he will become protagonist from chapter 13 onward."[65]

From this point on, the spiritual unity between Jesus and Saul ("Paul," from 13:9 on) is the highlight. Paul is the missionary *par excellence* who brings Jesus' light to the Jews and the nations. He states his role already in his speech at Pisidian Antioch (13:47) and Jesus' voice confirms it in a significant flashback (Acts 26:16–18).[66] Saul's life, as do the lives of the other disciples, reflects Jesus' light as "the dawn from on high."

Therefore, Theophilus's confidence in Paul as a reliable character is founded in this encounter with the resurrected hero on the road. As he observes Paul's character, overcoming opposition among the Jews and the nations, his faith is also strengthened. This prepares the reader for later uses of *hodos*, which illustrate Paul's teaching about Jesus and finally his open association with those whom the narrator later describes plainly as "the Way." Thus, from this episode on, a close connection between *hodos* and Paul begins and then culminates in his confession of faith in Acts 24:14.

Only one thoroughfare expression appears (*rumē* 12:10) between Paul's departure for Tarsus and the narratives about his missionary ministry (9:32–12:25). In this section, the reader returns to Peter's "acts" in particular his experience with Cornelius, his report to the leaders in Jerusalem, as well as his arrest by Herod and his escape from prison. The lack of thoroughfare terminology in relation to Peter (Acts 2:28; 5:15; 12:10) suggests again that these words are especially employed in Acts for the description of Paul's relationship with Jesus and his disciples. The discussion now turns to the occurrences that illustrate the message of Paul and his entourage in Jewish and Gentile contexts.

---

65. Marguerat, *Actes (1–12)*, 322.

66. Kurz (*Reading Luke-Acts*, 27) explains, "Acts 22 and 26 are increasingly retrospective personal flashbacks by Paul to emphasize this centrally important event and to show its further implications in the account of Paul's work and the spread of the word in Acts."

Paul and Missionary Entourage: Teachers of "the Way(s) of God/the Lord"

As stated, from Acts 13:10 on, *hodos* is the only thoroughfare term used until the end of the narrative. The next five occurrences illustrate the teaching or message of Paul and his missionary entourage. Characters and groups are posited according to their reception of the way(s) of the Lord. The subtitles below indicate whether reception or rejection of Jesus occurs and if the group in question is primarily Jewish or Gentile. The mention of place names in the subtitles has two functions. First, it indicates the forward movement toward the narrator's goal to highlight Paul's part in the hero's mandate on his way to Rome. Second, it shows how, paradoxically, the uses of *hodos* from this point, despite much journeying, never occur once to qualify Paul's physical movements in this stage. The last occurrence in 26:13 helps describe a physical setting, but it is part of an analepsis concerning Paul's conversion already narrated in Acts 9.

Jewish rejection, Gentile reception in Paphos: "the Straight Ways of the Lord" (13:10)

The next occurrence of thoroughfare imagery appears in the passage concerning Saul and Barnabas's preaching tour in Cyprus (13:4–12). Having departed from Salamis, they arrive at Paphos where they meet two characters, a Jew named Elymas the magician and a Roman proconsul named Sergius Paulus.[67] The narrator portrays Sergius Paulus through his own voice as "a man of intelligence" (v. 7). On the other hand, Elymas is described poignantly through Paul's voice (v. 10, see below). The comparison between the two continues until the end of the story, allowing the reader to understand clearly the narrator's point of view of their initial and final states.

The reader learns here for the first time that Saul was also called "Paul" (v. 9), who is "filled with the Holy Spirit" (v. 9) in contrast to what fills Elymas (v. 10). A complication arises when Sergius Paulus requests to hear the word of God (v. 7), but Elymas attempts to prevent him from receiving it (v. 8). Paul recognizes this opposition and harshly rebukes Elymas invoking upon him a temporary blindness. The expression *hodos* appears in the last part of verse 10 in the plural form as the direct object of the verb "make crooked" (διαστρέφω). It is qualified in two ways: by an adjective ("right" εὐθείας) and by a genitival construction with a noun without the article ("Lord" κυρίου):

---

67. Cf. Acts 8:9–11, 13, 18–24 for the description of another magician (Simon of Samaria) with similar language and ending.

He said, "O son of the devil, full of every deceit and fraud, enemy of all righteousness, why do you not cease to make crooked the right ways of the Lord?"

εἶπεν· ὦ πλήρης παντὸς δόλου καὶ πάσης ῥᾳδιουργίας, υἱὲ διαβόλου, ἐχθρὲ πάσης δικαιοσύνης, οὐ παύσῃ διαστρέφων τὰς ὁδοὺς [τοῦ] κυρίου τὰς εὐθείας;

Paul, in the first part of the verse, describes Elymas's character through a series of nominal phrases. In short, he is animated by the devil because he is corrupt, and even opposes righteousness. The reason for such pejorative appellations is revealed by way of a rhetorical question[68] in the last part of the verse: "Will you not cease to make crooked (pervert) the straight (right) ways of the Lord."[69] This is clearly exemplified by his opposition to the apostles' influence on Sergius Paulus.

To understand this figurative use of *hodos*, the meaning of the verb "make crooked" (διαστρέφω) must be explained. It is also used in 13:8 (but followed by the preposition "from" ἀπό) where Elymas tries to turn Sergius away from receiving the word of God.[70] The form of Elymas's opposition (v. 8a) is certainly in the area of speaking things against the apostles' teaching and would suit Paul's description of him. This verb occurs elsewhere three times, twice in the first volume, and once in the second, with the idea of misleading or being misled from what is known to be true. Jesus describes the people as an "unbelieving and perverse (misled) generation" (Luke 9:41) and Jesus is accused of distorting or perverting (misleading) "the nation" (Luke 23:2). Moreover, Paul warns the Ephesian elders that some men will come "teaching perverse things in order to draw away the disciples after them (λαλοῦντες διεστραμμένα τοῦ ἀποσπᾶν τοὺς μαθητὰς ὀπίσω αὐτῶν Acts 20:30). There it describes the work of the opposition in contrast with Paul's teaching. Here Elymas's opposition appears to be the same; he is set against the apostles' teaching

---

68. The question is expressed through "the volitive future, with mildly imperative force and an implied reproach." Bruce, *Acts*, 298. For the emphatic force of υἱὲ διαβόλου, a vocative in apposition, see Wallace, *Greek*, 70–71.

69. The variant without the article τὰς ὁδοὺς [τοῦ] κυρίου does not affect the interpretation. Also, the addition in D* of ουσας τὰς ὁδοὺς [τοῦ] κυρίου τὰς εὐθείας, would simply produce a relative clause, "the ways of the Lord that are straight," and not affect the meaning.

70. Barrett (*Acts*, 1:617) clarifies its use: "Luke now uses διαστρέφειν in a different sense from that of v. 8; it now means to pervert: Bar-Jesus is making straight roads crooked." The apostles' intent, however, is to bring people to God, conveyed through a related verb ἐπιστρέφω (14:15).

(cf. "the word of God" v. 7 and "the teaching of the Lord" v. 12).[71] Haenchen's concise explanation is right: "God's straight path leads the governor to conversion; but Bar-Jesus would like to distort this path."[72]

Further evidence for this view is the final state of the two individuals, one due to rejection of the teaching, the other due to reception of it. In the depiction of Paul's gesture to castigate Elymas, the familiar words "blind" and "darkness" reappear, serving to symbolize Elymas's spiritual state. This evokes the early image where darkness and light are in opposition (Luke 1:78-79). In addition, the thoroughfare motif appears with the themes of illumination and darkness as in other moments (e.g., the blind beggar, the Emmaus disciples, the Ethiopian eunuch, and Saul). Elymas has refused Jesus' light coming through his disciples that would lead him out of darkness and into the way of peace. He remains in that darkness because he is a "son of the devil" (Acts 13:10), because he has attempted to obstruct salvation reaching another person. Thus, Satan's presence is again evident in opposition to the realization of Jesus' mandate, now against his disciples. Though Satan's attempt here to sabotage the hero's mandate is not successful, he remains present in the background as he was in the raveling sequence.

The opposite consequence has resulted for Sergius Paulus, who has believed; it is further qualified by a participial phrase in which the means of transformation is the "teaching of the Lord" (13:12). This befits the narrator's portrayal. Therefore, based on the context of proclamation of the apostles' message and the meaning of "make crooked" (*diastrephō* διαστρέφω), the meaning of the expression "the straight ways of the Lord" is most likely "the correct (or right) teachings of the Lord" (". . . that lead to the Lord"). The two responses prepare the reader to interpret and experience subsequent accounts of reception and rejection among the Jews and the nations.[73] Again, irony is present, since an individual from the Jewish people rejected God's teaching while someone from the nations received it. One stayed in darkness, and, implicitly, the other came out of it by receiving Jesus' teachings.

---

71. Although the thoroughfare imagery is present, Tannehill's suggestion is not persuasive (*Narrative*, 2:163). He links this expression with John the Baptist's mandate εὐθείας ποιεῖτε τὰς τρίβους αὐτοῦ (Luke 3:4b). Yet, the contexts are too different to make this connection. The occurrences related to John describe the preparation for Messiah's coming; Acts 13:10 concerns the teaching(s) of the Lord.

72. Haenchen, *Apg.*, 343.

73. Talbert (*Reading Acts*, 119) finds here another example of Luke's "legitimation technique": "This story is another example of Luke's interest in the high social status of the converts to the Way."

Expanding Encounters: From Roads to "the Way"

Gentile Rejection in Lystra: the Nations and Their Ways (14:16)

The next appearance of *hodos* occurs in the episode of Paul and Barnabas in Lystra following the healing of a lame man (14:8–20). Very much in contrast to the reactions displayed in Jewish contexts, the Lystrans perceive that their gods have come down to them (Zeus and Hermes). It is not clear from the text which of the two apostles speaks, but in the short text that is available, what they say to the crowd is pertinent to this discussion. They describe their God and the motive for their preaching: ". . . bringing the Good News to you to turn away from the vain things to the living God" (v. 15). Then they describe how God dealt with the nations in the past: "In past generations he allowed all the nations to go (walk) in their ways" (ὃς ἐν ταῖς παρῳχημέναις γενεαῖς εἴασεν πάντα τὰ ἔθνη πορεύεσθαι ταῖς ὁδοῖς αὐτῶν· v. 16).

The apostles' God (i.e., Israel's God) is the creator of the heavens, the earth, and the sea. For this reason, in the past, he gave them a witness by providing rain and food, resulting in satisfaction and joy. The nations, however, did not recognize this, and consequently, "walked in their own ways," that is, they developed and practiced other belief systems by worshiping other gods (cf. vv. 11, 13, 15). The crowd's reaction to this divine intervention, the healing of a lame man, is symptomatic of this; they respond by worshiping their gods instead of the living God. The apostles explain that a message has now come that offers them another "way," which can be inferred as "the way of God" or "the way of the Lord."

The verb "allow" and its object "all the nations" demonstrate God's sovereignty over all nations despite the fact that they do not worship him.[74] In fact, he allowed them to "walk in their ways."[75] By means of this adverbial phrase with a "dative of rule," it answers the question: In conformity to what standard (or rule) did God allow the nations to live?[76] The answer is that he allowed them to live in conformity to their religious beliefs; hence, not according to the way of the God of Israel. Given the immediate context of religious interpretation and action based on a divine intervention, the

---

74. The verb ἐάω is a preferred Lukan expression, found in Luke-Acts nine of the eleven times in the NT. Schneider, *Apg.*, 2:160n55. God is the subject only in this occurrence, but cf. Luke 4:41 (Jesus) and Acts 16:7 (the Spirit of Jesus).

75. The use of the dative with verbs of movement is found elsewhere in Acts (9:31; 21:21). Both examples can be understood as figurative expressions for "to live." Cf. BDR, §198.5.

76. Wallace (*Greek*, 158) understands it as a dative of rule, i.e., "according to . . ." or "in conformity with . . ."; hence, his translation: "He allowed all the nations to walk in their own ways (= "according to their own ways")." So CP, 279.

expression "to walk in their own ways" certainly means more than customs.[77] There is a religious orientation to the use of "in their ways." Their ways do not lead to the one true God, Israel's God. A possible paraphrase could be "to live according to their beliefs in relation to the realm of spiritual beings, real or imagined." As the God of creation, he gave them the permission, as it were, to live according to their beliefs. The plural form of *hodos* here, from the narrator's point of view, expresses the variety of false religions in the pagan world as Tannehill explains:

> Paul in Lystra recognizes that various peoples have had various religions and does not harshly condemn their religious histories. He says, "In past generations [God] permitted all the nations to go in their ways" (14:16), but Paul assumes that he stands at a turning point in world religion. The time of ethnic permissiveness in religion, a time of ignorance and trust in "vain things," is drawing to a close. As Paul will say in Athens, now God "commands people that all everywhere repent" of their idolatry (17:30).[78]

In light of the portrayed scene and the thrust of the apostles' discourse, the ways of the nations are in direct contrast with the way of God as preached by Jesus and his disciples, as Schneider states, "The nations' *own* ways went in another direction than *God's* way (which Jesus taught, Luke 20:21; see Rev 13:10; 16:17; 18:25, 26)."[79]

The reader witnesses again immediate opposition from the Jewish population, which is sufficient to stop further proclamation of the gospel (v. 19). The result is a dual rejection in one scene, both Jews and non-Jews. The opposition from Jews and the nations means refusing to accept this way that the apostles know to be the only *hodos* that comes from God and leads to him. Though there is no apparent success in this episode for the apostles, the fact that Paul remains alive after being stoned (vv. 19–20) confirms for the reader that God's hand is upon him, and that his purposes cannot be thwarted by human or spiritual forces.

The observation of this event, featuring a clash of three religious perspectives, contributes to the Theophilus's understanding of his faith in contrast to other teachings available among the Jews and the nations. It contributes to Luke's strategy of normalization for the reader, namely, making

---

77. Johnson (*Acts*, 249) paraphrases it as, "to follow their own paths," and reduces the force of the expression to custom or moral behavior based on diachronic data.

78. Tannehill, *Narrative*, 2:179. Similarly, Barrett, *Acts*, 1:663–64.

79. Schneider, *Apg.*, 2:160–61. Also understood in a religious sense: Jervell (*Apg.*, 378) and Weiser, *Apg. Kapitel 13–28*, 352.

sense of this theocentric world and his part in it. The sense of belonging to the right group is strengthened; hence, his assurance grows accordingly.

Gentile Rejection in Philippi: "the Way of Salvation" (16:17)

After the episode in Lystra, the reader follows the apostles' preaching in Derbe and return through various towns on their way back to Antioch, thus ending their first missionary journey (14:21-28). Then, the reader learns about the decisions made in Jerusalem (15:1-30) regarding "those who are turning to God from the nations" (v. 19b). The church in Antioch receives this news favorably and Paul and Barnabas are sent out again, though in different directions (15:30-41). The spotlight continues to remain on Paul and his missionary entourage to the end of the narrative. Paul and Silas travel through Syria and Cilicia, arriving again at Derbe and Lystra where Timothy joins them (16:1-3). It is noteworthy that the narrator subtly informs the reader that he also has joined them, presumably at Troas (16:10). This is the first of the "we-passages" (i.e., first person plural narration), which enhances the rhetorical force of the narration.[80] Through divine direction, the apostles arrive in Macedonia, specifically at Philippi (16:4-12). This leads to the next appearance of the thoroughfare imagery in Acts 16:17.

In the passage Acts 16:11-40, the narrator ("we"), who is now within the narrative, recounts the events in Philippi (Lydia's conversion, healing of demon-possessed girl and ensuing trouble, and the jailor's conversion). This passage contains intense emotions due to pagan reception and rejection, accompanied by violent pagan opposition. This opposition is human, but the instigation of demonic forces lies behind it (16:16-21). Following the conversion of Lydia and her household, the narrator tells how he, Paul and others encountered a demon-possessed slave-girl over a number of days.[81] The passage especially characterizes Paul, but Silas is also specifically mentioned in the passage (vv. 19, 25, 29). Ironically, the girl's words (via the spirit) correspond to the narrator's portrayal of Jesus' group of disciples: "These men are servants of the Most High God, who are proclaiming to you the way of salvation" (οὗτοι οἱ ἄνθρωποι δοῦλοι τοῦ θεοῦ τοῦ ὑψίστου εἰσίν, οἵτινες καταγγέλλουσιν ὑμῖν ὁδὸν σωτηρίας (16:17b). The disciples are from a divine source, "the Most High God," from whom they bring a message, "the

---

80. Other occurrences are found in Acts 16:10-17; 20:5-15; 21:1-18 and 27:1—28:16.

81. The narrator emphasizes the presence of Paul and his own secondary presence expressed through the girl's accompaniment: "While she was following Paul and us . . ." (16:17a).

way of salvation" (16:17).[82] This utterance comes through the girl's voice (v. 17); yet, one infers that the demon is the source since Paul commands it to come out of her. This subsequently occurs (v. 18).[83] This recognition of truth through demons evokes similar scenes when Jesus encountered them (Luke 4:41; 8:28). Similar to the spies' truthful statement about Jesus' identity through deceitful flattery (Luke 20:21), the narrator ably uses the odd utterance to portray Jesus' disciples and enhance their part in the unfolding story.

Again, *hodos* is the object of a verb of communication "proclaim" (the reader has already seen this in two other examples, Luke 20:21; Acts 2:28). Thus, it represents something that can be communicated, a message or teaching.[84] Moreover, *hodos* is in a genitive construction qualified by an abstract term "salvation" (cf. "peace" Luke 1:79; "life" Acts 2:28). This indicates that the message is about "salvation." The reader has already encountered similar expressions that clarify this as spiritual salvation, deliverance from one's sins (Luke 1:77; 3:3, 6; 24:47). This concerns a turning to Israel's God.[85] Thus, by keeping the natural image of "way" or "path," the meaning is most likely, "the path that leads to salvation,"[86] namely, the message concerning the means for reconciliation with God.[87]

This would appear to be the most natural reading in light of the overall narrative. Saul's irritation might have been due to the demon's presence, not so much due to its words. Nevertheless, scholars suggest that when the expressions "the Most High God" and "way of salvation" are interpreted in light of ancient pagan context, they shed light on Paul's strong reaction. The idiom "way of salvation" is doubly anarthrous (no articles); therefore, it is possible that the demon is relativizing the disciples' message as only "a way of salvation." In addition, the demon's statement is not specifically

---

82. The expression τοῦ θεοῦ τοῦ ὑψίστου recalls similar qualifications through ὕψιστος in the first volume with reference to Jesus (1:32, 78; 8:28), the Holy Spirit (1:35), and John the Baptist (1:76).

83. Cf. Johnson, *Acts*, 298.

84. "Salvation is presented here as a message to receive and a way upon which to set forth." Bottini, *Luca*, 110.

85. This notion is often expressed through "turn (back)" (ἐπιστρέφω) in Luke 1:16; Acts 3:19; 9:35; 11:21; 14:15, 15:19; 26:18, 20; 28:27).

86. Wallace (*Greek*, 100–101) identifies it as a genitive of destination (a.k.a. direction) or purpose (destined for, toward). CP (p. 315) do not find Wallace's label helpful: "The idiomatic expression ὁδὸν σωτηρίας denotes, 'how you can be saved.'"

87. Schneider (*Apg.*, 2:215) summarizes it: "Proclamation of the faith is seen by Luke as a development of the 'path to salvation' (Acts 2:28; see the Macedonian's cry for help, 16:9, and the jailor's question, 16:30)."

Christological. Most commentators, however, translate the expression with the definite article "the way of salvation" and not "a way of salvation."[88] Paul Trebilco, however, argues that the latter is the most probable translation and is a misleading statement by the demon because of the vague referent of "the Most High God" in a pagan context that probably would have been interpreted as the supreme deity in a pantheon of gods.[89] Therefore, the demon's repetitive utterances through this girl could be seen as a taunting or teasing demonic refrain. Paul was not only annoyed; he was concerned that this continued outburst would mislead the people to understand that Paul and Silas were servants of the highest god in the hearer's pantheon. Trebilco's interpretation is suggestive but lacks convincing historical and textual support. Irina Levinskaya, for example, argues that, "the extent of pagan usage of the title has been strongly exaggerated and most of the pagan highest gods are merely the result of scholarly reconstruction."[90] Levinskaya concludes, "The demon was exorcised by Paul, not because of the content of his proclamation, but because the Christian mission did not need allies such as these."[91] This corresponds well to the narrator's portrayal of Jesus when he silences the evil spirits even when they tell the truth.[92]

Returning now to the reader's level, Bruce sums up the situation by recognizing that some ambiguity of meaning may have been present in the minds of those hearers in the original context, but not so for the reader of Acts: "σωτηρία [salvation] was a term current among Gentiles as well as Jews and Christians. Whatever the fortune-teller meant by it, Luke probably intends his readers to read the full Christian sense of σωτηρία into her words: Paul and his companions were indeed proclaiming *the* 'way of salvation.'"[93]

---

88. Barrett interprets the expression in light of the entire pericope: "ὁδός here however will refer not to a manner of life but to the way to, that is the way to acquire, salvation." Barrett, *Acts*, 2:787. So, Bruce, *Acts*, 361; and Jervell, *Apg.*, 423.

89. Trebilco states that when ὁδός occurs in Acts in a metaphorical sense, Luke almost always uses the article. He recognizes the exception in Acts 2:28 in ἐγνώρισάς μοι ὁδοὺς ζωῆς, but mentions that it is a citation from the LXX. Trebilco, "Paul and Silas," 60. Yet, he does not include the evidence in the Gospel of Luke where ὁδός is also used without the article εἰς ὁδὸν εἰρήνης (Luke 1:79). In each of these examples ὁδός occurs with abstract terms as the dependent genitive (εἰρήνης; ζωῆς; and here σωτηρίας) and are normally translated in English with the article. Therefore, internal evidence does not completely support his position. Witherington (*Acts*, 495n108) and Talbert (*Reading Acts*, 142) accept his argument.

90. Levinskaya, *Acts*, 98.

91. Ibid., 100.

92. Cf. Jervell, *Apg.*, 423.

93. Bruce, *Acts*, 361.

Given the internal evidence concerning *hodos* and Luke's interest in salvation through Jesus, Levinskaya and Bruce's conclusions are the most plausible.

Regarding the value of the expression for the plot, the irony is lucid: the hero's mandate is realized and one of Satan's emissaries confirmed it. "The way of salvation" that had been alluded to by Gabriel, Zechariah, Simeon, John the Baptist and Jesus is no longer a potentiality, but a reality, and it has come to the nations. *Hodos* helps express the Messianic benefits through him (peace, life, salvation). "The way of salvation" is available to the nations but also in confrontation with their religion(s). The image of "the way of salvation" with a clear soteriological sense evokes the early image about Jesus' identity as the "dawn" and his mandate to guide people into the "way of peace" (Luke 1:78–79). Fitzmyer summarizes its narrative value thus: "So the slave girl divines the import of the Christian message, using the distinctively Lucan *hodos sōtērias*, 'way of salvation'. She thus announces a prominent motif of Lucan redemptive history."[94] Satan's attempt to sabotage this "way of salvation" had failed (Luke 4:5–7); Jews and non-Jews have begun to respond to it favorably, thus entering the way of peace. This becomes clear later in the larger passage when "the way of salvation" through Jesus is exemplified in a pagan home through the proclamation of "the word of the Lord" (16:32) to the jailer, "believe on the Lord Jesus and you will be saved, you and your household (16:31).[95] The passage does not leave the reader in doubt; this message is from God, because even the demons acknowledge it and must obey the servants of the Most High. The passage confirms the theocentric world that Theophilus and others were called to live in.

Jewish Reception in Ephesus: Apollos and "the Way of the Lord/God" (18:25, 26)

The analysis now turns to the next two occurrences of *hodos* concerning missionary work in Ephesus, in the passage with Apollos, Priscilla and Aquila (18:24–28). Luke inserts this account as a brief interlude between the accounts regarding Paul's missionary work in Thessalonica, Berea, Athens, Corinth, Antioch, and Ephesus. The spotlight still follows Paul, who is fulfilling Jesus' mandate. In fact, the reader meets again Paul's collaborators, Aquila and Priscilla, who were introduced in the Corinth account (18:2). They had accompanied Paul to Ephesus and stayed there during his trip to

---

94. Fitzmyer, *Acts*, 586.

95. The word σωτηρία in Luke-Acts almost always refers to Jesus, directly or indirectly. Bottini, *Luca*, 111.

Expanding Encounters: From Roads to "the Way"

Antioch. Apollos, a Jew from Alexandria, appears only after Paul's departure. Apollos then meets Priscilla and Aquila. This is the first of two episodes concerning the integration of persons who knew John the Baptist's teaching but had not heard the full story concerning Jesus (the second is recounted in 19:1–7). This episode compares the time before and after Apollos's encounter with Paul's disciples: what he knew and taught before, and what he learned from them and subsequently taught. It is a brief story of individual transformation, since Apollos is sent to Corinth for missionary work only after his meeting with Aquila and Priscilla (18:27; 19:1). However, the use of the terms "Jewish" and "Christian" in commentaries tends to complicate the discussion about Apollos.[96] What is important for Luke is to indicate who had responded positively to God's revelation. Disciples of John, in this sense, were a part of this group, and thus—from the narrator's perspective—naturally *pro* Jesus. Consequently, they should become disciples of Jesus, because John and Jesus are inseparable in God's plan. The highlighted examples in Ephesus serve to demonstrate this. Comparable to John the Baptist and his disciples who had responded well to God's revelation, and were speaking accurately about Jesus, they were asked to respond again in faith when further revelation was given to them (cf. Luke 7:18–35).

In this portrayal of Apollos's transformation, two thoroughfare expressions occur with *hodos*: "the way of the Lord" and "the way of God." How do they contribute to the characterization of Apollos and the plot? Below are the two verses in which they are employed (18:25–26):

> He had been instructed (in) the way of the Lord, and, being fervent in spirit, he was speaking and teaching accurately things concerning Jesus, [yet] knowing only the baptism of John. And so he began to speak boldly in the synagogue. When Priscilla and Aquila heard him, they took him aside and explained the way [of God] to him more accurately.

> ²⁵ οὗτος ἦν κατηχημένος τὴν ὁδὸν τοῦ κυρίου καὶ ζέων τῷ πνεύματι ἐλάλει καὶ ἐδίδασκεν ἀκριβῶς τὰ περὶ τοῦ Ἰησοῦ, ἐπιστάμενος μόνον τὸ βάπτισμα Ἰωάννου· ²⁶ οὗτός τε ἤρξατο παρρησιάζεσθαι ἐν τῇ συναγωγῇ. ἀκούσαντες δὲ αὐτοῦ Πρίσκιλλα καὶ Ἀκύλας προσελάβοντο αὐτὸν καὶ ἀκριβέστερον αὐτῷ ἐξέθεντο τὴν ὁδὸν [τοῦ θεοῦ].

96. Fitzmyer (*Acts*, 637), for example, writes, "In both instances Luke is concerned to incorporate such 'Johannine Christians' into the mainstream Christian fold . . . ." Likewise, Jervell (*Apg.*, 470): "For Luke of course, a Jew who knows the Scriptures well can be only Christian, for he knows the story of Jesus from the Scriptures, 17:3, 11." Similarly, Schneider (*Apg.*, 2:260): "Apollos was, so to speak, a Jewish 'Jesus follower', but not yet a Christian."

Both expressions concern the instruction of Apollos: his training prior to his visit to Ephesus, and then under Priscilla and Aquila. Both expressions are direct objects of verbs of instruction. The first, "the way of the Lord," is the object of the verb "instruct" (κατηχέω), which here takes a double accusative (indication of *direct object*), the person being instructed and the content of instruction.[97] The second expression, "the way [of God]," is the object of the verb "explain" (ἐκτίθημι) whose subject is Priscilla and Aquila. What do these expressions mean? Are they synonymous?[98]

As stated, the reader has already met *hodos* in expressions meaning teaching or message, in other words, something to be communicated, taught or proclaimed (Luke 20:21; Acts 16:17). The reader finds the verb *katēcheō* ("inform," "teach") elsewhere only three other times (Luke 1:4; Acts 21:21, 24). In Acts 21:21 and 24, the meaning can be interpreted as "to inform" since it is not used in a didactic situation. In Luke 1:4, however, some ambiguity is present. Had Theophilus only been informed about things related to Jesus? Alternatively, had he already received instruction as a disciple about Jesus?[99] Based on internal evidence, the probable interpretation is the latter one, since the narrative manifests a didactic relationship between fellow disciples, Luke and Theophilus.[100] The latter had already received some instruction concerning Jesus, but he needed more. Apollos, on the other hand, is a Jewish teacher (v. 25 "he was speaking and teaching"), who, although he included Jesus (even "accurately" v. 25) in his teaching in the synagogue context, did not have a complete understanding about Jesus. Talbert's evaluation is correct: "At most, Apollos knew of Jesus' life before Jerusalem; at least, he knew only the teaching of John the Baptist ... If so, then Apollos is not fully a Messianist when he comes to Ephesus."[101] This significant problem—the *complication* in this micro-narrative—is expressed at the end of verse 25: "though he only knew the baptism of John." The probable rendering of this

---

97. Cf. Wallace, *Greek*, 181–82. It is an accusative of reference answering the question, With respect to what had Apollos been instructed? So CP, 356.

98. For example, McCasland ("The Way," 229) differentiates the expressions based on origins, one from Qumran through John the Baptist, and the other from Christians: "Apollos was probably still using 'the way of the Lord' as it was understood at Qumran. He had to learn the different meaning it had among Christians." He supports this with Matt 21:32 and 22:16.

99. Eisen (*Poetik*, 94) understands Apollos to be Christian through the link of κατηχέω in Luke and Acts 18:25.

100. See the discussion on various proposals concerning the identity of Theophilus in Chapter 2.

101. Talbert, *Reading Acts*, 166.

participial phrase is one of concession: "though he only knew . . . ." The phrase could be implicitly understood in the negative formulation, "but he did not know the baptism in the name of Jesus," and, consequently, nor the gift of the Holy Spirit through him. Johnson acutely describes the differences in portrayal between Apollos and other protagonists: "Apollos is 'ardent in the spirit' and 'eloquent' but he is not 'full of the Holy Spirit' nor does he speak 'God's word', or perform 'signs and wonders'. He is, the reader learns, not of the same rank as those called to be prophets by Jesus and the Spirit."[102]

Thus, based on what the narrator has told the reader so far, it can be deduced that Apollos probably did not know about the events in Jerusalem regarding Jesus, which became the basis for baptizing believers in his name.[103] Nonetheless, he did teach accurately what he knew about Jesus even though it was incomplete.[104] Apollos's predicament is the source of narrative tension, since the sympathetic reader hopes for a positive resolution. In light of the greater narrative, however, this complication can be interpreted as being easier to resolve than in other episodes, for the narrator's portrayal of John the Baptist and his disciples is positive. The narrator wants to highlight another type of reception episode in which followers of John's teaching receive more instruction about Jesus and become his disciples in the fullest sense. The fact that Apollos accepted John's baptism and certain teachings of or about Jesus meant that he was in some ways already a disciple, but before having knowledge of the events transpired in Jerusalem. The narrator's criterion for understanding God's purposes supports this, namely, the reception of John in relationship to Jesus.[105] In fact, in the following passage, the reader learns that the men who only knew John's baptism are also "disciples" (19:1).

How does "Lord" qualify the expression "the way" in 18:25? The closest expression to this occurrence is "the way for/of the Lord" in Luke 3:4 (from Isa 40:3) in the description of John the Baptist's mandate. Yet, it does not describe the content of his message, rather his function as forerunner for

---

102. Johnson, *Acts*, 335.

103. These verses contain references to the baptism in Jesus' name in connection with the reception of the Holy Spirit: 2:38 (Jerusalem); 8:16 (Samaria); 10:48 (Caesarea). Apollos's case is exemplified in the pericope immediately following this passage. Paul instructs the "disciples" about the meaning of John's baptism (19:3–4), baptizes them in the name of Jesus (19:5), and then the Holy Spirit comes upon them (19:6). This is the same order described for the Samaritan believers.

104. Cf. CP, 356.

105. That is, John the Baptist's baptism in relation to Jesus (Luke 7:29–30), Jesus' evaluation of John (7:24–28), and Jesus' response/question about John to the religious leaders (20:3–8).

Jesus. Moreover, other uses of *hodos* in relation to John the Baptist do not describe his message (Luke 1:76; 7:27). However, it could be the narrator's own reference to John the Baptist's teaching. Yet, the narrator's use of "Lord" in 18:25 is ambiguous, as in some occurrences, referring either to God or to Jesus. The natural reading for the referent "Lord" in Acts 18:25 is probably "God" (of Israel), since Apollos had been raised a Jew and was "mighty" in the Jewish Scriptures (v. 24). Given the interchangeable uses of "Lord" and "God," the expression in Acts 18:25 has a close semantic connection to the use in Luke 20:21 "the way of God" where it is also the object of a verb of instruction "teach" (διδάσκω). For this reason, the narrator's description of Apollos's prior instruction, though oriented toward the preparation for the Messiah's arrival, is not fully Christocentric. Nonetheless, he did know something about Jesus and he taught it accurately.

This problem that Apollos was unaware of (but signaled to the reader, v. 25) becomes evident on the action level in verse 26 when Priscilla and Aquila notice that something is missing in Apollos's teaching, which can be inferred through the phrase "they took him aside and explained the way [of God] more accurately." This is the transforming action on the action level. The encounter serves to fill in the gaps in his knowledge about the events concerning Jesus and his sending of the Holy Spirit. Subsequently, he had the necessity to be specifically baptized in the name of Jesus Christ. In fact, the two gaps that the reader must fill are: (1) that which Apollos did not know about Jesus and (2) the events that happened after Apollos had received further teaching about Jesus prior to his departure for Corinth.

This leads to the meaning of the second expression, "the way [of God] (τὴν ὁδὸν [τοῦ θεοῦ]). Accepting the recommendation that the fuller expression "the way of God" is closer to the original reading, the two expressions are probably synonymous in meaning.[106] They both represent teaching from God and lead to God. The reason for the difference is merely stylistic

---

106. The fuller expression τὴν ὁδὸν τοῦ θεοῦ is most likely the original reading based on overwhelming textual evidence. The shorter expression τὴν ὁδόν, which the narrator has used thus far only in Acts 9:2, is supported only by D gig. Schneider (*Apg.*, 2:261n21) views this as an attempt to harmonize the expression by making it explicitly the way (of Jesus). Metzger (*Textual*, 414) explains that this text is clearly secondary due to the expansion in the previous verse (18:25) where τὴν ὁδὸν τοῦ κυρίου is replaced by τὸν λόγον in the expression κατηχημένος ἐν τῇ πατρίδι τὸν λόγον τοῦ κυρίου. Yet, based on internal evidence (Acts 9:2; 19:9, 23; 22:4; 24:14, 22), the "Committee" placed τοῦ θεοῦ in square brackets, recognizing "the possibility that the Western text may be original." Pervo (*Acts*, 458), however, argues that D contains the closest variant (referring to Ropes, *Beginnings*, 178) and translates the phrase: ". . . they took him aside and expounded the Movement more fully."

in order to avoid repetition. The pragmatic force of the second expression indicates that Priscilla and Aquila's rendition of the events is trustworthy and in conformity with the way of God. However, it does not indicate an intrinsic qualitative difference in doctrine between "the way of the Lord" and "the way of God." The expression "the way of the Lord" expresses the teaching that Apollos had received up until John including his training in the Jewish Scriptures. This is an image of the teaching from the Lord, the God of Israel, and leads to him. Some teaching about Jesus was present. It was not wrong, only incomplete. Alternatively, the expression "the way of God" could have been used without changing the sense, since it is probably a synonym of the above expression, an example of the narrator's stylistic variety.[107] Priscilla and Aquila, who are Jewish, give him a more complete picture about what had happened in Jesus' life and their consequences. This type of situation is exemplified by another event in Ephesus recounted in the following passage (19:1–7).

If the order were reversed, that is, "the way of the Lord" in the second position, the reader would probably associate "Lord" with Jesus, thus a more specific reference to a teaching centered on Jesus through Priscilla and Aquila. Alternatively, supposing that the narrator had used the elliptical expression "the way" (τὴν ὁδόν as in certain manuscripts), this might have signaled to the reader, based on the parallelism in Acts 9:1–2, a more explicit Christological accent on the content of their teaching. In addition, the force of the article could have given it additional emphasis, *the* way, thus enhancing the corrective action taken by Priscilla and Aquila. Even so, with the current wording and order of the text, given the narrator's description of Apollos's essential deficiency, the overall meaning remains the same: Apollos needed to know more about Jesus' accomplishments and the consequences thereof. For this reason, the transformation necessary for Apollos was far less radical than for those of Jewish background who had not accepted John's teaching, or for those who were from a non-Jewish background.[108]

The reader must fill the second major gap: what happened after their encounter? It is clear from verses 27–28 that this is a reception scene, because Apollos received the correction given, and was most likely baptized

---

107. This seems the best interpretation, unless the expression was used for John the Baptist's ministry and teaching.

108. The narrator's portrayal of John the Baptist and his disciples is very positive, though he also includes those moments of doubt experienced by John (Luke 7:18). This portrayal of Apollos and John's disciples in the following passage (Acts 19) is further evidence of this evaluation: The fact that they accepted John's teachings meant that they were to some degree already "disciples" and expected to receive full teaching about Jesus.

in the name of Jesus, and possibly experienced a manifestation of the Holy Spirit. One infers from the results (the resolution) of the transforming action, which the narrator carefully shows: the church in Ephesus has enough confidence in him to send him to Achaia, and, once there, he is able to refute the Jews successfully based on his newly acquired knowledge about Jesus (v. 28). By comparison, it follows that that he was not able to do this in Ephesus, though he spoke boldly (v. 26).

Pragmatically, Luke wants to illustrate for Theophilus the importance of knowing accurately "the way of God," which is in conformity to Jesus' identity and accomplished mandate. This episode represents another type of reception scene that involves the thoroughfare imagery in a figurative sense. There is a before-and-after-portrait of Apollos, what he had been instructed and what he had taught, compared to what is instructed by Priscilla and Aquila and what he now teaches. The entire portraiture is positive: a triumph for Paul and his missionary entourage. For the reader, this scene could also serve as a *mise en abyme* (a story within a story epitomizing the thrust of the entire narrative) for the need to have a fuller picture of "the things accomplished among us" (Luke 1:1), a coherent narrative that makes sense of the past (*normalization*). Similar to John the Baptist and his disciples (Luke 7:18–23), Apollos also needed to be informed about what Jesus had actually accomplished. The audience might find in Apollos a positive example of someone who knew much, but not enough. There is irony here in that Apollos is "mighty (capable) in the Scriptures" (v. 24) and yet he needs further instruction. The reader might be somewhat like Apollos, and the narrator—assuming the role of teacher—is similar to Priscilla and Aquila, providing the desired instruction, "the way of the Lord/God." In the following section, another nuance of *hodos* is presented, beginning with two other occurrences that illustrate Paul's work in Ephesus (19:1–40).

Paul: Protagonist for the Collective Character, "the Way"

This section discusses how the reader encounters *hodos* with a different nuance. The idiom "the Way" begins to assume the value of a collective character in the story, based on a natural progression from a metaphor to a metonym.

Expanding Encounters: From Roads to "the Way"

Jewish Rejection in Ephesus: Speaking Evil of "the Way" (19:9)

After the integration of those in Ephesus who only knew John's baptism (Apollos and then the twelve "disciples"), the reader observes some of the events that occurred while Paul was established in Ephesus (19:8–41) before his departure for Macedonia (20:1). The narrator makes an important allusion to a turning point in Paul's missionary work: after his visit to Jerusalem, he has projected to go to Rome (19:21). The reader is thus prepared for the two main final movements in the plot, Ephesus to Jerusalem and Jerusalem to Rome. Paul's stay in Ephesus is important for Luke's portrayal of the progress of the gospel among the Jews and the nations as the final major showcase of reception and rejection in a particular geographical region.[109] It is the final long period of ministry as a non-prisoner. In two episodes described below, one among the Jews, the other among non-Jews, the narrator uses *hodos* for the first time with another nuance, which the reader has been prepared to interpret through previous uses of the word and/or prior knowledge of the expression.

The next appearance of *hodos* occurs in the brief passage in Acts 19:8–12, which recounts Paul's teaching in the synagogue of Ephesus, the ensuing conflict with the Jewish community, and Paul's separation from the synagogue with those who had received Jesus. The reader learns that Paul's training of the disciples lasted two years.[110] *Hodos* in verse 9 describes the conflict between the followers of Jesus and the Jewish community:

> When some were hardened and were not believing (but) speaking evil of the Way before the assembly, he [Paul], having withdrew from them, took away the disciples, reasoning daily in the hall of Tyranus.

> ὡς δέ τινες ἐσκληρύνοντο καὶ ἠπείθουν κακολογοῦντες τὴν ὁδὸν ἐνώπιον τοῦ πλήθους, ἀποστὰς ἀπ' αὐτῶν ἀφώρισεν τοὺς μαθητὰς καθ' ἡμέραν διαλεγόμενος ἐν τῇ σχολῇ Τυράννου.

After the successful integration of John the Baptist's disciples, the reader now encounters a less favorable situation among the Jewish community. Two groups are in opposition: those of the synagogue (τινες of the synagogue, v. 8) and the "disciples" who adhered to Paul's teaching (cf. 19:1, 7, 9). The two groups are illustrative of the rejection and reception pattern

---

109. Cf. Tannehill's chapter, "Ephesus: Climax of Paul's Mission as a Free Man" in *Narrative*, 2:230–40.

110. The lexical similarities between this passage and 28:23–31 are striking. Both take place in contexts of Jewish communities: witness (19:9; 28:23); two years (19:10; 28:30); resistant attitude (19:9; 28:27); rejection of Paul's teaching (19:9; 28:34).

highlighted for the reader.¹¹¹ Those who reject Paul's teaching are "hardened and unbelieving,"¹¹² having become openly hostile through public slander before the entire Jewish community (v. 9).¹¹³ The targeted party of the slander is described as "the Way." The word "slander" (or "speak evil" κακολογέω) occurs once in Luke-Acts.¹¹⁴ It has similar uses to "blaspheme" (βλασφημέω) in Luke-Acts, namely, against Jesus (Luke 22:65; 23:39) and against Paul in Pisidian Antioch (13:45) and Corinth (18:6). In summary, this group is reviled because of their association with the teaching that they hold.

This is the second occurrence of the unmodified *hodos* in Luke-Acts, after the occurrence in Acts 9:2. It is similar to the first occurrence because of the context of hostility against the "disciples," followers of Jesus. They are different, however, in that the first occurrence of *hodos* occurs as a dependent genitive in the expression "some . . . being of the Way" (τινας . . . τῆς ὁδοῦ ὄντας). Here Luke uses *hodos* alone, as the direct object. In the analysis of the occurrence in 9:2, the referent for "of the Way" (τῆς ὁδοῦ) is interpreted as the teaching of and about Jesus, as an ellipsis of "the way of God/the Lord" (ἡ ὁδὸς τοῦ θεοῦ/κυρίου). Therefore, the expression *tinas . . . tēs hodou ontas* is a construction that indicates their sense of belonging to this teaching of and about Jesus. Here in Acts 19:9, the same idea is present, but the narrator goes a step further by using a full metonymic expression, that is, the disciples are identified directly as "*the* Way" through their association with the teaching.¹¹⁵ They are not the "teaching," but those who adhere to

---

111. Fitzmyer (*Acts*, 648) rightly notes, "Obstinate refusal is a Lucan description, characteristic of his value judgments (cf. 13:6)."

112. A similar situation appeared in Iconium. The word σκληρύνω is a hapax in Luke-Acts, and ἀπειθέω occurs here and in Acts 14:2 in a similar situation of synagogal opposition through derogatory speech.

113. For the referent of πλῆθος, the synagogue community as a whole is the most plausible (CP, 363). Based on the context, it appears to be an ellipsis: the assembly (of the Jewish synagogue/community).

114. It occurs elsewhere in the NT only three times: in Mark 7:10 // Matt 15:4 concerning the warning for speaking evil of one's parents, and in Mark 9:39, "But Jesus said, 'Do not hinder him, for no one who performs a miracle in my name will be able to speak evil of me soon afterward.'" BDAG (p. 50) defines it: "speak evil of, revile, insult τινά someone."

115. Caird clarifies the confusion regarding related terms: "Some linguists classify synecdoche and metonymy as metaphor, on the ground that all three consist in the transfer of a name from one referent to another. This usage, however, blurs one important distinction: in synecdoche and metonymy the link between the two referents is one of contiguity and in metaphor it is one of comparison. Metaphor is best understood when it is studied along with other forms of comparative language." Caird, *Language*, 137. So Aletti et al., *Vocabulaire*, 93.

it.[116] Nor are they *like* the teaching as a metaphor would suggest. Thus, the expression is based on association (metonymy) and not on similarity (metaphor). The next four occurrences of the unmodified *hodos* have this same metonymic value. Based on intrinsic data, the process of Luke's construction of this particular expression can be described as follows:

1. "The way of God/the Lord" (ἡ ὁδὸς τοῦ θεοῦ/κυρίου) occurs as a figure or image in a metaphoric sense to describe "the instruction of God/the Lord" or "that which God has revealed." The implicit comparison is based on the picture that the thoroughfare image communicates. The instruction or teaching of God is like a "way" or "road" in that it leads to God (Luke 20:21; cf. Acts 18:25, 26). It is about him, from him, and leads to him. Conceptually, it could be called "God's instruction," or "the divine way."

2. With this expression established, Luke is able to employ an elliptical expression, from "the way of God/the Lord" to "the Way" (Acts 9:2). It is "*the* way," that is, none other than "the way of God." The ellipsis maintains the same meaning, but adds emphasis: "the Way," the only "way" among other "ways" that is worth mentioning and thus worthy of an ellipsis.

3. The notion of adherence or belonging to this teaching is expressed through a genitival construction "some belonging to the Way" (τινας ... τῆς ὁδοῦ ὄντας): hence, the people who follow Jesus' teaching are described as "those of the Way" (Acts 9:2b) in contrast to Saul who represents the interests of the opposing Jewish leadership (9:1–2a).

4. Through the ellipsis and the sense of belonging, the narrator expresses the disciples' full identification or association with Jesus' teaching through a metonymic expression, "the Way" (Acts 19:9, 23; 22:4; 24:14, 22). This is a more forceful rhetorical expression through direct association, not only "those of the Way" but plainly, "the Way." They are portrayed in contrast with the unbelieving Jews of the synagogue of Ephesus (19:9) and the worshipers of Artemis (19:23). In Paul's defense speeches, he associates openly with "the Way" before the mob in Jerusalem (22:4) and before Felix in Caesarea (24:14, 22).

In summary, each occurrence of *hodos* prepares the reader to interpret other nuanced expressions used to enhance the plot. What then is the pragmatic force of this metonymic expression in this context? Narratively,

---

116. Contra Schneider (*Apg.*, 2:268n11): "It refers to the (new) religious teaching and way of life in the broadest sense."

the image begins to assume the value of a collective character in the story (similar to "disciples," "saints," and "church").[117] Other figurative expressions in the absolute are not used in this manner to describe Jesus' followers (e.g., "the word," "the kingdom," "the law," etc.). This use of *hodos*—implied as "the way of God/the Lord"—continues to characterize those associated with Jesus as being in harmony with God's revelation and activity. Other expressions in Acts do this as well, as Gaventa notes, "God's comprehensive role means that it should come as no surprise that two small phrases pepper the story: Word of God and Plan of God."[118] Consequently, this expression adds to the sympathetic reader's identification with this collective of disciples. As the plot progresses, his sense of belonging to "the Way" is strengthened and he is able to relive these events with greater empathy. This idiom is clearly an *avoidable* expression (in Freedman's terms) since a concrete expression could have been used.[119] It draws the reader's attention as an assertion of uniqueness, "the Way," namely, those who really know the way of God, among all the other religious groups, Jewish and non-Jewish. The spiritual unity between Jesus, his teaching, and his disciples, already established in 9:1-2, is again emphasized: "the Way" is opposed and maligned (Acts 19:9). Thus, the pattern of reception and rejection continues through another parallel between Jesus and the collective group of disciples. Through this didactic narrative, Luke and Theophilus are united with this group through their relationship with Jesus.

In light of these observations on the above metonymic use of *hodos*, the discussion turns to a similar use in the next occurrence (19:23) in another passage about hostility towards "the Way" in a pagan context in Ephesus.

Gentile Rejection in Ephesus: "no little disturbance concerning the Way" (19:23)

The thoroughfare motif reappears shortly after the previous occurrence in the spotlight of a rejection episode among the nations during Paul's extended stay in Ephesus (19:21-41). His plans to leave for Macedonia and Achaia (v. 21) en route for Jerusalem are precipitated by the riot of Artemis's worshippers reacting violently to the religious and economic effects caused by Paul's

---

117. Another expression (but without metonymy) is the personified λόγος (Acts 6:7; 12:24; 13:49; 19:20).

118. Gaventa, *Acts*, 31. Cf. "the word of God" and "the word of the Lord" in Acts 4:31; 13:7, 44; 16:32.

119. E.g., "the disciples of the Lord" (Acts 9:1) and "church" (Acts 8:1, 3; 12:1) in contexts of opposition.

ministry (e.g., his miracles; the evil spirit and Sceva's sons; the burning of books of magic). Paul has already sent Timothy and Erastus ahead of him (v. 22). Now, Luke underlines the progress of the gospel by expressing the culmination of the growing tension between the pagan community and "the Way."[120] Verse 23 summarizes this conflict: "There arose at that time not a little trouble concerning the Way" ('Εγένετο δὲ κατὰ τὸν καιρὸν ἐκεῖνον τάραχος οὐκ ὀλίγος περὶ τῆς ὁδοῦ.).

Thus, the function of verse 23 is to introduce the episode's *complication* with a characteristic litotes, "not a little trouble," for "the Way" is seen as the source of this disturbance, which is explained in verses 23-34. This time, the unmodified *hodos*, as the object of the preposition "concerning" (περί), answers the question: With respect to what (or whom) was there no little disturbance?[121] Again, via metonymy, the expression signifies the people associated with the teaching of the way of the Lord/God (Israel's God).[122] Thus, they are portrayed again as a collective character.[123] Now the reader learns through the voice of Demetrius, the chief antagonist, about the perceived religious and economic threats that "the Way" has brought (vv. 25-27). For Demetrius, "the Way" must be attacked because they are the channels of this teaching that is in contrast with the values of the worship and activities pertaining to Artemis. It concerns a clash of two groups holding conflicting worldviews: the people associated with Artemis and the people associated with the way of the Lord, "the Way."[124] Jervell sums up well the situation in Ephesus: "The effectiveness of Paul is so successful that the pagan cult is threatened ... and here, vv 23-40, a real threat of paganism comes through Paul, which shows once more the Christians as the true people of God."[125]

---

120. Cf. Tannehill, *Narrative*, 2:242-43.

121. It is a prepositional phrase of reference. Alternatively, if *hodos* is the logical subject: "Around that time, 'the Way' became the source of much disturbance."

122. This description then concurs with the Haenchen's interpretation that the absolute ὁδός here as in 19:9 serves as a "self-designation of the Christian community." This is not the case, he opines, for τοῦ ὁδοῦ in Acts 9:2, where it does not refer to the Christians as a "community." Haenchen, *Apg.*, 268, 506.

123. It is clear that Paul is not alone, based on the various general and specific references to disciples and fellow missionaries in the pericopes concerning Ephesus (19:7, 9, 18-19; Timothy and Erastus, 19:22; and Gaius and Aristarchus, 19:29; the Asiarchs, 19:31; 20:1).

124. BDR (§495n4) is not accurate enough by designating the unmodified *hodos* here as a metonymy for teaching (*Lehre*). It is fundamentally a metaphor for teaching (an ellipsis of "the way of God/the Lord"). This makes metonymy possible for those associated with the teaching.

125. Jervell, *Apg.*, 489. The fundamental source of this threat is again Paul and his

Consequently, similar to the conflict with the owners of the slave-girl in Philippi, Paul, the leader of "the Way," is not only forced to separate from the synagogue in Ephesus, he is now forced by the pagan community to depart for Macedonia since his life was at risk (inferred from verses 30–31 and from his immediate departure, 20:1). Therefore, before leading the reader to follow Paul's journey back to Jerusalem, Luke has provided two illustrations in which "the Way" has been received and rejected by Jews and non-Jews in Ephesus. In both cases, the primary cause is the message or teaching brought by Paul for the Jews (19:8, 9b) and for the nations (19:26).[126]

Pragmatically, by employing this figurative use of *hodos*, the narrator enhances the identity of Jesus' disciples and the identity of the reader. By highlighting "the Way" as superior to the major religious powers in Ephesus, the "disciples" are depicted as the true people of God. The discord with the Jews recalls the foreshadowed opposition through Simeon (2:34), only now it has extended to the nations. Ephesus thus serves as a showcase in which Jesus, through "the Way," is depicted as received and rejected as a light for revelation to the nations and for the glory for Israel. In fact, the protest scenes in Acts have emotive value: "The scenes of protest in the narrative heighten dramatic tension and also highlight issues of conflict between the new way and its environment."[127]

At the end of the passage, the reader understands that people from both groups remain in darkness and in the shadow of death, because they have refused the light that would have brought them into the way of peace. The reader observes occasions and reasons explaining why the people of the way of the Lord are not universally accepted. The reader admires Paul's role as the chief envoy and defender of "the Way," which prepares him for the final five occurrences of the thoroughfare motif illustrating Paul's role as defender of "the Way" in various situations in Jerusalem and Caesarea, the last geographical sequence of Luke-Acts. The discussion now turns to these.

Paul's Defense of "the Way" in Jerusalem and Caesarea (22:4; 24:14, 22; 25:3; 26:13)

Through the narration, the reader travels from Ephesus to Jerusalem through a series of visits in Macedonia, Greece, and again through Asia Minor, then

---

colleagues (e.g., Gaius and Aristarchus, v. 29).

126. For the thesis that Ephesus is the climax of Luke's portrayal of universal mission in Acts, in which Jews and Gentiles both receive the gospel, see Pereira, *Ephesus*.

127. Tannehill, *Narrative*, 242.

Palestine (20:1–21:14). Narrative tension rises as Paul's death appears to be imminent (20:22–23, 36–38; 21:10–14), because he finds himself immersed in immediate conflict with the Jewish community. Opposition to Paul is so intense that, ironically, he finds refuge in the hands of the Romans, fulfilling Agabus's prophecy (21:11). In fact, all of the last five occurrences of *hodos* concern Paul's defense before the Jews while in Roman custody. For this reason, they will be treated together in this section. Three are figurative uses of the unmodified *hodos* (22:4; 24:14, 22). The other two uses have literal meanings, one in a planned ambush to kill Paul (25:3) and the other in an analepsis of Paul's encounter with Jesus (26:13).

Jewish Rejection in Jerusalem: Paul's confession, "I persecuted this Way" (22:4)

The thoroughfare motif appears again in the context of Paul's defense before the mob in Jerusalem at the temple (21:27—22:29). Narrative tension grows steadily as Paul moves toward Jerusalem and continues to increase in the first days of his visit. The church wanted to protect Paul by having him perform certain rituals to show his attachment to Jewish customs. The opposite occurs, since some Jews from Asia stirred up the inhabitants of Jerusalem against him with the intention to kill him without trial (21:31a). Despite torture, Paul finds strength to address the violent mob protected by Roman soldiers. His story has now come full circle; some time before he was doing the same thing against those of "the Way" in Jerusalem. There are leaders in Jerusalem who can still testify to this (22:5). In fact, Paul constructs his defense on the solidarity with his listeners as a former persecutor (22:1).[128] Paul identifies with the Jewish people, but more importantly with those called "the Way" by confessing that he had previously persecuted them. There is a sort of play on identification with Paul's listeners to gain their hearing, and, at the same time, also with those of "the Way."[129] Thus, this occurrence appears in an analepsis about his encounter with Jesus. Since this passage reviews the events recounted in Acts 9, only the most relevant elements of his defense is presented for this discussion (22:4–5):

---

128. Pesch, *Apg.*, 2:233.
129. Kurz (*Reading Luke-Acts*, 129) acutely observes the role of the ideological point of view in Paul's defense. For "the atmosphere of Scripture and Jewish tradition," see Tannehill, *Narrative*, 278–79.

I persecuted this way to death binding and delivering both men and women to prison, as the chief priest also can bear witness and the whole council of elders, from whom I received letters and went to the brothers in Damascus in order to lead even those at that place bound to Jerusalem so that they might be punished.

⁴ὃς ταύτην τὴν ὁδὸν ἐδίωξα ἄχρι θανάτου δεσμεύων καὶ παραδιδοὺς εἰς φυλακὰς ἄνδρας τε καὶ γυναῖκας, ⁵ ὡς καὶ ὁ ἀρχιερεὺς μαρτυρεῖ μοι καὶ πᾶν τὸ πρεσβυτέριον, παρ' ὧν καὶ ἐπιστολὰς δεξάμενος πρὸς τοὺς ἀδελφοὺς εἰς Δαμασκὸν ἐπορευόμην, ἄξων καὶ τοὺς ἐκεῖσε ὄντας δεδεμένους εἰς Ἰερουσαλὴμ ἵνα τιμωρηθῶσιν.

It is noteworthy that this is the first of two occurrences of *hodos* expressed through Paul's voice. It functions simultaneously as a public confession of guilt as a former persecutor and as a confession of association with "the Way" as a witness (22:15, 18) and apostle of Jesus (22:21). The use of the demonstrative "this" (οὗτος) in "this way" (ταύτην τὴν ὁδόν) serves to refer to what has been mentioned in the mob's accusations (a gap for the reader), namely Paul's teaching and association with Jesus' disciples (21:28; cf. also 21:21).[130] The verb "persecute" clarifies the meaning of "this way"; the object of his persecution is the people ("both men and women") because of their association with the teaching of and about Jesus.[131] Thus, "this Way" is also a metonymy for "those who adhered to the way of the Lord" (cf. 9:2). Moreover, in this context, "this Way" refers to Jesus' persecuted disciples in Jerusalem, not those of Damascus, since he had not begun persecuting those in Damascus.[132] Paul mentions the spiritual unity between Jesus and his persecuted disciples in verses 7-8, which again illustrates the theme of persecution in Luke-Acts.[133]

---

130. Most English translations render the demonstrative and capitalize *way* for emphasis: "this Way" (cf. various languages: "cette Voie" (Bible de Jérusalem 1973), "questa Via" (La Sacra Bibbia Nuova Riveduta 1994); "die neue Lehre" (Lutherbibel 1984). Likewise, in commentaries: so Barrett, *Acts*, 2:1029; and Fitzmyer, *Acts*, 702. And "diesen Weg," Roloff, *Apg.*, 318; Jervell, *Apg.*, 540; Pesch, *Apg.*, 2:228; Weiser, *Apg. 13-28*, 604; and "cette voie," Boismard and Lamouille, *Les actes*, 152; "cette Voie," Delebecque, *Les actes*, 106. But also "den (neuen) Weg," Schneider, *Apg.*, 2:316.

131. The phrase τοὺς ἐκεῖσε ὄντας (22:5) could be an ellipsis of τοὺς ἐκεῖσε ὄντας τῆς ὁδοῦ and parallel to τινας εὕρῃ τῆς ὁδοῦ ὄντας in 9:2.

132. The object of his journey is expressed through a future participial clause ἄξων καὶ τοὺς ἐκεῖσε ὄντας δεδεμένους εἰς Ἰερουσαλὴμ (22:5) and followed by a ἵνα clause ἵνα τιμωρηθῶσιν (not mentioned in 9:2; cf. 26:11 ἠνάγκαζον βλασφημεῖν).

133. Cf. the objects of the verb διώκω: the prophets (Luke 11:49); Jesus' disciples via his prolepsis (Luke 21:12); the prophets (Acts 7:52); Jesus in unity with his disciples (Acts

In this way, here the figurative use of *hodos* helps provide continuity in the story of Paul's relationship with Jesus and his disciples. Tannehill rightly explains its strategic placement: "The triple narration of this event is an indication of its key importance for understanding Paul's mission. The placement of the three accounts supports this observation. The first appears at the beginning of Paul's mission as its foundation, the second and third in the two major defense speeches at the beginning and end of the defense sequence in Acts 22–26, all prominent positions."[134]

Thus, for the reader, Paul's narration greatly enhances this reliving of events on Damascus road. Paul is not ashamed to acknowledge this in such a hostile Jewish context. In fact, the paradoxical confession of persecution of and identification with "the Way" places Paul in greater danger. The irony is evident: Saul the persecutor of "the Way" in Jerusalem is now Paul "the persecuted" in Jerusalem.[135] He risks the same treatment that he gave to Stephen.[136] Thus, his present identity is marked by his unity with Jesus and the other disciples. His speech underlines this as it begins with the identification with his own people (22:1–3) and ends, abruptly, with the blasphemous statement—for the Jewish mob's sensibilities—about a mandate from the risen Jesus to go to the nations (22:21). The reader relives this event through Paul, who functions as the narrator's link between Jesus, the Jews and the nations. His former persecution of "the Way" and his being persecuted for them prepares the reader for the next two occurrences of *hodos* in Paul's defense before Felix.

Gentile and Jewish Rejection in Caesarea: Paul, Felix and "the Way" (24:14, 22)

On the action level, time passes quickly from the mobbing in Jerusalem to Paul's appearance before the council (22:30—23:10), and then to his removal to Caesarea due to the plot to kill him (23:12). Jesus reassures Paul that he will be safe and be brought to Rome as his witness (23:11). No consensus is found about charges against Paul (23:7–9). The letter from Claudius Lysias

---

9:4–5; 22:7–8; 26:14–15); and the disciples (26:11).

134. Tannehill, *Narrative*, 2:275.

135. Talbert (*Reading Acts*, 191) finds a chiastic pattern in Luke's rendition of Paul's speech in which element B "Paul persecuted the Way" (vv. 4–5a) is parallel to B' "Paul speaks of his days as a persecutor (vv. 19–20)."

136. This last stage includes also suffering for the name of Jesus, which evokes Jesus' words (Acts 9:16).

to the governor Felix also contains no charges (23:29); hence, the story goes forward confirming his innocence. Paul's recurring defense is based on the resurrection motif (22:6–8, 15; 23:6). In his defense before Felix and his Jewish accusers (24:1), who call him "the ringleader of the sect of the Nazarenes" (24:5b), Paul does not use the strategy of telling his past as a zealous Pharisee, because the context now is different. Rather than a confession of past deeds and his encounter with the resurrected Jesus, Paul makes a confession of faith emphasizing his association with "the Way" and its conformity to Jewish Scriptures (24:14–15):

> I confess this to you that according to the way, which they call a sect, I worship our ancestors' God, believing everything according to the law and written in the prophets, having hope in God, which these men also accept, the resurrection that is going to come for the righteous and the unrighteous.

> ¹⁴ ὁμολογῶ δὲ τοῦτό σοι ὅτι κατὰ τὴν ὁδὸν ἣν λέγουσιν αἵρεσιν, οὕτως λατρεύω τῷ πατρῴῳ θεῷ πιστεύων πᾶσι τοῖς κατὰ τὸν νόμον καὶ τοῖς ἐν τοῖς προφήταις γεγραμμένοις, ¹⁵ ἐλπίδα ἔχων εἰς τὸν θεὸν ἣν καὶ αὐτοὶ οὗτοι προσδέχονται, ἀνάστασιν μέλλειν ἔσεσθαι δικαίων τε καὶ ἀδίκων.

The central point of his confession is "I worship my ancestors' God."[137] It is qualified by three complex subordinate phrases: (1) "according to the Way . . ."; (2) "believing everything . . ."; and (3) "having hope in God . . . ."

The first subordinate serves as a premise: Paul worships according to the teaching of "the Way," a metonymy for the followers of Jesus. The expression represents Paul's new religious orientation, which his accusers call a sect, "the sect of the Nazarenes" (24:5b).[138] Paul prefers the expression "the Way," because it is the teaching from God that leads to him. An implicit comparison is noticeable between the two points of view; the narrator's purpose is to vindicate Paul's position. His opponents relate Paul's faith only to the teaching of Jesus and that of the Nazarenes. Paul, on the other hand, even as a part of "the Way," can affirm the faith that was revealed to his fathers and the

---

137. Talbert (*Reading Acts*, 201–2) states, "He worships the Jewish God, albeit according to the Way (v. 14b) . . . . He is a Jew, a certain kind of Jew: one who believes in the resurrection of the dead."

138. The word αἵρεσις occurs six times in Luke-Acts, all in the second volume: 5:17 (for the Sadducees); 15:5 (Pharisees); 24:5 (Christians); 24:14 (Christians); 26:5 (Pharisees); 28:22 (Christians). BDAG (p. 28) suggests that the three occurrences for Jesus' followers incline toward the sense of "heretical sect" whereas the others have the value of "sect," "party," and "school." BA (p. 43) proposes "school" (*Schule*) or "party" (*Partei*) for the occurrences in 24:5 and 28:22, but "doctrine" (*Lehrmeinung*) for 24:14 in the occasion of Paul's defense.

Expanding Encounters: From Roads to "the Way"

faith that was revealed by and in Jesus. For Paul, they are not contradictory but complementary. Delebecque captures the irony of the scene: "... what for a moment seems the announcement of an avowal is going to crush the hope of the Jewish accusers: they are far from expecting the profession of faith that the accused is going to make on the spot."[139]

The second subordinate phrase begins with "believing," which has two objects "everything according to the law" and "the things written in the prophets." The phrase reinforces Paul's attachment to the Jewish Scriptures, the basis for his religious and cultural heritage. Paul's adherence to this tradition represents his assertion that "the Way" is as much a true form of Judaism as the others are. Yet, the ellipsis, "the Way," goes beyond this general claim by affirming that his faith in Jesus is indeed *the* way of God, as Johnson states, "The critical difference here is the messianic claim to represent a legitimate (indeed, *the* authentic) form of Judaism."[140] Therefore, far from taking distance from his Jewish roots, Paul incorporates it into his defense, showing that the Way is the true fulfillment of Jewish aspirations.[141]

The third subordinate focuses on Paul's hope for the resurrection, which he knows is shared by the Pharisees. The placement of "resurrection" under "hope" serves to stress their syntactic and semantic relationship: "having hope in God, that is, a resurrection that is going to come for the righteous and unrighteous." In short, these three subordinates elucidate what Paul means by "I worship the God of my ancestors." The object of his worship remains the God of Israel. Tannehill correctly summarizes the situation: "Paul's confession is ironic, for there should be nothing wrong, especially in the eyes of the accusers, with what Paul is confessing... The ironic tone reappears in vv. 20–21, where Paul defines his "crime" (ἀδίκημα, RSV: "wrongdoing") as his declaration before the Sanhedrin that he is on trial concerning resurrection of the dead."[142]

One phrase, however, certainly agitated Paul's audience: "according to the Way." This element connects him to Jesus of Nazareth and makes his confession implicitly Christocentric.[143] Through this successful defense, the

---

139. Delebecque, *Les actes*, 116n14.

140. Johnson, *Acts*, 413.

141. "Thus, the other important correction of the opposing allegation is prepared: Christianity is simply not a Jewish sect, but the true fulfillment of Judaism." Roloff, *Apg.*, 337. So Fusco, *Premières communautés*, 244.

142. Tannehill, *Narrative*, 2:298.

143. The connection to the Nazarene was also the tactic of Stephen's accusers (Acts 6:14).

narrator has presented Paul as the defender of the Way, who "possessed an official Jewish legitimation."[144] This confession and the preceding occurrences of *hodos* depict Paul as the representative *par excellence* of the Way, its teaching and, through metonymy, the people. As the story progresses, the narrator invites the reader to view Paul as a trustworthy source for teaching and conduct. Undoubtedly, this particular use of *hodos* emphasizes the movement's ideological and sociological composition as Haenchen describes:

> We see here why Lukas uses 'the Way' expression so fondly; this expression describes the new Jesus religion as greatness yet it does not tear it away from Judaism. It recalls most strongly Old Testament phrases like "the ways of the Lord," which presented Judaism as the true, living religion. Paul has not led this Way out of Judaism: he believes everything in the Law and the Prophets (26:22 will make this more apparent).[145]

This expression then underlines the perceived continuity from Moses, the prophets, John the Baptist, Jesus, Paul and the Way, and finally to the narrator and reader. This leads to the next occurrence of *hodos* in verse 22 where the reader discovers that even Felix knows something about the Way. In fact, the only element in Paul's defense speech that is implicitly Christocentric is the expression "the Way." It is assumed that Paul's accusers must know something about "the Way," and, surprisingly, Felix has a good understanding of this group. The scene ends, without a clear verdict, with these words (Acts 24:22–23):

> Felix, knowing accurately things concerning the Way, adjourned them (the trial) saying: "When Lysias, the tribune, comes down, I will decide your case." He ordered the centurion to guard Paul but to allow him some freedom and not to prevent any of Paul's friends from serving him.

²² ἀνεβάλετο δὲ αὐτοὺς ὁ Φῆλιξ, ἀκριβέστερον εἰδὼς τὰ περὶ τῆς ὁδοῦ εἴπας· ὅταν Λυσίας ὁ χιλίαρχος καταβῇ, διαγνώσομαι τὰ καθ' ὑμᾶς· ²³ διαταξάμενος τῷ ἑκατοντάρχῃ τηρεῖσθαι αὐτὸν ἔχειν τε ἄνεσιν καὶ μηδένα κωλύειν τῶν ἰδίων αὐτοῦ ὑπηρετεῖν αὐτῷ.

The reader learns that Felix reached his decision because of his knowledge of the Way. What he knew is not reported, but his understanding was enough to cause him to postpone the hearing due to a lack of condemning evidence. What does the narrator mean by "more accurately" (ἀκριβέστερον

144. Jervell, *Apg.*, 279n6.
145. Haenchen, *Apg.*, 586.

v. 22)? Some commentators suggest that it has an elative (superlative value "very much") while others suggest a comparative value.[146] The first reading would merely indicate Felix's accurate understanding about the movement called "the Way." The second reading requires a comparison. What does Luke want to compare? Perhaps he wants to illustrate Felix's increase in knowledge in time. Does he have a better understanding than he did before the trial? Alternatively, as Witherington suggests, Felix actually knew more than Paul's Jewish accusers did.[147] This would certainly add a touch of irony to the passage. The expression could even have the value of "more exactly (than one thought)."[148] The most natural reading is that Felix's accurate understanding of "the Way" came through Paul's explanation through his defense and perhaps through private conversations.[149] One might also infer that the source of Felix's knowledge of "the Way" was his wife Drusilla, a Jewess (24:24).[150] This would support the notion that Felix had prior knowledge of "the Way" before the proceedings.[151]

The Jewish opponents are not in an advantageous position. The result of the hearing supports this. "The Way" is not a group of troublemakers, and Paul is not guilty of any of their charges. For this reason, Felix allows some of them to assist Paul and for him to enjoy some degree of freedom. Despite his accurate knowledge of "the Way," and apparently some interest in it (inferred from his or Drusilla's request to hear 24:24b), he rejects it because of Paul's discussion about "righteousness, self-control, and the coming judgment" (24:25). Thus, Paul's defense before a Roman governor—who knew the Way—further confirms Jesus' mandate reaching the nations through Paul, which evokes Jesus' words about Paul bringing Jesus' name before kings (9:15b) and being light for the nations (13:47).[152] This episode further

---

146. Cf. these uses of ἀκριβέστερον with the notion of comparison of completeness, "more accurately," "more thoroughly" (Acts 18:26; 23:15, 20). Cf. also 26:5 with ἀκριβεστάτην (in "the strictest sect of our religion").

147. Witherington, *Acts*, 713.

148. Delebecque (*Les actes des apôtres*, 118) explains this nuance: "'exactly enough': the comparative can mean 'more exactly' (than one thought); Drusilla was able to inform her husband about the religion of the Jews."

149. CP, 469.

150. So Fitzmyer, *Acts*, 739; Schneider, *Apg.*, 2:349n71; and Jervell, *Apg.*, 572.

151. Bruce (*Acts*, 482) understands the sense here as elative "rather accurately" (cf. κάλλιον, 25:10).

152. Tannehill (*Narrative*, 2:304) also suggests this: "The narrator may well have been concerned to show that Paul used his imprisonment to bear witness to high officials, which would help to account for a scene in which Felix allows Paul to preach."

illustrates Jewish and non-Jewish rejection of "the Way." Thus, the two occurrences of the unmodified *hodos* illustrate the full circle that Paul has come, from being violent persecutor of "the Way" to being their defender.

The occurrences of the unmodified *hodos* end here. Pragmatically, Theophilus receives assurance that Paul is a trustworthy teacher through the link that connects him to "the Way" and the Law and the prophets. Like Paul and the others of "the Way," the reader can also claim adherence to the group, their teaching, and remain attached to the Jewish Scriptures. In addition, based on Felix's verdict, the reader knows that his faith is legal in Roman courts, because it is as "Jewish" as other existing groups.

The discussion now turns to the final two occurrences of thoroughfare terminology in the unraveling sequence, both in the long section concerning Paul's imprisonment under Festus (25:1—26:32).

Gentile and Jewish Rejection in Caesarea: Paul's Account before Festus, Agrippa and Bernice (25:3; 26:13)

The audience finds again *hodos* in the background information about the transition between Felix and Festus and the Jews in Jerusalem who attempt to convince Festus that Paul should be brought to Jerusalem for trial (25:1–5). Their plot is similar to the one that brought Paul from Jerusalem to Caesarea (cf. 23:12–15): their intent is assassination. This time the context for the murder would be "along the road" (or "on the way" κατὰ τὴν ὁδόν)[153] somewhere between Caesarea and Jerusalem:

> ... requesting a favor against him (Paul) that he might send him to Jerusalem, planning an ambush to kill him on the way. (Act 25:3 ESV)
>
> αἰτούμενοι χάριν κατ' αὐτοῦ ὅπως μεταπέμψηται αὐτὸν εἰς Ἰερουσαλήμ, ἐνέδραν ποιοῦντες ἀνελεῖν αὐτὸν κατὰ τὴν ὁδόν.

Festus does not allow this to happen, but invites them to bring their accusations against him in Caesarea in conformity with Roman custom (25:16). Luke expresses his evaluation clearly through an aside: "the Jews ... bringing many serious charges against him that they were not able to prove" (25:7). Thus, the thoroughfare imagery depicts here, in a literal sense, a planned action but not accomplished. Paul would have been murdered "on

---

153. Some perceive κατὰ τὴν ὁδόν as a Lukan expression (cf. Luke 10:4; Acts 8:36; 26:13). Delebecque, *Les actes*, 120 and Barrett, *Acts*, 2:1124.

the way" as an innocent Roman citizen and a follower of Jesus at the hands of his fellow Jews. Ironically, his life would have ended on a thoroughfare, the direct opposite of the result of his encounter with Jesus. Therefore, another plan by the Jews is thwarted by the will of God: Paul will go to Rome according to Jesus' words (23:11).

The story of Paul's imprisonment under Festus continues. Paul, as a Roman citizen, has appealed to go to Rome for fear of a mistrial by Festus and his Jewish accusers, but perhaps also to be transported safely to Rome under Roman protection.[154] The reader then encounters Agrippa and Bernice who are paying a visit to Festus. Festus requests Agrippa to evaluate Paul's case so that Festus might send a clear report to Rome. Hence, another hearing is organized, and Paul, once again, is permitted to bear witness of his conversion and faith before rulers. He begins with the resurrection and continues with a report of his former hostile life against "the name of Jesus of Nazareth" (26:9). Instead of referring to the disciples as "those of the Way" (9:2) or "this Way" (22:4), he calls them "saints" whom he had persecuted (26:10). Instead, the thoroughfare motif reappears in its literal form in Paul's second rendition of his transformational encounter with Jesus "on the road" (26:13):

> At midday, along the road, I saw, o King, a light from heaven, brighter than the sun, shining around me and those traveling with me.
>
> ἡμέρας μέσης κατὰ τὴν ὁδὸν εἶδον, βασιλεῦ, οὐρανόθεν ὑπὲρ τὴν λαμπρότητα τοῦ ἡλίου περιλάμψαν με φῶς καὶ τοὺς σὺν ἐμοὶ πορευομένους.

The accounts in Acts 9:1–9 and 22:1–22 do not mention the thoroughfare context; it is assumed and stated in the analepses through Ananias and Barnabas. This particular detail is now made explicit through Paul's voice.[155] Two other aspects receive greater emphasis in this analepsis: the light around Paul and the commission from Jesus. In this account, this light is so powerful that all fall on the ground (26:14a), whereas only Paul is said to fall in 9:4

---

154. This was in Jesus' plans for him (he "must (δεῖ) also bear witness in Rome" 23:11). Tannehill (*Narrative*, 2:308) suggests also the latter factor in this decision: "Release from his arrest is not Paul's only goal. Bearing witness in Rome and to Caesar (27:24) is itself a controlling purpose. Paul acts to make this possible whether it improves his chances of acquittal or not."

155. In this way, it contributes in a final way to the several explicit thoroughfare reception scenes in the raveling sequence (would be disciples, the blind beggar, Zacchaeus, the crowd of disciples), the pivot (the Emmaus disciples), and the unraveling sequence (the Ethiopian eunuch).

and 22:7. Similarly, Fitzmyer compares the references in 9:3 and 22:6: "The description of the 'light from heaven' grows with each mention of it."[156]

Still, another noteworthy element is that the reader encounters again another junction of the illumination theme and the thoroughfare motif. Together they evoke the transformational image in Luke 1:78–79, which confirms Tannehill's forceful synopsis: "The whole of the Messiah's saving work can be represented as proclaiming light, a light that reaches both Jews and Gentiles."[157] Paul in effect is transformed in order to carry further Jesus' mandate as "the dawn from on high" leading people from the shadow of death to the way of peace, which is the basis of Jesus' commissioning of Paul—the missing (and suspense creating) element in the other two accounts of Paul's conversion.[158]

The occurrence of *hodos* in 26:13 marks the final occurrence of thoroughfare imagery in the unraveling sequence and the last occurrence in Luke-Acts. Consequently, the next section provides a summary of relevant occurrences of the motif in the unraveling sequence.

Summary of the Thoroughfare Motif in the Unraveling Sequence

The thoroughfare motif enhances the unraveling sequence for the reader by illustrating transformations that take place through Jesus' transforming actions, especially in relation to Paul. First, however, the motif appears in the spotlight on Peter's successful ministry in Jerusalem. Immediately after the third transforming action of the pivot sequence, the reader receives instruction through Peter's appropriation of Psalm 15 to buttress his argument regarding Jesus' resurrection in relation to the sending of the Holy Spirit. The expression "the ways to life" (Acts 2:28; LXX 15:11), overtaken from a credible source, adds to the cumulative force of the thoroughfare motif as an image of spiritual transformation, that is, from death to life. Next, the literal use of *plateia* (wide street) in Acts 5:15 helps depict the dramatic effects of Peter's ministry on the inhabitants and outsiders of Jerusalem who desperately seek healing. By bringing transformation into the streets of Jerusalem, Peter perpetuates and extends Jesus' mandate into public spaces (cf. Luke 10:10; 13:26; 14:21).

---

156. Fitzmyer, *Acts*, 758.

157. Tannehill, *Narrative*, 2:324.

158. For the rhetorical effects of this disclosure of Paul's mandate, see Hedrick, "Paul's Conversion/Call," 427.

Expanding Encounters: From Roads to "the Way"

Second, the narrator highlights for the reader another cluster of thoroughfare reception scenes, one from the nations (the Ethiopian eunuch) and the other from the Jews (Saul of Tarsus). Both episodes provide continuity in the plot as tangible examples of people transformed through Jesus' illumination as the dawn who leads them into "the way of peace." They signal an important shift in the narrator's focus on movement toward the nations. Saul's encounter is the most significant thoroughfare reception scene in Luke-Acts, related again by Ananias, Barnabas, and twice by Paul. Through this encounter with the hero, Saul also meets "those of the Way," an ellipsis for "those of the way of God/the Lord," which emphasizes their spiritual attachment to the teaching of and about Jesus (cf. Luke 20:21). This enhances the clash with Saul the Pharisee and subsequent conflicts with groups and individuals from a different religious orientation.

Third, various expressions with *hodos* illustrate how Paul and his missionary entourage extend Jesus' mandate by bringing light to the Jews and the nations as teachers of the way of God/the Lord in various localities (Paphos, Lystra, Philippi, Ephesus). Jewish and Gentile characters and groups are posited according to their reception or rejection of their teaching: "the straight paths of the Lord" (13:10); "the way of salvation" (16:17); "the way of the Lord/God" (18:25, 26). Paul's teaching is contrasted with the ways of the nations, which do not lead to the living God, Israel's God (14:16). It may be inferred that he teaches "the way of God/the Lord."

Fourth, the narrator then uses five occurrences of *hodos* in a metonymic expression for the group of followers, "the Way" (Acts 19:9, 23; 22:4; 24:14, 22), based on the ellipsis of the metaphor "the way of God/the Lord" in Acts 9:2.[159] It makes a stronger affirmation of the disciples' association with Jesus and his teaching, thus illustrating their role as a collective protagonist. Paul is thus portrayed as the defender of "the Way" in scenes of opposition in Ephesus, Jerusalem and Caesarea, which culminates in his public confession of the faith of "the Way," which the Jews call a sect (*hairesis* αἵρεσις 24:14). Thus, this confirms Paul as a reliable source of certainty for the reader as the plot unravels.

The thoroughfare motif enhances the unraveling sequence by contributing to the decrease in narrative tension as the reader's certainty and a sense of closure grows through his identification with the characterization of Jesus' followers as, "those of the Way," and teachers of the way of God/the Lord,

---

159. In comparison, Völkel finds the same meanings but locates them differently: "Christian teaching" (19:23; 22:4; 24:22) and "Christians as a group" (9:2; 24:14). He does not indicate a meaning for ὁδός in 19:9. Völkel, "ὁδός," 1203.

and later emphatically, "the Way." The reader receives greater confidence by observing the superiority of "the Way"—through implicit and explicit comparison—over other religious groups. This expression of continuity between the beliefs of Israel and the teaching of Jesus is supported by intertextual expressions involving thoroughfare imagery. Thus, the existence of this group of disciples, from the Jews and the nations, who have figuratively entered "the way of peace" through Jesus' light, adds to the cumulative force of the thoroughfare motif, as the two strands of the motif—for Jesus and his collaborators—have been successfully developed and brought to closure.

7

Final Encounter: "The Way" in Rome via Paul

(Acts 28:16–31)

THE FINAL ORIENTATION DESCRIBES in cursory form Paul's sojourn in Rome. The reader had learned, through the voice of Agrippa, that Paul could have been released if he had not appealed to Caesar (26:32). Yet, this was not Jesus' plan for his apostle to the nations. That which could have happened—murder and release from prison—does not happen, because Paul must go to Rome to bear witness before Caesar. Now he has arrived in the heart of the Roman Empire and he continues to bear witness to Jesus' revelation as savior. As indicated in the statistics in Chapter 1, no occurrences of thoroughfare imagery appear in this brief section. In fact, they cease completely during the travel description from Caesarea to Rome, quite understandably since Paul and companions are mostly traveling by sea (27:1—28:16). Despite this fact, some important links with the thoroughfare motif reappear in the final orientation sequence, which merit a brief discussion.

Paul and "the Way" before the Jewish Leaders in Rome

Again the encounter of two points of view appear in this final scene, Paul meets the leading Jews in Rome. Here the reader observes Paul who represents Jesus and his disciples, "the Way." The Jews, however, perceive him to be one of the "sect" (*hairesis* αἵρεσις 28:22), that is opposed everywhere (28:21). This recalls Simeon's prolepsis about Jesus, who was "a sign that is opposed" (Luke 2:34). Paul has already been called the ringleader of the

Nazarenes (24:5). On the other hand, no negative report about Paul has reached the Jewish leaders. They have heard about the opposition to the sect but nothing directly against Paul. Once more, Paul's innocence is confirmed for the reader. This situation allows Paul to expound the way of the Lord, teaching the kingdom of God and of Jesus in conformity with the Jewish Scriptures (ἀπό τε τοῦ νόμου Μωϋσέως καὶ τῶν προφητῶν (28:23). Similar scenes of exploring Scriptures have been highlighted (e.g., Jesus and the Emmaus disciples; Philip and the Ethiopian eunuch; Paul and the Bereans). In addition, the pattern of reception and rejection is confirmed, "and some were persuaded by what he said while others did not believe" (28:24). Paul's rebuke follows by way of the prophet Isaiah (28:25–27). Here the familiar blindness theme reappears with *seeing* and *not seeing* (28:27). The "salvation of God" has been realized; the Jewish people and the nations are called to receive it (28:28). Jesus has become the cause "for the fall and rise of many in Israel" (Luke 2:34). Figuratively speaking, the "dawn from on high" has come to Rome through Paul, but not all have seen and received it. The consequences are plain: some leave the darkness and enter the way of peace through Jesus' light, while others remain in the shadow of death (28:25–28). The point then is that the people of God, "the Way," include disciples from the Jewish people and any other nation.

Summary of the Thoroughfare Motif in the Final Orientation

Although the narrator does not use specific occurrences of thoroughfare imagery in the final orientation, other narrative links closely related to the thoroughfare motif are present allowing for some plausible deductions. "The Way," known as an opposed sect by the Jews, arrives in Rome through the apostle Paul. He brings their teaching about the kingdom of God and Jesus. Thus, the light of Jesus has come to Rome, the plot's final destination, to the Jews and to the nations. Some receive it and enter into the way of peace; others reject it and remain in darkness because they are spiritually blind (28:26–27). As various narrative strands come together in this last highlighted episode, Theophilus is prepared to leave the storyworld more confidently than when he entered it, because his identity as one of "the Way" is confirmed through the testimonies of Paul, Isaiah and the Holy Spirit (28:25).

PART THREE

The Thoroughfare Motif's Narrative and Theological Value for Luke-Acts

8

The Thoroughfare Motif's Narrative Performance

THIS CHAPTER SUMMARIZES THE narrative performance of the thoroughfare motif within the plot's development. I present the primary conclusions first and then additional observations pertinent to the literary study of Luke-Acts.

Preliminary Remarks

Before proceeding to the evaluation, I restate the main questions we have explored. What narrative value does the thoroughfare motif add to Luke-Acts? How does it contribute to a pragmatic and theological reading of this long narrative? I have sought answers by observing how and where thoroughfare expressions (especially *hodos*) appear and form a motif as a part of the plot, the reader's encounter of the story. Does it enhance the plot of Luke-Acts? If so, what is the progressive and cumulative effect of the thoroughfare motif on the work and the reader? A narrative approach has been used to describe the unifying plot in Luke-Acts in order to explore the progressive development of the thoroughfare motif within the plot's main sequences. I present the primary literary results in three parts: the motif's performance as a part of the plot's five major sequences, the motif according to Freedman's five criteria for an effective motif, then a synthesis of these results. This chapter, in turn, underlies the description of the theological contribution of the thoroughfare motif presented in Chapter 9.

Thoroughfare Motif within the Plot's Sequences

This first evaluation brings together results using the narrative sequence model as a literary framework. This model was supplemented with additional narrative theory in order to illustrate the implied reader's progressive and passionate encounter with the forces for and against the spiritual transformations foreshadowed so early in the narrative.

Initial Orientation Sequence (Luke 1:5–3:38). The thoroughfare motif helps orient the reader in the storyworld through the characterization of Jesus (the hero) and John the Baptist (his forerunner). These represent the two strands of the motif that develop in various sequences of the plot. The first strand begins with John the Baptist and continues with Jesus' disciples. The second strand contributes to the characterization of Jesus. The order reflects the *forerunner-hero* relationship that runs through the work.

Through Zechariah's voice (Luke 1:76–79), the reader encounters the two interconnected strands of the thoroughfare motif that shape the proleptic portraits of Jesus and John (what they will be and do). Both strands appear as a response to the initial state: the Jewish people are in spiritual darkness and must return to their God to receive forgiveness of their sins. The narrator foreshadows for the reader a better spiritual state, "the way of peace," for those who would allow themselves to be led out of "the shadow of death" through Jesus, "the dawn from on high" (Luke 1:78–79). This collective proleptic image helps the reader to anticipate the responses to Jesus and the transformations that are highlighted throughout the narrative. It prefigures the convergence of the thoroughfare motif and the illumination theme in various moments in the story. Given the emphasis of spiritual transformation in the following sequences, this is the clearest image in the initial orientation in which the hero, his mandate, and its beneficiaries are depicted. It contributes to other proleptic images about Jesus' identity and mandate toward which the story moves to bring closure for the reader. This study has attempted to give more attention to its proleptic and programmatic value than in previous research.

The first strand continues to develop in the initial orientation by showing that John the Baptist is already accomplishing his mandate of spiritual preparation. To describe this, the narrator recontextualizes Isaiah's words in Isa 40:3–5 (LXX) by applying it to John as the forerunner of Jesus, who goes before him and invites the people to prepare "the way for the Lord" (Luke 3:4–5). Consequently, John prepares for the Lord "his ways" (Luke 1:76) by preparing the people to receive him. For the second strand, however, the reader must wait for the beginning of the hero's mandate in the raveling sequence.

Therefore, regarding the initial orientation, the two strands of the thoroughfare motif appear early in the narrative and contribute to the reader's growing awareness that the plot will be centered on Jesus and not on John the Baptist. They stimulate the reader's curiosity raising questions and expectations requiring further enlightenment and fulfillment. The stage is set for the reader's experience, having a privileged position to view the unfolding drama. This demonstrates the *complicity* between the narrator and the reader, as the latter becomes aware of events or explanations about which many of the actors in the story are not yet aware. To satisfy the reader, the two strands develop in the following sequences. For the above reasons, the very early appearance of the thoroughfare motif concerning the hero is strong evidence that this is a plot-intensive motif.

Raveling Sequence (Luke 4:1—23:56). The two interrelated strands of the motif continue to help guide the reader to experience the increasing narrative tension in the raveling sequence. The hero has begun to implement his mandate, which is now overtly opposed by spiritual and human forces (Luke 4:1–13, 33–36, 41; 5:21–23, 30; 6:1–11). His mandate risks being sabotaged. The motif, however, continues to be very positive, as it revolves around the hero fulfilling his mandate despite this intense opposition.

The first strand of the motif reappears when the narrator brings positive closure to John the Baptist's role as the hero's forerunner. This comes through Jesus' voice in a quotation of Mal 3:1 in Luke 7:27. This intertextual element reinforces for the reader the forerunner-hero relationship, already described in similar terms by Gabriel (1:17), Zechariah (1:76), and the narrator through Isaiah (3:4–5). Then, a new element appears in the first strand: Jesus' disciples become protagonists in the hero's mandate thus extending John the Baptist's ministry into the public spaces of the Jewish people. Literal uses of thoroughfare terms describe the transition between John the Baptist and Jesus' disciples, as Jesus sends them *on the road* to preach in Jewish towns where he is going to pass through (9:3; 10:4) and to announce divine judgment in their streets in case of rejection (10:10). Both actions parallel John's role as the hero's forerunner, thus providing unity in the development of this first strand.

The development of the second strand illustrates the fulfillment of Jesus' mandate. However, despite the importance of traveling in this sequence, thoroughfare terms seldom occur to describe physical movement of the hero on the action level. Rather, they appear in illustrations, highlighted reception scenes, and an ironic confirmation of Jesus' identity in Jerusalem. First, thoroughfare imagery occurs in illustrations that have proleptic value. Jesus assumes the role of the "head of the house" as the rejected teacher in their streets in the Parable of the Narrow Door (13:26). He refuses to let people enter based on their claim that they heard him teaching in their streets. Likewise, in the Parable of the Great Supper, the head of the house sends his servant to invite the outcasts scattered on thoroughfares inside and outside the city (Luke 14:21, 23). Both depict Jesus' mandate for the benefit of the Jewish people, the growing tension between them, and the external prolepsis of judgment. The cluster of thoroughfare terms in the latter parable contributes to the reader's progressive awareness that Jesus' mandate will be extended to include the nations.

Second, Theophilus encounters tangible examples of the hero's reception in thoroughfare settings in the climactic movement from Jericho to Jerusalem. Three thoroughfare receptions feature a blind beggar outside Jericho, Zacchaeus in Jericho, and the crowd of disciples just outside Jerusalem. These scenes evoke the images of the servant going to the outcasts and the dawn coming to those in darkness. They contrast with the thoroughfare rejection with the three would-be disciples (Luke 9:57–62). Furthermore, they are a part of a literary pattern that includes three other thoroughfare reception scenes: the Emmaus disciples, the Ethiopian eunuch, and Saul of Tarsus. These scenes feature the hero, since Jesus is physically present in five of six encounters, except the encounter between Philip and the Ethiopian. In the latter, however, Jesus is still the center of attention since he is *present* in the interpretation of the passage in Isaiah. Moreover, these scenes appear in key moments of the plot: the climactic movement to Jerusalem, the dramatic pivot, and the shift of focus on the evangelization of the nations. Despite much travel, rather than illustrating Jesus physically moving along roads, the spotlight is on Jesus in thoroughfares as settings for transformational encounters.

In addition, the thoroughfare motif helps to portray Jesus as the teacher of Israel by confirming the spies' insincere, but true statement that Jesus teaches "the way of God" (Luke 20:21). Thus, the early image of Jesus being "the dawn from on high"—a guide from divine origin—is also confirmed with great irony. The people see this, but the leaders do not see it, because they are spiritually blind and consequently have not entered the way of peace (cf. Luke 19:42).

Thus, the two strands of the thoroughfare motif are positive and central in the raveling sequence by contributing to the portraiture of the hero and protagonists: Jesus, John the Baptist, and Jesus' disciples. This reinforces Theophilus's certainty as a follower of Jesus. He gradually receives answers to his questions about Jesus' mandate as well as confirmation for his expectations. This leads to a heightened experience of Jesus' tragic death at the hands of the Jewish people and the nations in Jerusalem.

Pivot Sequence (Luke 24:1–Acts 2:13). The pivot sequence depicts for the reader the fulfillment of Jesus' mandate by featuring the resurrected Jesus in another thoroughfare reception scene. On the road from Jerusalem to Emmaus, the hero encounters two disciples who are to some extent spiritually blind. The thoroughfare motif thus reappears in another crucial moment of the plot: the turning point from defeat and desperation to victory and joy. The two strands of the motif converge as a tangible illustration of the proleptic image of Jesus as the dawn leading people into the way of peace. The hero is back on the road for the spiritual transformation of his two disillusioned disciples. Through this enlightenment, these disciples understand that he is more than a prophet; he is the Christ. Thus, narrative tension begins to decrease for the reader as he witnesses the interaction between Jesus and his disciples. Through his identification with the Emmaus disciples, he observes with pleasure the transformation that takes place in them for their greater involvement in Jesus' mandate. In addition, due to its placement and its link with the other thoroughfare reception scenes (three preceding it and two following it in the second volume), this reception scene contributes greatly to the plot's unity and cumulative effect on the reader.

Unraveling Sequence (Acts 2:14—28:15). Narrative tension continues to decrease in the unraveling sequence, as the reader views the gradual fulfilling of the hero's mandate and the disciples' participation in it. The thoroughfare motif enhances the reader's experience by characterizing Jesus' disciples through their attachment to him and his teaching. As they begin to extend his mandate among the Jewish people and the nations. Thus, it contributes principally to the development of the motif's first strand regarding spiritual transformation in and through them. Moreover, despite the mention of much journeying in the raveling sequence, thoroughfare terms seldom describe physical movement on the action level. This parallels the sparse usage of thoroughfares in other sequences to describe physical movement on the level of action. The figurative uses of *hodos* become increasingly more important in this part of the narrative, especially in the characterization of Paul and his missionary team.

First, however, the reader follows the spotlight on Peter's successful ministry in Jerusalem. Immediately after the account of the third transforming action (the sending of the Holy Spirit), the reader receives instruction through Peter's appropriation of Psalm 15 to support his argument about Jesus' resurrection and its relation with the manifestation of the Holy Spirit on the day of Pentecost. The intertextual expression, "the ways to life" (Acts 2:28; LXX 15:11), adds to the motif's cumulative force in the plot's emphasis on spiritual transformation, that is, moving from the realm of death to life. Next, the literal use of *plateia* (wide street) in Acts 5:15 helps depict the extraordinary expectations of the inhabitants of Jerusalem—as well as outsiders—in response to Peter's extension of Jesus' mandate in public spaces.

Second, the motif reappears in the shift of focus on the hero's effects on the nations by highlighting a cluster of two thoroughfare reception scenes, one from the nations (the Ethiopian eunuch) and the other from the Jews (Saul of Tarsus). Both episodes are tangible examples of Jesus leading individuals into the way of peace and illustrate Luke's constant interest in the Jewish people and the nations. Saul's encounter is the most significant thoroughfare reception scene in Luke-Acts, evoked later by Ananias, Barnabas, and twice by Paul. This repetition strengthens the motif's cumulative effect on the reader. Through this encounter with the hero, Saul is depicted as meeting "those of the Way." This is the first occurrence of the unmodified *hodos*, an ellipsis for "those of the way of God/the Lord." It emphatically expresses their attachment to the teaching of and about Jesus (cf. Luke 20:21). This peculiar, emphatic characterization of the group enhances the clash between Jesus and Saul the Pharisee as well as subsequent conflicts with groups and individuals among the Jews and the nations. In this respect, Theophilus reflects on the disciples' unique identity and, consequently, his identity as well.

Then the reader comes across various expressions with *hodos* in relation to Paul that illustrate the extension of Jesus' mandate. Paul and his missionary entourage bring Jesus' light to the Jews and the nations as teachers/preachers in various localities (Paphos, Lystra, Philippi, and Ephesus). Parallel to the pattern of reception and rejection, Jewish and Gentile individuals and groups are posited according to their response to the apostles' teaching: "the straight paths of the Lord" (13:10), "the way of salvation" (16:17), and "the way of the Lord/God" (18:25, 26). Paul and Barnabas's teaching in Lystra—inferred as the way of God'—is contrasted with "the ways of the nations," which do not lead to the living God (14:16). This adds to the reader's awareness that the disciples are bringing Jesus' light to groups among the Jewish people and the nations.

Additionally, five occurrences of the unmodified *hodos* appear as a metonymic expression, "the Way" (19:9, 23; 22:4; 24:14, 22). It is based on the ellipsis of the metaphor "the way of God/the Lord." It makes a stronger and more direct affirmation of the disciples' association with Jesus and his teaching and their role as a collective protagonist. Paul is portrayed as the defender of "the Way" in scenes of opposition in Ephesus, Jerusalem and Caesarea, which culminates in his public confession of the beliefs of "the Way," which the Jews call a sect (αἵρεσις 24:14). The reader has observed the full circle that Paul has made in his life: from a persecutor "of those belonging to the Way" in Jerusalem to a persecuted defender of "the Way." Consequently, Paul in particular becomes a source of certainty for Theophilus as the plot unravels.

Thus, the thoroughfare motif enhances the unraveling sequence by decreasing the narrative tension as the reader's certainty and a sense of closure grow. This occurs through his identification with the characterization of Jesus' followers as, "those of the Way," as teachers of the way of God/the Lord, and then more emphatically as "the Way." The two strands of the motif have developed successfully and have achieved closure in this sequence through the confirmation of the existence of this group of disciples, from the Jewish people and the nations, who have entered "the way of peace" through Jesus' light. Their spiritual unity with Jesus is confirmed for Theophilus. Therefore, this demonstrates the cumulative, pragmatic force of the thoroughfare motif.

Final Orientation Sequence (Acts 28:16–31). Although specific occurrences of thoroughfare do not occur in this final sequence, other narrative links closely related to the motif are present and confirm its cumulative value for the work and the reader. The reader observes with pleasure how "the Way," known as an opposed sect by the Jews (28:22), arrives in Rome through the apostle Paul. He brings their teaching about the kingdom of God and Jesus (28:23, 31). Thus, the light of Jesus has come to the Jews and to the nations even in Rome, the long-awaited final destination. By inference, some receive Paul's teaching and enter the way of peace; others reject it and remain in darkness because they are spiritually blind (28:26–27). This confirms the narrative-long pattern of reception and rejection. As various narrative strands come together in this last episode, the reader as one of "the Way" leaves the storyworld with greater assurance because the testimony of Paul, Isaiah, and the Holy Spirit confirm his belonging to the group (28:25).

Having considered the progressive performance of the thoroughfare motif as a part of the plot's main sequences, the next section evaluates the motif applying Freedman's theory.

Thoroughfare Motif's Efficacy via Freedman's Five Criteria

The thoroughfare motif's performative value can also be assessed using Freedman's criteria for evaluating the cumulative effect of a motif in a single literary work (cf. Chapter 1). These measures are the following: (1) frequency of recurrence, (2) avoidability, (3) significance of contexts, (4) degree of coherence, and (5) symbolic correlation. This evaluation is principally synchronic, staying within the limits of Luke-Acts. The intertextual value will be further discussed in Chapter 9.

Frequency. The effective motif achieves maximum strength just short of "the point where unlikelihood begins to shade into unsuitability or frequency into tedious repetition."[1] Again, this question depends on the length and nature of the work. As for the thoroughfare motif, it is frequent enough to be felt throughout the narrative, in all of the sequences, except in the brief *final orientation*. The forty-nine occurrences of thoroughfare expressions are spread out quite extensively, from Luke 1:76 to Acts 26:13. They occasionally appear in clusters (e.g., Luke 1:76–79; 3:4–5; 14:21, 23; Acts 8:26–36; 18:25–26). Interestingly, *hodos* occurs forty times, twenty in both volumes. Yet, I have not sought to explore an eventual numerological or symbolic value for this statistic; I understand it as coincidental, and not intentional. Other expressions account for nine occurrences: *tribos* (path); *plateia* (broad street); *rumē* (narrow street); and *phragmos* (hedgerow path).

The presence of the occurrences is neither inconspicuous nor overused. This judicious use of the motif's components, both literal and figurative uses, maintains the tension between making the motif too subtle or overused, rendering it less effective. Thus, it has the frequency of an effective motif. The only weak point is that it does not occur explicitly in the last part of the work, the *final orientation*.

Avoidability. An effective motif does not develop through occurrences based on complete coincidence or necessity. In other words, the context might require them or perhaps there is a sense of randomness or coincidence in their use. However, if the interpreter can identify a number of occurrences as avoidable, he or she provides stronger evidence that the narrator has a specific purpose for their use beyond the necessary. In Luke-Acts, few occurrences describe physical movement on the action level despite much journeying in both volumes. The narrator could have used thoroughfare imagery much more in circumstances where it would have been quite natural to find it, especially for the description of itinerant preachers. This suggests

---

1. Freedman, "Motif," 126.

that Luke does not use these terms arbitrarily. Evidence for this is that there are twenty-seven literal uses (several used in illustrations) and twenty-two figurative uses.

Some of the literal uses form a literary pattern illustrating thoroughfare reception scenes. Furthermore, the cluster of literal uses in the Parable of the Great Supper suggests purposeful design for effect. Figurative uses are abundant in Luke-Acts and are often avoidable. They are particularly important in the characterization of John the Baptist and Jesus in the initial orientation and raveling sequences. In addition, the figurative uses of *hodos* become increasingly important in the unraveling sequence to describe the teaching and identity of Jesus' disciples. Luke could have used other non-figurative expressions to describe them (e.g., "church," "saints," "disciples"). These observations suggest that there is a high degree of intentionality in the development of the thoroughfare motif. It does not develop from mere coincidence or necessity, but purposefully, as a part of Luke's *emplotment* for the reader's experience.

Significance of Contexts. An effective motif appears in significant moments of the plot. It does not describe only peripheral issues in the narrative. Rather, it appears often in relation to central characters and in significant moments of the plot's progression. It begins in the early proleptic portraits of John the Baptist and Jesus, helping to prepare the reader to experience the responses to the hero and the transformations that take place through him. It reappears in the positive closure of John the Baptist's role and transition to Jesus' disciples in the hero's mandate. Moreover, six thoroughfare reception scenes all appear in significant moments of the plot: the climactic movement from Jericho to Jerusalem, the turning point with the Emmaus disciples, and the shift of focus on Paul and the evangelization of the nations. Finally, the motif reappears consistently in the characterization of Paul and his missionary entourage as messengers of God's teaching. This signals the forward movement of the effects of the hero's mandate in various localities among the Jewish people and the nations. The culmination of Luke's emphasis on this aspect is the use of the emphatic metonymic expression, "the Way," in Paul's association with Jesus' followers (24:14).

Cohesion. This criterion concerns the degree to which the occurrences fit together. From the narrator and reader's point of view, the motif is remarkably positive. It centers almost entirely on various phases of the development of the hero's mandate. The majority of thoroughfare expressions appear as two interrelated strands: the characterization of the hero (Jesus) and protagonists (John the Baptist, Jesus' disciples, Paul and his missionary entourage).

Thoroughfare imagery rarely describes individuals or groups outside these two strands. When used in this sense, it is still in conjunction with the hero and Paul's mandate and implies an opposing point of view (e.g., Elymas, Acts 13:10; the nations, Acts 14:16). In this sense, the motif does not ramify in too many directions but forms an "associational cluster" that works together for a cumulative effect. This leads to the object of the fifth criterion.

Symbolic correlation. This step seeks to understand if the motif has a particular symbolic value and the degree to which the motif correlates with its referent. This is the key criterion links the literary to the theological (Ch. 9). Figure 8.1 illustrates the symbolic force of the motif and the correlation between thoroughfares and its primary referent, salvation, which is the fundamental narrative need that seeks closure. The motif's two strands work together toward a common purpose: to portray, concretely and figuratively, the different phases in Jesus' mandate to bring salvation to the Jewish people and the nations.

The proleptic image through Zechariah's voice in Luke 1:76–79 signals to the reader an early and complete picture of the events on the action level toward the realization of salvation. It is a picture of what happens on the action level thus revealing subtly what the incidents tell directly.[2] As the narrative progresses, this proleptic image expands in three ways: (1) content concerning Jesus' mandate (cf. 2:30–35; 3:16–17; 4:18–19); (2) extent concerning the beneficiaries including the nations (e.g., illumination theme, Luke 2:31–32; Acts 26:23); and (3) protagonists (e.g., disciples as a light, Acts 13:47; 26:17–18). The human sphere is characterized as being in a spiritual state of darkness and the shadow of death (i.e., under Satan's oppression). The object of "the dawn from on high" is to lead people into a better spiritual state, "the way of peace." The passage out of "the shadow of death" into "the way of peace" becomes the central problem or need in Luke-Acts that must be resolved by the hero. Spiritual transformation will either succeed or fail. Narrative tension revolves around the exploration of this question.

The steps toward the success of the hero's mandate require the involvement of various protagonists, which results in the passage from the divine sphere to the human sphere then back to the divine. First, the motif describes a preparation of the people by John the Baptist ("1" in fig. 8.1, "the prophet of the Most High") for the coming divine intervention. Second, the motif expresses the idea of the divine "dawn" ("2" in fig. 8.1) that brings light to those in spiritual darkness in order to lead them into "the way of peace" (a visitation from the divine sphere, Luke 1:78; 19:44).

2. Cf. Freedman, 124.

The Thoroughfare Motif's Narrative Performance

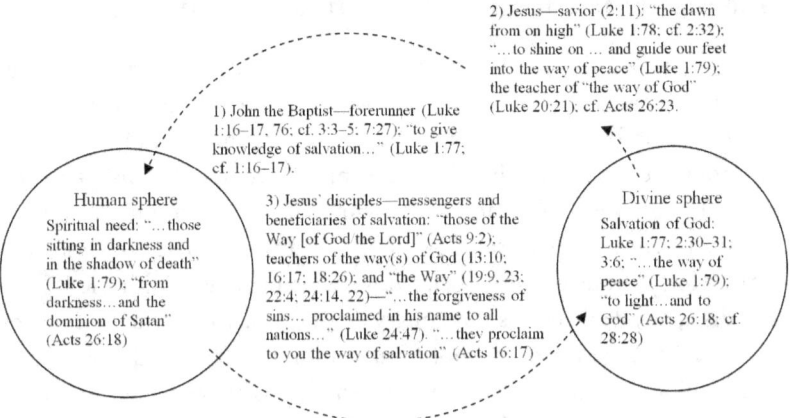

Figure 8.1 Symbolic Correlation
between the Thoroughfare Motif and Salvation

Third, various characters (such as Jesus' followers) leave the "the shadow of death" and enter "the way of peace" ("3" in fig. 8.1). The various expressions involving *hodos* in the second volume confirm this link between Jesus and his disciples, who belong to his teaching and are teachers of God's way(s). Through this association, their identity is "the Way." This unusual name contributes to the construction of the collective character of the church in Acts.[3] Like Jesus, they also bring illumination to those sitting in darkness in order to lead them into the way of peace.

Therefore, the cumulative correlation between the thoroughfare motif and its symbolic referent (salvation) is the reconnection between the human and divine spheres. The correlation is appropriate to the referent because of the intrinsic value of thoroughfares as links between two entities. Symbolic movement goes from need to provision. This correlation links the point of departure, "the shadow of death" with the destination, "the way of peace." The latter is expressed through the emphatic metonymic expression "the Way," which describes the result of Jesus' mandate, a confirmation of the individuals who have entered salvation. Luke's constant emphasis on the spiritual union between Jesus and his disciples reinforces this.

---

3. As Richard Thompson has shown in his work on the church's characterization in Acts, "... the Christian community or church functions as a central character among the cast of characters in the Acts narrative, and through a variety of ways the characterization of the church throughout that narrative emphasizes certain features that compare and contrast significantly with other depicted characters." Thompson, *Keeping*, 241.

Synthesis of the Thoroughfare Motif's Narrative Value

Having observed the motif's narrative performance and other qualities, these observations show that the thoroughfare motif is an effective, plot-intensive motif for several reasons. First, the literal and figurative meanings of thoroughfare imagery that form the motif occur judiciously—neither too subtle nor overused— and reveal cumulative, purposeful design, not arbitrary or coincidental usage. Second, it mainly characterizes Jesus (the hero) and key protagonists associated with his mandate (John the Baptist, Jesus' disciples, Paul and his missionary entourage). These strands converge often in Luke-Acts. Third, the motif acts within the center of the plot, as the reader explores questions related to the hero, Jesus as savior, and responses to him. The two interrelated strands symbolically illustrate the realization of spiritual transformation (salvation), the passage from a needy spiritual state to a fulfilled one with God. Fourth, the motif appears in key moments of the plot to accentuate the increase or decrease of narrative tension related to the hero and the main protagonists associated with him. Finally, the motif is meaningful to the sympathetic reader—inferred as one of "the Way"—giving him greater certainty about his faith and identity in Jesus (Luke 1:4). He is a part of a group who knows and teaches "the way of God/the Lord" just as Jesus did; hence, the collective identity of Jesus' disciples is strengthened. In addition, the pragmatic effects are reinforced via intertextual voices from the Jewish Scriptures, which were authoritative for Luke's audience: Luke 3:4–6 (Isa 40:3–5); Luke 7:27 (Mal 3:1); and Acts 2:28 (Ps 15:11).

Thus, the thoroughfare motif is an effective, plot-intensive motif. It accentuates the progressive and cumulative effect on the reader's interpretation and experience, performing a valid role in the dual teleological function of the plot that works progressively toward narrative closure of the work and toward its pragmatic intent on the reader by providing a coherent and meaningful narrative. Like the role of an instrument in a complex orchestral composition, the thoroughfare motif is a significant literary element in Luke-Acts, playing a part in its total transformational perspective by pervading its cognitive, emotive and aesthetic atmosphere for a heightened reading experience. Due to the performance of the thoroughfare motif, Luke-Acts provides a more vivid depiction of the revelation of Jesus as savior and the responses to him.

Additional Literary Contributions

The Plot of Luke-Acts. Although the plot of Luke-Acts (Chapter 2) was not the focus of this study, it received significant attention. Indeed, a fuller treatment of the plot in Luke-Acts was lacking, and the main research questions required the elaboration of a pragmatic narrative framework. Several studies were assessed for their value in determining the unifying plot of Luke-Acts. Parts of the plot and literary and narrative features reveal patterns and links within the plot's progression. I incorporated some of these intuitions and supplemented them by using current narrative theory. A somewhat surprising result is the identification of Jesus as the hero, not only of the Gospel of Luke, but also as the hero of Luke-Acts. Plainly stated, there would be no narrative if Jesus were removed. If Luke-Acts is indeed one story, then a central theme about someone or a group of persons unifying the plot must be present. This is a crucial step in the identification and formulation of the unifying plot. In particular, the third sequence (the pivot), which spans the two volumes, highlights the effects of three transforming actions accomplished by Jesus (resurrection, ascension, and sending of the Holy Spirit). Furthermore, Jesus remains active in the story even after his ascension. In fact, Luke continuously emphasizes the spiritual unity between Jesus and the disciples. The result is a Christocentric plot based on the implied reader's passionate exploration of questions relating to Jesus and his disciples and responses to them. Consequently, this research offers a fresh look at the plot of Luke-Acts, that is, from the reader's perspective in historical context. In addition, it provides a method for analyzing the narrative or performative value of an element within the dynamics of the reader's encounter (plot). Thus, the plot synopsis and supporting evidence are useful for examining: (1) the implied reader's progressive exploration regarding Jesus in Luke-Acts; (2) Luke's literary, historical and theological interests and emphases; and (3) the narrative value of pericopes, characters, and literary elements (e.g., motifs or themes).

Narrative Unity of Luke-Acts. The narrative unity of Luke-Acts is clearly one of the underlying assumptions of this thesis. Although this hypothesis is well documented, it still requires demonstration. Through this research, the plot and the thoroughfare motif in Luke-Acts—both centered on Jesus as hero—provide additional evidence that the two volumes were intended to be read together as a single narrative, regardless of the fact that they have been read separately in the greater part of Church history. Certainly, readers can study and benefit from Luke and Acts separately. However, in light of the evidence provided here and elsewhere, it is more profitable to study the two volumes as a literary whole. This appears to have been the author's intention for the first readers (and hearers) of the two scrolls dedicated to Theophilus. This study—along with many others—has shown the importance of Luke's use of material in the earliest stages of the narrative for the purpose of orienting his readers and listeners to anticipate what is going to be the central focus of the narrative, the revelation of Jesus as savior, responses to him, and the consequences. Furthermore, from a literary perspective, the pivot sequence (Luke 24:1—Acts 2:13), which surrounds the traditional *hinge* of Luke-Acts (Luke 24:36–53—Acts 1:11), extends the commonly established textual limits that unite the two volumes. Consequently, the spiritual union between Jesus and his disciples and the latter's transformation is at the heart of the scrolls. Finally, this literary framework confirms the position that Luke-Acts ends with closure—despite the gap concerning Paul's trial—concerning the reader's main questions and expectations raised early in the first volume.

The Origins of the Unmodified Hodos. The intent of this study was not to solve the question of the origin of the unmodified *hodos* ("the Way"). Michaelis had shown that this particular use was not found elsewhere in literature before or immediately after the redaction of Luke-Acts.[4] The literature review also confirms that no study has demonstrated conclusively its precise origins. The question remains whether Luke borrowed this particular emphatic use or if he is responsible for its existence. Luke's familiarity with the Jewish Scriptures in Greek could have been a sufficient source of inspiration for adapting certain uses of thoroughfare imagery. Related to that conclusion, this study provides evidence to support the position that this emphatic form might be the fruit of Luke's literary creativity. Besides his fondness for similar elliptical expressions in Luke-Acts (e.g., "word," "law," "spirit," and "kingdom"), Luke's interest in thoroughfare imagery and prophetic expressions from the LXX to tell this story may have been the inspiration for coining this metonymy for the group of Jesus' disciples. This explanation, however, does not preclude the probability that various thoroughfare expressions—including *hē hodos*—were being used by Christian communities. Luke chose to record many of them. Yet, he might have gone a step further in abbreviating "the way of God/the Lord" to "the Way."

François Bovon, following his critique of Eero Repo's work, suggests that a *"redaktionsgeschichtlich* analysis of the Lukan notion of the Way is

---

4. Michaelis, "ὁδός," 95.

still lacking."[5] Such a study would have two main inquiries: "Does Luke voluntarily take over an archaic expression? If not, how does one explain the scarcity of the term in the literature after Luke?"[6] Perhaps another redaction-critical work could shed some light on these questions. Yet, this narrative-critical study presents plausible evidence that should also be taken into consideration.

In conclusion, the performance of the thoroughfare motif in the plot of Luke-Acts enhances the reader's encounter with the hero's mandate of spiritual transformation through concrete and figurative thoroughfare imagery. The primary and secondary literary results illustrate Luke's literary art that support his pragmatic and theological project. Due to these qualities, Luke and Acts have made a significant difference in history: "It is not wholly inappropriate that Luke should have come to be claimed as the patron saint of artists, given the intrinsic connection between the artistic tradition and the liturgical tradition. And in the world of virtual history, we may fairly claim that both might have looked very different if Luke had not met Theophilus."[7] Accordingly, given the intrinsic link between literary, theological, and pragmatic levels, the discussion now turns to the contribution of the thoroughfare motif for appreciating Luke's theological interests and emphases.

---

5. Bovon, *Luke the Theologian*, 363.
6. Ibid.
7. Alexander, "What if Luke," 170.

9

The Thoroughfare Motif's Theological Contribution

TRACING THE THOROUGHFARE MOTIF'S performance within the plot is also constructive for a theological reading of Luke-Acts. Some preliminary discussion addresses the relevancy of this study for theological study of Luke-Acts. This thematic approach complements the previous chapter's focus on narrative progression. It exemplifies the intersection between the author's emplotment that allows the reader to explore the narrative's central questions about God's intervention and responses to him (*plot*). Consequently, a continued religious encounter or experience is made possible leading eventually to a recurring experience or revisitation of Luke-Acts (*explotment*). In this sense, Luke-Acts tells about divine intervention and human response working on the levels of action and discourse inviting ancient and modern readers to enter and explore the story.

Preliminary Remarks

This discussion brings together notions presented in previous sections "Thoroughfare Motif's Performance: What Narrative and Theological Value?" (Ch. 1) and "Plot Theory and the Analysis of Nonfiction" (Ch. 2). Throughout this work, allusions emerged concerning the motif's value for a theological reading of Luke-Acts. Here the questions change somewhat since the focus shifts from the narrative's internal dynamics to the world outside, from the implied reader's exploration (*plot*) to the author's composition (*emplotment*). What does the motif reveal about Luke's theological interests and emphases? How does it play a part in the theological program that Luke wanted to communicate to Theophilus? Moreover, do answers to these questions reveal something about his pastoral concerns for his audience? In brief, this discussion attempts to shed light on the *expressive* aspect of Luke-Acts (cf. Ch. 1).

It is true that a motif can be developed even unconsciously in the course of narration. The narrator may or may not be aware of it, since elements of the motif can be so ingrained in his or her manner of description. On the other hand, an effective motif usually betrays a certain degree of intentionality. Yet, when one speaks about an author's theological program, it is usually meant that the author has deliberately advanced one or more theological emphases. True, it is not possible to ascertain this fully when studying authors who are no longer available for discussion. Nonetheless, when scholars speak of "theological program," the text functions as a window to the author's theology, whether explicitly or implicitly expressed.[1] For example, Joel Green, who treats Lukan literature with great narrative sensitivity, perceives the mind of an individual who is profoundly interested in communicating his understanding of Jesus and his followers:

> For Luke, though, this is much more than a good story. For him, this is the way things "were" and "are," for the divine purpose and the conflict to which Luke's account bears witness was at the time of his writing still ongoing. Situated in the latter third of the first century CE, he relates the story of Jesus for more than entertainment, just as he does so for more than antiquarian interest or fidelity. His is an engaged and engaging accounting of the ministry of Jesus and Christian beginnings.[2]

Although historical knowledge about Luke' remains vague, Green's description of this personality behind the texts appears accurate in light of the present study and it informs the discussion below.

To reflect this change of focus from the motif's poetic value to its referential value, different terms are necessary. The focus shifts from the storyworld through which the implied reader progresses to the world of the real author and real reader at the time of the composition (cf. fig. X). Instead of speaking of the "unifying plot," one may speak of the author's "theological program," or "hero" and "savior," and "closure" and "fulfillment." In addition, a verse or passage (or another element) may be *proleptic* for later developments in the

---

1. For example, Cadbury (*Making*, 213–368) dedicates significant space to such *expressive* questions in Part III "The Personality of the Author" (e.g., "Theological Attitudes") and Part IV "The Purpose of the Author" (e.g., "The Object of Luke-Acts").

2. Green, *Theology*, 22.

plot, but also *programmatic* as evidence of the author's theological program underlying the work. The discussion below demonstrates that the literary and theological levels are interrelated and consequently that literary techniques can provide evidence for the author's theology.

The summary of previous research demonstrates that scholars have long noticed that Luke appears to have a particular predilection for thoroughfare vocabulary, especially *hodos*. Beyond this, these expressions give the impression that Luke has a particular function in mind in his theologically motivated project. Scholars have suggested that Luke uses these elements in the development of a salvation history for various stages in the development of God's movement to the Jewish people and to the nations.[3] They have used various terms to express this function: "theology of the Way" (*Weg-theologie*), "*hodos* conception," *Weg-konzeption*, and *Wegmotiv*. To support these overarching concepts (or "umbrella terms") scholars use particular uses of *hodos*, but also other elements such as toponymy, verbs of movement, and data outside Luke-Acts. Discussions often begin with the idea that Luke was inspired by Mark's use of the citation in Isa 40:3 concerning John the Baptist (Mark 1:3). Several scholars attribute major programmatic value to this passage, as it highlights "the way of God, a new, divine intervention in salvation history. Undoubtedly, the importance of this passage is paramount for orienting the reader, similar to Simeon's prophecy and Jesus' discourse in Nazareth.

The proposal below also explores how the thoroughfare motif sheds light on Luke's Christology, soteriology, and ecclesiology (indivisible in Luke's narrative). Yet, it underlines other aspects that are not treated sufficiently in previous research. First, this proposal seeks to discern Luke's unique portrayal of salvation by paying closer attention to its narrative development. Second, not only individual words or expressions are discussed, but also their collective function as a motif in relation to the plot. Third, for thoroughfare expressions, this proposal goes beyond the usual starting point with "the way for the Lord" in Luke 3:4–5 by beginning with Zechariah's prophecy in Luke 1:76–79. Fourth, the two strands of the motif illustrate Luke's description of key persons involved in bringing salvation to the Jews and the nations in terms other than those of expiation. Finally, this evidence provides some indication of the main *point* that Luke wanted to

---

3. Hans Conzelmann created much discussion about how a Lukan salvation history can be best explained, especially his proposal of a three-staged history. Cf. Conzelmann, *Die Mitte*, 9–11. Other proposals came through Robinson, Brown, and Navone, who, as stated, use thoroughfare expressions as evidence. Cf. also Löning, "Lukas," 213–15.

communicate to his readers. Before elaborating these points, I discuss the relevance and value of plot and motif analysis for a theological reading of Luke-Acts.

The Value of Plot and Motif Analysis for Theological Studies

This discussion works with the premise that Luke-Acts is neither a manual of theology nor a story without theology. Rather, the author presents "a theologically developing story in his Gospel and in its sequel, and not merely an editor assembling disparate pieces of material."[4] Luke-Acts is not a philosophical treatise on soteriology, Christology, or ecclesiology; rather, it is a narrative revealing and portraying salvation, its agent and beneficiaries.[5] Consequently, Luke's understanding of Jesus should be interpreted narratively—along with other appropriate methods—as a part of the overall assessment.[6] This marks the clear juncture between literary and theological analysis, which Bock relates to the research of Christology in Luke-Acts: "Perhaps in no other place in Lukan theology and study does the issue of method become so prominent in how the text is being read."[7]

We return for a moment to the question of emplotment (cf. Chapter 2). Jean-Michel Adam provides some intimation about the process of emplotment and the author's understanding of the world: "Merely describing and narrating actions without emplotment [*mise en intrigue*], to refuse the story, is to take a poetic position which is the expression of a worldview."[8] Adam's observation is intriguing, because it underlines the notion that when

---

4. Bock, "Luke," 355.

5. Several studies attempt to demonstrate Luke's theological thought through a narrative reading. See, for example, the approaches in Gaventa, "Toward a Theology," 157; Aletti, *Il racconto*, 223; Talbert, *Reading Acts*, xxv; and Brawley, *Centering*. Tannehill expresses some reservation about seeking to formulate a Lukan theology from the two books, preferring rather a description of its rhetorical force (or "system of influence"). Tannehill, *Narrative*, 1:8. Somewhat different is Jervell's formulation: "His theology is to be found not within, but behind his narrative account, where we have his theological presuppositions." Jervell, *Theology*, 10.

6. Darrell Bock indicates a methodological error concerning Christology in the works by Evans (*Luke*) and Tuckett ("Christology," 133–64), which leads them to conclude that Lukan Christology is not consistent. Bock argues that their focus on sources distorts the reading of the document as a unit, thus they do not take sufficient consideration of the gradual development of characters. The construction of a Christology in Luke-Acts must be done in light of its narrative progression. Bock, "Luke," 354–55.

7. Ibid., 354.

8. Adam, "Décrire," 21.

writers choose *not* to identify one or more central questions and tie various elements together, they forfeit the occasion to explain to the reader *how* and *why* events occurred. They fail to express their interpretation of the story, its causes and consequences, and, implicitly or explicitly, its significance for the reader. Thus, by not identifying at least one unifying question to explore, according to Adam's argument, no narrative is produced, but only a chronicle or journal. Conversely, authors who implement the process of emplotment, assume a *poetic position* as the expression of their interpretation of the world being described.

When applied to nonfictional narrative, Adam's observations illustrate the inextricable link between the author's thought and his manner of expressing it. It is a reminder that the theoretical distinction between literary and theological analysis of a work is artificial, for theological, historical and literary aspects intertwine to form a unique tapestry.[9] Consequently, this step from literary to theological analysis attempts to avoid the caveat stated by Gaventa: "Yet the many unsuccessful efforts to separate Luke's theology from its narrative home should convince us that that enterprise is doomed. Lukan theology is intricately and irreversibly bound up with the story he tells and cannot be separated from it. An attempt to do justice to the theology of Acts must struggle to reclaim the character of Acts as a narrative."[10] Indeed, Luke relates not only what happened but also how and why the events happened from his theocentric perspective. He has in mind a receiving consciousness for which he provides instruction as well as an experience. For these reasons, Luke composed this theologically motivated, literary act through narrative (*diēgēsis* Luke 1:1).[11] This represents Luke's "rhetoric of the real" for his audience. As William Robinson expresses: "Luke's literary abilities served theological as well as aesthetic aims . . . literary aspects were meaningful for Luke as demonstrating the realization of God's plan in a continuous, ongoing *Heilsgeschichte*."[12] In this sense, plot analysis has value for understanding Luke's theology, because it seeks to trace the progressive

---

9. The distinction between these various elements is useful in research in that one comes to the text with a limited number of questions, and even necessary when treating large portions of text.

10. Gaventa, "Toward a Theology," 150.

11. Since the author—from his perspective—wrote Luke-Acts as nonfiction, it may also be deduced that the author and the reader have an intellectual investment in the narrative's content. For this reason, Tannehill (*Narrative*, 1:8) makes a valid point when he suggests that Luke-Acts should be read as "a literary system of influence" as a part of the author's "narrative rhetoric."

12. Robinson, "Theological Context," 22.

exploration of the narrative's questions, enabling the reader to move from perplexity to lucidity.[13] Again, this is the pragmatic aim of *normalization* (cf. Chapter 2).

Moving from the macro level of narrative to its constituent elements, motifs can also contribute to a theological reading of Luke-Acts. As common forms of repetition, motifs can be signs of the "meaningful" in a literary work.[14] As such, the identification of motifs can "help enormously in establishing what a work is about and where its focus lies, and that in turn can be used to eliminate some interpretations and to lend support to others."[15] The claim here is that the thoroughfare motif is a literary indicator of what is meaningful to Luke, and by inference, to his audience. Accordingly, since the symbolic function of motifs reveals to the reader "subtly what the incidents perhaps tell him bluntly," the motif points to something greater than itself.[16] It is at the service of Luke's theological and pragmatic objectives. The literary results sustain the view that the need for an explanation of salvation in Christ for the Jews and the nations is the main theological concern that motivated Luke's composition. Luke primarily seeks to recount spiritual transformation that is divinely projected and realized.

Thus, plot and motif can be used as evidence for the author's poetic position, the expression of his unique understanding of the world and the events concerning Jesus and his disciples. In this sense, Luke-Acts rightly merits Adam's criteria for narrative (*récit*). It can also become a window to the author's theological thought; his understanding of a theocentric worldview out of which the story emerges.[17] It follows then that an interpreter might want to go a step further by asking the question: "What is the *point* of this narrative?" Indeed, what point does Luke want to make through this massive project? William Labov describes *point* in relation to the *evaluation* of a narrative:

> Beginnings, middles, and ends of narratives have been analyzed in many accounts of folklore or narrative. But there is one important aspect of narrative which has not been discussed—perhaps

---

13. Ricoeur, *Temps et récit*, 1:89–90
14. Abbott, *Narrative*, 241.
15. Ibid., 95.
16. Freedman, "Motif," 124.
17. "Overarching Luke-Acts is a divine story. Within that divine story, there are human stories that move toward a teleological purpose. Accordingly, divine action does not consist of external interventions into history. Rather, divine action is coexistent with history." Brawley, *Centering*, 106.

the most important element in addition to the basic narrative clause. That is what we term the *evaluation* of the narrative: the means used by the narrator to indicate the point of the narrative, its raison d'être: why it was told, and what the narrator is getting at. There are many ways to tell the same story, to make very different points, or to make no point at all. Pointless stories are met (in English) with the withering rejoinder, "So what?" Every good narrator is continually warding off this question; when his narrative is over, it should be unthinkable for a bystander to say, "So what?" Instead, the appropriate remark would be, "He did?" or similar means of registering the reportable character of the events of the narrative.[18]

It seems obvious that Luke must have had one or more points that he wanted to demonstrate to his audience. However, what is the central point among others, at least one overarching theological interest or concern that motivated Luke's writing of two long scrolls? What is the main theological *raison d'être* of this account?

Theological Implications from a Christocentric Plot and Motif

The following discussion attempts to shed light on the above question, fully aware of the necessity to respect Luke-Acts as a multifaceted narrative, its "narrative complexity," which is capable of bearing various items of interest and in tension from beginning to end.[19] Admittedly, the risk of this step is to be reductionist, exalting one theme over the others.[20] Nevertheless, the literary results suggest that Luke wishes to bring closure to several interrelated questions that can be regrouped under one principal conclusion that Luke wanted to draw for his readers.

Luke's Soteriology via the Plot and the Thoroughfare Motif

Two main literary conclusions from this study suggest implications for the theological analysis of Luke-Acts: the plot is Christocentric and the thoroughfare motif contributes to its development. This claim does not deny

---

18. Labov, *Language*, 366.
19. Gaventa, "Toward a Theology," 157.
20. This is one of Gaventa's critiques about methodologies used to construct a theology of Acts without considering its narrative nature. Ibid., 149.

the underlying and consistent activity of God and the Holy Spirit in both volumes; it is in reality a story of divine activity with its own logic on the divine plane.[21] Jean-Noël Aletti rightly observes that the reader cannot *not* hear what is repeated throughout the narrative, that is, the constant presence of the divinity (Father, Son, and Holy Spirit), but also the logic on the divine plane underlying the whole story.[22] Steve Walton's essay, for example, provides significant evidence that brings God out of the backstage. He concludes that God can be considered the main topic and actor of Acts, because "Acts is a book about God and what God is doing." What is certain is that Luke maintains close and consistent contact between God, Jesus, and the Holy Spirit throughout the narrative.[23] Jervell summarizes this idea: "The significance of the Jesus-event is, first and foremost, salvation. The saviour is God himself and salvation is God's own gift (Acts 28:28; Luke 1:47; 2:30; 3:6)."[24]

Nevertheless, from a narrative perspective, the plot of Luke-Acts is thoroughly Christocentric, because it centers on the reader's exploration of the revelation of Jesus as savior and the contrasting responses to him on the spiritual and human planes. This is what carries the narrative from beginning to end. The conclusions on plot provide evidence that salvation through Jesus can be considered the center of Luke's theological focus in both volumes. In fact, the narrative presupposes a theocentric worldview, but the outworking of the plot from a narrative perspective is *primarily* Christocentric. Jesus is the hero in Luke-Acts because transformation comes through him. It confirms that Luke wanted to demonstrate to his audience the difference Jesus' coming into the world actually made, explaining the reasons for Jewish rejection of salvation and the nations' inclusion. Therefore, if Jesus is removed from the story, then there is really nothing to tell in either volume and a very new story would need to be told. The *raison d'être* of the story, in Labov's terms, would be lost. In this regard, Bo Reicke elucidates the active role of the risen Christ in Acts: "According to the short introduction to Acts given in 1:1–2, this book was meant to be a direct continuation of the

---

21. John Carroll is right in keeping the balance between the theological focus on God and Christ in his proposal: ". . . Luke-Acts is simultaneously theocentric and christocentric. The saving initiative of Israel's God in human history comes to sharp focus in the person and work of Jesus." Carroll, "God of Israel," 92.

22. Aletti, *Il racconto*, 69.

23. Walton, "The Acts – of God?," 291–306. Burridge, however, challenges Walton's position with statistics on verbal subjects in relation to the literary genre of Acts. Burridge, "Genre of Acts," 12–16.

24. Jervell, *Theology*, 94.

Gospel of Luke. In the Gospel, the acts of the Lord had been described. This is precisely what Luke intends to do in Acts also. It is a description of what *the risen Lord did for his church through the apostles*."[25] This assessment is correct as long as the activity of God and the Holy Spirit—both implicit and explicit—is not neglected.[26] Yet, Luke's concern was not to prove whether God is active in history—this is assumed—but whether God had realized what he had projected through Jesus and his disciples. Luke also emphasizes the Holy Spirit's presence, from beginning to end, as evidence that God was indeed behind the activities of Jesus and his disciples.[27] Yet, in both volumes, Jesus remains the vital link between God and the characters in the story, as well as between Luke and his audience. Salvation in Jesus for the Jewish people and the nations is the point or *raison d'être* of Luke's theologically motivated project.[28] The description of the Christocentric plot of Luke-Acts confirms this conclusion.

Second, as seen in the preceding chapter, the thoroughfare motif is also Christocentric, because it primarily illustrates Jesus' mandate as savior and those associated with him as a part of the narrative's progression. It is a positive motif for Luke and Theophilus, because it highlights two sides of the same coin: the agent and beneficiaries of salvation. More specifically, the two strands of the thoroughfare motif illustrate the gradual construction of Jesus' identity and the group's identity that he was forming on earth and then

---

25. Reicke, "Risen Lord," 157; emphasis added. So Marshall, "One Theme," 348. Despite the significant changes in verbal subject between Luke (Jesus) and Acts (the disciples), Richard Burridge identifies their generic resemblances and acknowledges the continued, active presence of Jesus: "If Luke's first volume (Τὸν μὲν πρῶτον λόγον) is all about 'what Jesus *began* to do and teach' in his life and ministry (ὧν ἤρξατο ὁ Ἰησοῦς ποιεῖν τε καὶ διδάσκειν), then the second part is what Jesus *continues* 'to do and teach' through the deeds and words of Peter, Paul and the early church." Burridge, *Genre of Acts*, 28.

26. For example, in addition to John Carroll's work, Diane Chen responds to the neglect of the study of God in Luke-Acts by proposing that the fatherhood of God could be considered the hub of Lukan theology, since, "For Luke, the God who orchestrates the plan of salvation is the Father of Israel, Jesus, and Jesus' followers." Chen, *God as Father*, 240. These points are already introduced by Gaventa (*Acts*, 28–31).

27. For these reasons, Maddox (*Purpose*, 16) describes Luke-Acts as a "theological history," because "... Luke is an historian, but he is at the same time a theologian: he uses history to express theology." Others describe it as a "divine story" (Brawley, *Centering*, 106), "theological narrative" (Aletti, *Il racconto*, 223), and "narrative theology" (Talbert, *Reading Acts*, xxv, and Green, *Theology*, 1, 21).

28. See Marshall ("One Theme," 357) for the description of thematic continuity in Luke-Acts based on Jesus, "the Proclaimer and Proclaimed" as the central figure in both books.

exalted in God's presence. Therefore, the results about the plot of Luke-Acts and thoroughfare motif help formulate an answer to the question: "What is the main theological concern that Luke wants to address for Theophilus?" The discussion below proposes answers to this question by observing the second strand of the motif concerning Jesus as the agent of salvation, then the first strand about the messengers and beneficiaries of his salvation.

The Agent of Salvation: Jesus as the Teacher of the Way of/to God

As stated above, the literary results guide the reader to this theological point: salvation through Jesus for the Jews and the nations explaining in particular the tensions resulting from Jewish rejection of this salvation and the nations' inclusion in it.[29] Jacques Dupont and Daniel Gerber, among other scholars[30], have articulated it in terms of the author's responses *to the reader's questions*.[31] While Dupont focuses on the value of the conclusion for the entire work, Gerber concentrates on its beginning (especially Luke 1–2). Both scholars reveal in complementary ways how Luke sought, among other objectives for the reader, to make sense of God's revelation of Jesus, the savior for the Jewish people and the nations.[32] Based on the relevance of the ending of Luke-Acts, Dupont concludes, ". . . the unbelief of the Jews as well as accession of the Gentiles to salvation is presented as accomplishing the Scriptures. The two facts do not explain each other, but both are manifested from God's design through the prophecies."[33] In effect, the conclusion shows that Luke works toward this goal from the beginning of the first volume. He

---

29. Marshall's description of the theology of Acts certainly mentions the main emphases of the book, but it lacks the indication of the key questions that Luke wants to clarify for Theophilus, namely Jewish rejection and the inclusion of the nations. He writes, "The theological centre of Acts lies in God's gift of salvation through Jesus Christ, the task of proclaiming it, and the nature of the new people of God empowered by the Holy Spirit." Marshall, "How does One Write," 3.

30. Cf. Marshall, "'Israel' and the Story of Salvation," 342; Bovon, *Luke the Theologian*, 273–328; 515–19; Flender, *Heil*; Green, *Theology*, 24; Martens, "Salvation Today," 100–126; and Chrupcała, "La storia lucana," 107–36. Likewise, cf. an extensive section in *Witness to the Gospel: The Theology of Acts*, which focuses on the theme of salvation. Marshall and Peterson, *Witness*, 17–166.

31. I refer to Dupont, "La conclusion" and Gerber, "*Il vous est né*."

32. McKnight states succinctly what has been demonstrated throughout this present work: "Luke, like Matthew, begins and ends both of his works with an emphasis on the universal implications of the Gospel (Lk 1:48; 1:79; 2:14, 30–32; 3:6; 24:47; Acts 1:8; 28:28)." McKnight, "Gentiles," 262.

33. Dupont, "La conclusion," 510.

responds to questions concerning Jewish rejection of Jesus and the inclusion of the nations in salvation.

Luke's project also provides an answer concerning this salvation and the new group formed by Jesus: "Is it [Paul's group] not just a *hairesis* that is contested and contestable from Jewish perspective, or is it to be considered the realization of the 'hope of Israel', 'the salvation of God' that the Law and the Prophets promised? This is the question that Luke wants his reader to respond to."[34] This link between salvation and its beneficiaries—soteriology and ecclesiology—is discussed below. The point is that Luke leads his audience to certain conclusions regarding Jesus as savior and its consequences for humanity, in particular for Jesus' disciples.

Likewise, Gerber, through his focus on the soteriological meaning of the coming of Jesus, suggests the conclusion that Luke wanted to draw for his readers:

> To assure his readers that the offer of the salvation of God was addressed, as foreseen, to Israel and to the Gentiles, these two entities, so different from their histories, cultures and belief systems, but equally concerned by the coming of the Nazarene, such was therefore one of the objectives the author of the work to Theophilus intended by telling how salvation prepared by God for the "glory of Israel" has also become, thanks to missionary activity, "light for the revelation of the Gentiles."[35]

Dupont and Gerber's contributions demonstrate that it is possible to uncover Luke's theological interests without treating Luke-Acts as a manual of theology. Likewise, the literary results of this study corroborate their conclusions in that both the plot and the thoroughfare motif are Christocentric.[36]

Consequently, how does the thoroughfare motif contribute to the main point that Luke wants to make for his audience? Since this discussion builds on the evidence presented in the preceding chapter, especially the symbolic value of the motif (cf. fig. 8.1), these aspects are expressed in cursory form below. The motif participates in Luke's portrayal of the savior's work by highlighting: (1) the people's spiritual need; (2) the manifestation of the solution (salvation); (3) the progressive realization of the solution; and (4) the various responses to Jesus as savior among the Jewish population and

---

34. Ibid., 473.

35. Gerber, *"Il vous est né,"* 259.

36. Tannehill (*Narrative*, 2:357) essentially agrees with Dupont's conclusions except for his insistence that Luke-Acts "does not provide a solution to the problem of Jewish rejection."

the nations. This narrative construction of salvation supplements Robinson's contributions and refines his use of thoroughfare terms as "stage markers" in Luke's history of salvation. Moreover, it provides additional evidence for those who explore Lukan themes, for example, a divine movement theme similar to Georg Geiger's proposal. As the motif illustrates the transformations highlighted by the plot, moving from the state of potentiality to the state of reality, Luke confirms for Theophilus what Jesus has become—not just what was said about him—and what his disciples have become through the realized salvation in him.

Concerning Jesus specifically, Luke uses the motif's second strand to illustrate Jesus as savior. This supplements the few explicit images and expressions of propitiation (cf. Luke 22:20; Acts 20:28). In other words, Luke seems to prefer to speak of Jesus as savior using various concepts or images—other than, for example, "cross," "blood," "sacrifice"—to show that Jesus accomplishes salvation by leading people to God. These aspects are further defined below.

Programmatic Image: Jesus and the way of peace (Luke 1:79). Luke's use of Zechariah's prophecy (Luke 1:78-79) reveals his understanding of Jesus as savior in the form of a spiritual leader (guide). This early use of prophecy is evidence for the *promise-fulfillment* model that scholars have observed in Luke-Acts.[37] In effect, Luke uses Zechariah's utterance in order to demonstrate that Jesus is from God and is able to lead people to God. This portrayal of Jesus as the "dawn from on high" has proleptic value since it hints to the reader that Jesus' mandate will lead people into the way of peace. Theologically, this image contains programmatic value in Luke's project (along with verses 76-77) to demonstrate Jesus as savior. This builds on and confirms Luke's claim through Zechariah that God had raised "a horn of salvation" in the house of David (Luke 1:69) and that John would "give knowledge of salvation to his people through the forgiveness of their sins" (Luke 1:77). Accordingly, Farris describes the importance of Zechariah's hymn for understanding Luke's theology: "As such the hymn is one of the most magnificent examples of the explosion of praise of God that surrounded the coming of Jesus Christ and is testimony to Luke's theology of the significance of the coming of Jesus Christ."[38]

---

37. For the question of promise and fulfillment and intrinsic examples within Luke-Acts, see Litwak, *Echoes of Scripture*, 15n57. For variations of this interpretative model, cf. Talbert, "Prophecy," 91–103; Bock, *Proclamation*; Strauss, *Promise*; and Peterson, "Motif of Fulfillment," 83–104.

38. Farris, "Zechariah's Song," 896.

This metaphorical image represents the act of leading people out of their needy spiritual state and demonic oppression and guiding them to the God of Israel (Luke 1:78–79). Thus, Jesus is able to save people by being their light so that they might see and return to God. Christoph Stenschke relates the "dawn" image to Luke's portrayal of human need for forgiveness: "It is not so much salvation from national and/or personal enemies but salvation from the coming judgement through the forgiveness of sins.... Salvation includes the forgiveness of sins and goes beyond this need in that it has the whole state of people in view. God graciously grants what men cannot attain themselves, as they sit in darkness, in the shadow of death and do not know the way of peace. This is why people need to be saved."[39] In brief, this image encapsulates—as a key programmatic passage—the central theme of salvation in Luke-Acts: Jesus has led people to God, both Jews and non-Jews. Luke then confirms this prophetic utterance through various examples of Jesus' acts and teaching. This reflection on this early programmatic passage is pertinent to Lukan theology since it has not received adequate attention for its progressive and cumulative value.[40]

In addition, Luke attributes much importance to the relationship between the resurrection and salvation. The use of Ps 15:11 (Ps 16.11 LXX) sustains the belief that Jesus has made known the "ways to life," that is, his return to life allows others to experience life with God as well (Acts 2:28). Again, it concerns an image of transformation, movement from death to life. The point is "the way of salvation" is available (Acts 16:17). Luke confirms this interpretation of Jesus as savior through the resurrection by quoting Paul: ". . . that the Christ was to suffer, be the first from the resurrection of the dead, and to proclaim light to the people and to the nations" (Acts 26:23). Furthermore, as savior, Jesus' coming to the world is characterized by peace, which he is able to provide (Luke 1:79; 2:14; 7:50; 8:48; 19:38, 42; Acts 10:36). According to Luke, many in Israel forfeited this peace because they did not recognize Jesus as their savior (19:42–44).

Confirmation of the Programmatic Image: Jesus and People on Thoroughfares. As a part of his theological program, Luke provides tangible examples how Jesus meets people on thoroughfares and leads them to God, out of darkness into light. In these scenes, Jesus brings light to people, and they

39. Stenschke, "Need for Salvation," 133.

40. Bovon (*Luke the Theologian*, 62) provides an example of this flawed procedure in his discussion of Karl Löning's article, "Lukas Theologe der von Gott geführten Heilsgeschichte (Lk, Apg)": "The reader is surprised that Löning, like Conzelmann, pays so little attention to the infancy narratives (Luke 1–2). This negligence is detrimental to the study of Christology."

experience some transformation, either physical or spiritual. This progressive work of salvation (i.e., leading people to God) on thoroughfares occurs before (blind beggar, Zacchaeus, crowd) and after his resurrection (Emmaus disciples, Ethiopian eunuch, Saul). Thus, Luke confirms that Jesus is able to lead people out of Satan's oppression into the kingdom of God through his teaching and interventions. This interpretation is confirmed by the parallels between the dawn image and the repetition of Paul's encounter with Jesus and the presence of light (Acts 9:3; 22:6, 9, 11; 26:13), as well as Paul's statement of Jesus' mandate (Acts 26:23). In addition, the Parable of the Great Supper—also containing a cluster of thoroughfare expressions—figuratively exemplifies Jesus' movement toward the people, especially the marginalized.

Confirmation of the Programmatic Image: Jesus, the teacher of the way of God (Luke 20:21). The episodes after Jesus' arrival in Jerusalem underline his superiority over the religious leaders. Luke affirms that Jesus is the teacher of Israel through his vigorous presentation of Jesus in the face of rejection. This is part of Luke's purpose to present Jesus as the teacher of Israel, a leader-prophet like Moses, since the themes of rule and direction are central in Luke-Acts.[41] This aspect emerges early in the narrative in the scene with young Jesus among the teachers of Israel in Jerusalem (Luke 2:46–50). Then, the expression "but you teach the way of God according to truth" confirms Jesus' identity. Just as Jesus knows and preaches "the word of God," he also knows and teaches "the way of God." He provides an instruction that is both from God and leads to him. In this way, this use of the thoroughfare motif confirms the programmatic value of Luke 1:78–79: Jesus leads people to God through his teaching. The verb "teach" with this thoroughfare expression provides a literary link with other thoroughfare expressions and verbs of communication or instruction in Acts.[42] In other words, this "way of God" can be communicated. Luke establishes an unbroken continuity between Israel's prophets, John the Baptist, Jesus and his disciples.[43] Jervell probably exaggerates by elevating Paul to the status of "teacher of Israel," in light of the apologetic discourses.[44] Nevertheless, given Luke's predilection for parallelisms, Paul's discourses correspond to Jesus' role as teacher by teaching the way of God and defending his people, "the Way." This leads to the next

---

41. Bock, "Luke," 356–57.

42. Cf. γνωρίζω (ὁδοὺς ζωῆς, 2:28); καταγγέλλω (ὁδὸν σωτηρίας, 16:17); κατηχέω (τὴν ὁδὸν τοῦ κυρίου, 18:25) and ἐκτίθεμαι (τὴν ὁδὸν [τοῦ θεοῦ], 18:26).

43. Cf. Luke 9:30–31; 10:24; 18:31; 24:27, 44; Acts 3:18, 21, 24; 10:43; 11:27; 13:1; 15:15–16; 24:14.

44. Jervell, *Luke*, 153–77.

point: the contribution of the motif's first strand to an understanding of the relationship between Lukan soteriology and ecclesiology.

The Messengers and Beneficiaries of Jesus' Salvation: "The Way"

Luke-Acts is also about human response to divine intervention. From beginning to end, Luke continually develops two general categories, those who respond positively and those who respond negatively. The thoroughfare motif contributes to the development of these two antithetical categories. I begin with the first group.

On the discourse level, in light of the explicit purpose stated in Luke 1:4 and the plot's development, it is inferred that Luke's readers, like Theophilus, needed this narrative for their individual assurance and for their collective identity. The narrative works on two levels to confirm the Way's identity as the people of God: the action level and the reader's level. Luke's ecclesiology gradually takes form as he demonstrates how Jesus' disciples—Jews and non-Jews—become a part of the people of God (cf. Acts 15:14).[45] Luke uses various terms to describe those who have responded positively to Jesus ("saints," "disciples," "church," "those who call upon the Lord," etc.). Thoroughfare expressions also add to this developing identity in Luke-Acts.

The first strand of the thoroughfare motif describes the beneficiaries of this salvation, their participation in Jesus' divine mandate, individual and collective transformation, and formation of distinct religious groups throughout the Roman Empire among other Jewish and non-Jewish groups. In this sense, Luke shows his pastoral concerns, responding relevantly to his audience's interests and needs. This corresponds with Larivaille's observation that most narratives are anthropomorphic, centered on the "human adventure," that which tends to interest humans the most.[46] Theologically, Luke-Acts is not unlike this, since it explores a fundamental human need met through Jesus, thus including also the "divine adventure." As a part of the author's project of normalization for the reader (cf. Chapter 2), Luke wants Theophilus to know *how* and *why* this new group emerging from Judaism can represent this salvation of God for the Jews and the nations. Thus, Squires rightly summarizes that Luke seeks to provide his audience with a

---

45. Similar to the interests expressed by Richard Thompson (*Keeping*, 3–5; 241) for understanding Luke's narrative development of the identity of churches, Christian communities, or groups of believers in Acts.

46. Larivaille, "L'analyse (morpho)logique," 384.

confirmation of faith, encouragement to be witnesses, and training for the defense of their faith.[47]

Beneficiaries of Jesus' salvation. The motif symbolically illustrates those who enter Jesus' salvation. This point has emerged extensively. The human need of reconciliation with the divine realm is assumed by Luke, rather than argued. Various expressions describe it in the two volumes: "forgiveness of sins," "salvation," "return to God," "enter the kingdom of God," "turn from darkness to light and from the dominion of Satan to God." In this way, Luke contributes to the development of the Church's identity by using the motif to illustrate how people are reconciled with God. It may be inferred that these beneficiaries enter "the way of peace" and confirms Zechariah's prophecy. In order to demonstrate that Jesus is able to save any person who is "in darkness and in the shadow of death," Luke shows how salvation comes—on thoroughfare settings— to a blind beggar, a chief tax collector, an Ethiopian eunuch, and a murderous Pharisee. Yet, Luke is careful to note that those who were already following Jesus were also in need of further enlightenment. Although Jesus is received as king entering Jerusalem (19:36–40), the crowd of disciples on the road only had a partial understanding of Jesus' identity (clearly alluded to in 18:31–34). This is dramatically depicted on the road to Emmaus (Luke 24:32–35) and confirmed by the following scene in Jerusalem (24:36–49). This is further impressed upon Theophilus through Luke's favorite thoroughfare encounter, repeated three times: Jesus and Saul of Tarsus. Through these interpretative signals, Theophilus understands his identity better as a part of "the Way," those who adhere to Jesus' teaching. Thus, the literary results also provide evidence for exploring Luke's ecclesiological interests and pastoral concerns in Luke-Acts.

The messengers for Jesus' mandate of salvation. Luke uses the motif's first strand to claim the participation of other individuals in God's plan of salvation, which is initially articulated at the beginning of the first volume (1:76–77). John the Baptist and Jesus' disciples perform the ministry of preparation for Jesus' mandate. As God sent John before Jesus (1:17, 76; 3:4), so Jesus sends his disciples before himself (9:3, 57; 10:3–4; 9:52; 10:1). They are Jesus' messengers for his mandate of salvation or forerunners preparing people to receive him. Yet, the communication of salvation through Jesus presupposes some knowledge of it. Luke takes pleasure in showing that Jesus' followers must also grow in their understanding of Jesus' mandate and its consequences. The examples are so numerous that one perceives a pragmatic intent for the learning reader. Luke enjoys underlining these examples

---

47. Squires, *Plan of God*, 192.

for Theophilus's edification: John the Baptist (cf. Luke 7:20–23), the disciples in Emmaus and Jerusalem, the Ethiopian, Peter with Cornelius, Apollos, and other "disciples" in Ephesus (19:1–7). Even after the resurrection, Jesus must give the disciples further explanation about the events that transpired in Jerusalem (24:26–27, 44–45; Acts 1:3). This results in the disciples' attachment to Jesus' teaching, since it confirmed for them that Jesus was the teacher of Israel, the one who truly teaches "the way of God." Several thoroughfare expressions illustrate Luke's emphasis on the spiritual union between Jesus and his disciples after the resurrection (e.g., Acts 9:2, 4–5; 22:7–8; 26:14–15). While the disciples are described as "those of the Way"—adherents to Jesus' teaching—Jesus is described as being persecuted through them.[48] Thus, the "disciples"—this term continues in the second volume—have an identity that is inseparable from Jesus' teaching and presence.

Having experienced Jesus' salvation, the disciples become teachers and preachers of "the ways to life" (the resurrection, Acts 2:28), "the way of salvation" (Acts 16:17), "the way of God" (Acts 18:26). Again, perhaps the strongest evidence for linking Jesus' role as "the dawn" and its extension to his disciples is the announcement in Pisidian Antioch (Acts 13:47) and the statement of Paul's mandate in relation to Jesus' role as savior (Acts 26:16–18, 23). This narrative construction of the identity of Jesus' followers underlies Luke's emphatic description of the disciples as "the Way." Luke perceives their identity as being so attached to the teaching of and about Jesus that he uses the expression as an "identity marker"[49] to claim Israel's heritage—possibly as other groups did.[50] The various uses of *hodos*—implied as being from God/the Lord—characterize those associated with Jesus as being in tune with God's revelation and activity, similar to other expressions in Luke-Acts, "the word of God/the Lord" (Acts 4:31; 13:7, 44; 16:32) and "the plan of God" (Luke 7:30; Acts 2:23; 20:27). In Luke's thought, the disciples were not an insignificant sect,[51] rather "*the* Way," "Judaism with its ancient belief and hope fulfilled."[52] This element points to the group as the true fulfillment of Jewish aspirations. Thus, the motif's first strand provides

---

48. The spiritual union communicated through expressions of *hodos* and other data is the focus of Lyonnet's essay "'La voie'" (discussed in Chapter 1).

49. Pao argues that Luke uses it primarily in an ecclesiological sense as an "identity marker" related to their understanding as the people of God via the new Exodus theme. Pao, *New Exodus*, 68.

50. Cf. the contributions of Repo and McCasland in Chapter 1.

51. Michaelis, "ὁδός," 93.

52. Pathrapankal, "Christianity," 534.

continuity in the line of messengers for Jesus' mandate of salvation before and after Jesus' resurrection. Jesus is savior and his disciples enter and extend his salvation to the Jewish people and the nations well beyond the land of the Jews, by preaching the light of Jesus and forming assemblies (ἐκκλησίαι) of those who receive him (Acts 13:47; 26:16–18). A people have been formed through a new phase in salvation history.[53]

Here the intertextual element helps understand the force of the thoroughfare expressions. In Jewish Scriptures, expressions with *derek* (way, *hodos* in LXX) occur as the object of verbs of instruction with the meaning of "will of God," "commandment," and "instruction" (e.g., Ps 24:8; 27:11; 50:15; 67:2; 86:11).[54] Abraham knew God's way and admonished his family to keep it (Gen 18:19). Consequently, these expressions are also used in reproaches to the people and leadership for not knowing "the way of the Lord" (Jer 5:4–5; Wis 5:7) and turning from "the way" (Exod 32:8; Deut 9:12, 16; Mal 2:8). God revealed his instruction, this *divine way*, to his people so that it might be taught and observed on the human plane.

Therefore, this link with ancient expressions from Jewish Scriptures further illustrates Luke's claim to Israel's spiritual heritage. For him, this passage from ancient to new is continuous—from the saints of the past to those of the present. This group "the Way" provides instruction that comes from God and leads to him. It is yet another link between the former covenant and the new covenant—the continuity and discontinuity in God's plan for humanity.

"Some were persuaded by what was said, but others did not believe" (Acts 28:24)

Luke's summary in Acts 28:24 describes well the final episode in Rome, as well as the reception and rejection pattern that runs through the two volumes. Much of the discussion above has revolved around the uses of thoroughfare expressions in the portrayal of Jesus and his disciples. For this reason, I have

---

53. Bottini, interpreting retrospectively Luke-Acts, summarizes Luke's intent in including Isaiah 40:5 (Luke 3:6) in the description of John the Baptist's ministry: "Thus, Luke not only presents God's salvific action as the winding of a journey, but also shows that such a journey does not stop at the preparation of the Jewish people in view of Jesus' coming and activity. Nor does it limit itself to the time of his public life, but interests also the Church and its mission, as it results from Acts 28:28 and alludes to Isa 40:5, showing also that universal salvation, of which the prophetic text speaks, is realized definitively in the conversion of the pagans." Bottini, *Luca. Aspetti teologici*, 501.

54. When *derek* is used in the plural, it often indicates individual laws and commandments (cf. Deut 26:17; 1 Kgs 2:3). Cf. Morgan, *derek YHWH*, 10–11.

described the motif as "positive" (from the author's point of view). The motif is never used as a means of criticism for the movement toward which Luke is obviously favorable. On the contrary, certain expressions depict, explicitly or implicitly, those who did not adhere to this new phase in God's plan. These expressions take part in the construction of antithetical categories that develop from an assumed theocentric world to an explicit Christocentric world (cf. Luke 9:62; 11:23; 22: 21–22). This theological (narrative) argumentation becomes more evident in Luke's second volume after the defining moments of Jesus' resurrection, ascension, and sending of the Holy Spirit. Furthermore, these categories can be subtle as in the antithetic prophecy of "the rising and falling of many in Israel" (Luke 2:34) or blunt as in the Nazareth scene where Jesus was nearly murdered (Luke 3:28–29).

In relation to the thoroughfare motif, the expression "those of the Way" implicitly means that it was possible not to be of "the Way," that is, to be outside the group or not yet within it. The implication from the scene in Lystra is that the nations are being confronted with this new reality and that to continue walking in their "ways" meant not walking in "the way of God" (Acts 14:16). Accordingly, concrete and figurative thoroughfare expressions permit a construction of this portrayal of resisting or opposing characters. The would-be disciples meet Jesus on the road, but they have other priorities than to benefit from their encounter with Jesus who invites them to follow him as disciples (Luke 9:57–62). The flattering spies sent by the religious leaders miss their chance to receive the true teacher of the way of God (Luke 20:20–26). Saul's folly to attack "those of the Way" is repeated several times to highlight this conflict of antithetical values (Acts 9:2; 22:4; 26:11–13). To oppose the disciples meant opposing Jesus, as well as God who sent him as savior. Likewise, Elymas opposes in vain the gospel and thus makes crooked "the straight paths of the Lord" (Acts 13:10). Similarly, "the way of salvation" is opposed in Philippi because of commercial interests (Acts 16:17–19). Finally, religious and political groups resist "the Way" in Ephesus (19:8–10) and Caesarea (24:1–22). This pattern of reception and rejection is then sealed in the *evaluation* regarding the "sect" that Paul represented in Rome: some believed and others did not. Consequently, Luke's narrative echoes a familiar refrain in biblical literature, which Nötscher encapsulates: "That God's ways and the ways of men might be identical is a biblical ideal, that they might go together or at least not contradict each other. This ideal, however, is already not reached according to the Old Testament or in everything even reachable."[55] Luke-Acts portrays this predicament from beginning to end.

55. Nötscher, *Gotteswege*, 7.

Conclusion: The Divine Way and Human Response in Plot and Explotment

If Luke-Acts is about God's activities and human responses to them, then a theological reading means observing what happens on the two aforementioned levels: action and discourse. On the first level, all agree that Luke-Acts is about Israel's God who continues to accomplish his purposes in the spiritual and human realms. On the discourse level, Luke appropriates God's activity for himself and his audience. By explaining what, how, and why God accomplished certain things, he provides a theological foundation upon which Theophilus's (and others') faith can grow. Not only, according to the definition of plot that I have used, Luke provides the means for an encounter through the reading experience, private or collective, with those events "fulfilled among us" (Luke 1:1). This gives a sense of *being there*—watching and participating. This experience raises questions and expectations in the minds of curious readers about the recounted events as well as issues in their own lives. In this sense, although Luke-Acts certainly exhibits features of ancient biography and historiography, Luke undoubtedly wishes to extend the Scriptures of his times. He writes for a group of people who desire to live with God, explaining to them "the divine way"—God's instruction that is about him, comes from him, and leads to him. To be people called "the Way" means that they are people of "the way of God" (or "the way of the Lord"). This, among other interpretations, illustrates the disciples' attachment to Jesus and his teaching, their spiritual union with him.[56]

Consequently, while scholars have given much attention to Luke and Acts for their literary, historical, and theological value, literature on Lukan spirituality appears to be neglected as a part of Luke's theology.[57] In this regard, I suggest that the present research offers some material to consider for the spiritual life or religious experience that it exhibits on the level of action and encourages on the level of discourse. In other words, Luke-Acts displays what God is doing and how people are responding to him and living out their faith. Yet, this narrative also features what God is saying to Luke's audience and—why not—other types of readers. This reading experience can also fall in the domain of religious experience because of the implicit and explicit universal claims that Luke-Acts affirms. The narrative invites readers

---

56. See Walton regarding "the apostles' teaching" as a response to God in "A Spirituality of Acts?," 196.

57. Cf. Resseguie, *Spiritual Landscape*, 121n2; and Walton, "A Spirituality of Acts?," 186.

to enter and explore its questions within its storyworld, which has various degrees of affinity with today's cultures.[58]

For those who read Luke-Acts as Scripture, perhaps ideas for contemplation and application have come to mind while considering various occurrences of the thoroughfare motif. As one part of Luke's theological project, its synecdochic function suggests paths to explore. Indeed, others have already related aspects of this motif (as well as the journey theme) to contemporary thought and practice.[59] This type of reflection implies a dialogical relationship between Scripture and life, described above as *explotment*, the counterpart of *emplotment* and *plot*. When applied to biblical texts, explotment describes the continued interaction between narratives and readers by which they re-experience testimonies of God's transformational acts.[60] Consequently, how do readers understand, integrate or resist theological values of the thoroughfare motif in their own life contexts? For example, how could this motif be meaningful to nomadic Christians among the Tuaregs in Africa or the Roma people in Europe, who in their respective histories know well thoroughfares, both literal and figurative? Alternatively, what does it mean to be a Christian community living and teaching "the way of God" in Islamic and Buddhist contexts where the path symbol has a long tradition? Likewise, how do Christians live and worship according to "the Way" (Acts 24:14) in secular contexts, which often resist or oppose claims of truth? Finally, is it still possible to enter and experience "the way of peace" as described by Zechariah? These are only a few points that Christian individuals and communities can ponder and unravel in their contexts, the "living plots" that they participate in daily.

---

58. An example of this type of exploration is the book *Anfang ist jetzt. Junge Christen lesen die Apostelgeschichte* (Köppen et al.). University students in Germany wrote and edited this work seeking to explore existential and faith questions raised through a fresh reading of Acts. I am grateful to Markus Lau, co-author of this work and my colleague at the University of Fribourg, who gave me a copy of this admirable project.

59. For various interpretative techniques and applications of thoroughfare expressions in modern contexts, see, for example, the contributions of Brox (*Der Glaube*), Gros (*Je suis la route*), Pathrapankal ("Christianity"), Göllner ("'Weg'").

60. See Minear ("Dear Theo," 149–50) who relates Theophilus's situation and Luke's "kerygmatic intentions" with the modern church in America in the 1970s. His application is stimulating: "But an awareness of this situation may force upon us the realization that the role of Luke as a pastoral theologian is as essential today as it was in the first century. The name of Theophilus today is Legion. Where are the legitimate successors of Luke? And how will they fulfill their vocation of helping Christians know the certainty of the things in which they have been instructed? Those are questions for other Lukes to answer, some of whom may be among the readers of this Journal." Ibid., 150.

The Thoroughfare Motif's Theological Contribution

Returning to Theophilus, obviously, it is empirically impossible to speak of his explotment, because we know little about this personage and nothing about any continued relationship between him and Luke-Acts. Nevertheless, we can imagine that the *point* of Luke-Acts did not leave Theophilus and others indifferent. On the contrary, as readers/hearers belonging to "the Way," one can suppose that the narrative and the thoroughfare motif were meaningful to them because of their positive portrayal of Jesus as savior and his transformed followers. Among other motifs and themes, this motif exemplifies Luke's primary theological concern to explain how the salvation of God has come through Jesus to the Jewish people who in part rejected it and to the nations who are included in it. In so doing, Luke connects the present of his readers with the divinely led events that began in Jerusalem and ended in Rome.

Indeed, by the end of the narrative, the *evaluation* of Luke-Acts appears quite clear: salvation has come through Jesus to the Jewish people and the nations. It is thus reasonable to conclude—referring to Labov's quote—that Theophilus and friends did not express the dreaded "So what?" Rather, similar to the believers in Pisidian Antioch (Acts 13:46–48), they probably joyfully responded with gratification for this encounter of spiritual transformation that Luke researched and constructed. His work allowed them and countless others to ponder, participate in, and relive passionately Jesus' revelation and contrasting responses to him and his disciples. The thoroughfare motif contributes to Luke's work meaningfully, giving to Theophilus, and any sympathetic reader, a greater degree of certainty and reading pleasure.

Bibliography

Abbott, H. Porter. *The Cambridge Introduction to Narrative*. 2nd ed. Cambridge: Cambridge University Press, 2008.
Abrams, Meyer Howard. *A Glossary of Literary Terms*. 7th ed. Fort Worth, TX: Harcourt Brace, 1999.
Adam, Jean-Michel. "Décrire des actions: raconter ou relater?" *Littérature* 95 (1994) 3–22.
Aletti, Jean-Noël. *L'art de raconter Jésus-Christ. L'écriture narrative de l'évangile de Luc. Parole de Dieu*. Paris: Éditions du Seuil, 1989.
———. *Il racconto come teologia. Studio narrativo del terzo vangelo e del libro degli atti degli apostoli*. Translated by C. Valentino and R. Fabbri. 2nd ed. Bologna: EDB, 2009.
Aletti, Jean-Noël, et al. *Vocabulaire raisonné de l'exégèse biblique*. Paris: Éditions du Cerf, 2005.
Alexander, Loveday. *The Preface to Luke's Gospel: Literary Convention and Social Context in Luke 1.1–4 and Acts 1.1*. SNTSMS 78. Cambridge: Cambridge University Press, 1993.
———. "Reading Luke-Acts from Back to Front." In *The Unity of Luke-Acts*, edited by J. Verheyden, 419–46. BETL 142. Leuven: Leuven University Press/Peeters, 1999.
———. "What if Luke had never met Theophilus?" *Biblical Interpretation* 8:1–2 (2000) 161–70.
Archer, Gleason L., and Gregory Chirichigno. *Old Testament Quotations in the New Testament*. Chicago: Moody, 1983.
Aristotle, *The Poetics*. Edited and translated by Stephen Halliwell. Loeb Classical Library 199. Cambridge, MA: Harvard University Press, 1995.
———. *Poetics*. Translated by Malcom Heath with an introduction and notes. Penguin Classics. London: Penguin, 1996.
Aune, David E. *The New Testament in Its Literary Environment*. Philadelphia: Westminster, 1987.
Baban, Octavian D. *On the Road Encounters in Luke-Acts: Hellenistic Mimesis and Luke's Theology of the Way*. PBM. Milton Keynes, UK: Paternoster, 2006.
Baldick, Chris. *The Oxford Dictionary of Literary Terms*. 3rd ed. Oxford: Oxford University Press, 2008.
Bar-Efrat, Shimon. *Narrative Art in the Bible*. London: T&T Clark, 1989.
Baroni, Raphaël. *La tension narrative. Suspense, curiosité, surprise*. Paris: Seuil, 2007.
Barrett, C. K. *A Critical and Exegetical Commentary on the Acts of the Apostles*. Vol. I, ICC. Edinburgh: T&T Clark, 1994.
———. *A Critical and Exegetical Commentary on the Acts of the Apostles*. Vol. II, ICC. Edinburgh: T&T Clark, 1998.
Barthes, Roland. "Par où commencer?" *Poétique* 1 (1970) 3–9.
———. *S/Z*, Points Essais. Paris: Seuil, 1976.
Bassin, François. *L'Évangile selon Luc*. Vol. 1. Vaux-sur-Seine: ÉDIFAC, 2006.

Bibliography

Bauckham, Richard. "James and the Jerusalem Community." In *Jewish Believers in Jesus: the Early Centuries*, edited by Oskar Skarsaune and Reidar Hvalvik, 55–95. Peabody, MA: Hendrickson, 2007.

Baum, Armin D. *Lukas als Historiker der letzten Jesusreise*. Brockhaus: Wuppertal, 1993.

Bock, Darrell L. *Proclamation from Prophecy and Pattern: Lucan Old Testament Christology*. JSNTSup 12. Sheffield: JSOT Press, 1987.

———. *Luke: 1:1—9:50*. BECNT. Grand Rapids: Baker, 1994.

———. *Luke: 9:51—24:53*. BECNT. Grand Rapids: Baker, 1996.

———. "Luke." In *The Face of New Testament Studies*, edited by Scot McKnight and Grant R. Osborne, 349–72. Grand Rapids: Baker Academic, 2004.

———. *A Theology of Luke and Acts*. BTNT. Grand Rapids: Zondervan, 2012.

Bockmuehl, Markus. "Why not Let Acts be Acts? In Conversation with C. Kavin Rowe." *JSNT* 28 (2005) 163–66.

Boismard, Marie-Émile, and Arnaud Lamouille. *Les actes des deux apôtres. I. Introduction et textes*. Etudes bibliques 12. Paris: Gabalda, 1990.

Bonz, Marianne Palmer. *The Past as Legacy: Luke-Acts and Ancient Epic*. Minneapolis: Fortress, 2000.

Borgman, Paul. *The Way according to Luke: Hearing the Whole Story of Luke-Acts*. Grand Rapids: Eerdmans, 2006.

Bottini, Giovanni Claudio. *Introduzione all'opera di Luca. Aspetti teologici*. SBF 35. Jerusalem: Franciscan Printing Press, 1992.

Bovon, François. *L'Evangile selon Saint Luc (1,1—9,50)*. CNT IIIa. Geneva: Labor et Fides, 1991.

———. *L'Evangile selon Saint Luc (15,1—19,27)*. CNT IIIc. Geneva: Labor et Fides, 2001.

———. *Luke 1: A Commentary on the Gospel of Luke 1:1—9:50*. Translated by M. Christine Thomas. Hermeneia. Minneapolis: Fortress, 2002.

———. *Luke the Theologian: Fifty-five Years of Research (1950–2005)*. 2nd ed. Waco, TX: Baylor University Press, 2006.

Brawley, Robert L. *Centering on God: Method and Message in Luke-Acts*. LCBI. Louisville: Westminster/John Knox, 1990.

Brown, Raymond E. *The Birth of the Messiah: A Commentary on the Infancy Narratives in the Gospels of Matthew and Luke*. New updated ed. ABRL. New York: Doubleday, 1999.

Brown, Schuyler. *Apostasy and Perseverance in the Theology of Luke*. AnBib. Rome: Pontifical Biblical Institute, 1969.

Brox, Norbert. *Der Glaube als Weg nach biblischen und altchristlichen Texten*. Munich: Pustet, 1968.

Bruce, F.F. *The Acts of the Apostles: The Greek Text with Introduction and Commentary*. 3rd revised and enlarged ed. Grand Rapids: Eerdmans, 1990.

Bruggen, Jakob van. *Lucas*. Commentaar op het Nieuwe Testament. Kampen: Kok, 1993.

Burke, Kenneth. *The Philosophy of Literary Form: Studies in Symbolic Action*. Revised ed. New York: Vintage, 1957.

Burridge, Richard. "The Genre of Acts—Revisited." In *Reading Acts Today: Essays in Honour of Loveday C.A. Alexander*, edited by Steve Walton et al., 3–28. LNTS 427. London: T&T Clark, 2011.

Cadbury, Henry J. "Names for Christians and Christianity in Acts." In *The Beginnings of Christianity*, edited by F.J. Foakes-Jackson and Kirsopp Lake, 375–92. Part I, The Acts of the Apostles, Vol. 5, Additional Notes to the Commentary. London: Macmillan, 1933.

———. *The Making of Luke-Acts*. 2nd ed. 1958. Reprint, Peadbody, MA: Hendrickson, 1999.

Caird, G.B. *The Language and Imagery of the Bible*. Philadelphia: Westminster, 1980.

Carroll, John T. "The God of Israel and the Salvation of the Nations: The Gospel of Luke and the Acts of the Apostles." In *The Forgotten God: Perspectives in Biblical Theology*, edited by A. Andrew Das and Frank J. Matera, 91–106. Louisville: Westminster John Knox, 2002.

Charlesworth, James H. "Intertextuality: Isaiah 40:3 and the Serek ha-Yaḥad." In *The Quest for Context and Meaning: Studies in Biblical Intertextuality in Honor of James Sanders*, edited by Craig A. Evans and Shemaryahu Talmon, 197–224. Leiden: Brill, 1997.

Chatman, Seymour. *Story and Discourse: Narrative Structure in Fiction and Film*. Ithaca, NY: Cornell University Press, 1978.

Chen, Diane G. *God as Father in Luke-Acts*. SBL 92. New York: Peter Lang, 2006.

Chrupcała, L.D. "La storia lucana della salvezza come illuminazione. Rilettura di Isaia in Luca-Atti." *Studium Biblicum Franciscanum Liber Annuus* 60 (2010) 107–36.

Colijn, Brenda. *Images of Salvation in the New Testament*. Downers Grove, IL: InterVarsity, 2010.

Conzelmann, Hans. *Die Mitte der Zeit. Studien zur Theologie des Lukas*. 6th ed. Tübingen: J.C.B. Mohr, 1977.

Dannenberg, Hilary P. "Plot." In *Routledge Encyclopedia of Narrative Theory*, edited by David Herman et al., 435–39. London: Routledge, 2008.

Delebecque, Edouard. *Les actes des apôtres*. Paris: Les Belles Lettres, 1982.

Denaux, Adelbert, and Rita Corstjens. *The Vocabulary of Luke: An Alphabetical Presentation and a Survey of Characteristic and Noteworthy Words and Word Groups in Luke's Gospel*. BTS 10. Leuven: Peeters, 2009.

Dibelius, Martin. *Studies in the Acts of the Apostles*. Translated by Mary Ling and Paul Schubert. London: SCM, 1956.

Downing, Gerald. "Theophilus's First Reading of Luke-Acts." In *Luke's Literary Achievement*, edited by C.M. Tuckett, 91–109. Sheffield: Sheffield Academic, 1995.

Dreyfus, François. Review of *Der 'Weg' als Selbstbezeichnung des Urchristentums eine traditionsgeschichtliche und semasiologische Untersuchung*, by Eero Repo. *Revue biblique* 76 (1969) 290–92.

Dupont, Jacques. "Le salut des Gentils et la signification théologique du Livre des Actes." *NTS* 6 (1960) 132–55.

———. "The Meal at Emmaus," in *The Eucharist in the New Testament: A Symposium*, edited by P. Benoit et al., 105–21. London: Geoffrey Chapman, 1964.

———. "Je t'ai établi lumière des nations (Ac 13,14.43–52)." In *Nouvelles Etudes sur les Actes des Apôtres*, edited by Jacques Dupont, 343–49. LD 118. Paris: Cerf, 1984.

———. "La conclusion des Actes et son rapport à l'ensemble de l'ouvrage de Luc." In *Nouvelles Etudes sur les Actes des Apôtres*, edited by Jacques Dupont, 457–511. LD 118. Paris: Cerf, 1984.

Eck, John van. *Handelingen*, Commentaar op het Nieuwe Testament. Kampen: Kok, 2003.

Eckey, Wilfried. *Die Apostelgeschichte. Der Weg des Evangeliums von Jerusalem nach Rom. Teilband I 1,1—15,35*. Neukirchen-Vluyn: Neukirchener, 2000.

———. *Das Lukasevangelium. Unter Berücksichtigung seiner Parallelen. Teilband I: 1,1—10,42*. Neukirchen-Vluyn: Neukirchener, 2004.

Bibliography

———. *Das Lukasevangelium. Unter Berücksichtigung seiner Parallelen.* Teilband II: 11,1– 24,53. Neukirchen-Vluyn: Neukirchener, 2004.
Eisen, Ute E. *Die Poetik der Apostelgeschichte. Eine narratologische Studie*, NTOA 58. Fribourg: Academic Press Fribourg, 2006.
Evans, C.F. *Saint Luke*, TPINTC. London: SCM, 1990.
Farris, Stephen C. "Zechariah's Song." In *DJG*, edited by Joel B. Green and Scot McKnight, 895–96. Downers Grove, IL: InterVarsity, 1992.
Filson, F.V. "The Journey Motif in Luke-Acts." In *Apostolic History and the Gospel: Biblical and Historical Essays Presented to F.F. Bruce on His 60th Birthday*, edited by W. Ward Gasque and Ralph P. Martin, 68–77. Exeter: Paternoster, 1970.
Fitzmyer, Joseph A. "Jewish Christianity in Acts in Light of the Qumran Scrolls." In *Studies in Luke-Acts*, edited by Leander E. Keck and J. Louis Martyn, 233–57. Philadelphia: Fortress, 1966.
———. *The Gospel according to Luke (I–IX): Introduction, Translation and Notes.* 2nd ed. AB 28. Garden City, NY: Doubleday, 1985.
———. *The Gospel according to Luke (X–XXIV): Introduction, Translation and Notes*, AB 28a. Garden City, NY: Doubleday, 1985.
———. *The Acts of the Apostles*, AB 31. New York: Doubleday, 1998.
Flender, Helmut. *Heil und Geschichte in der Theologie des Lukas.* Beiträge zur evangelischen Theologie 41. Munich: Chr. Kaiser Verlag, 1965.
Fokkelman, Jan P. *Comment lire le récit biblique. Une introduction pratique.* Le livre et le rouleau 13. Brussels: Lessius, 2002.
Freedman, William. "The Literary Motif: A Definition and Evaluation." *Novel: A Forum on Fiction* 4:2 (1971) 123–31.
Fusco, Vittorio. *Les premières communautés chrétiennes. Traditions et tendencies dans le christianisme des origines.* LD 188. Paris: Les Éditions du Cerf, 2008.
Gaventa, Beverly Roberts. "Toward a Theology of Acts: Reading and Rereading." *Interpretation* 42:2 (1988) 146–57.
———. *Acts*. ANTC. Nashville: Abingdon, 2003.
Geiger, Georg. "Der Weg als roter Faden durch Lk-Apg." In *The Unity of Luke-Acts*, edited by J. Verheyden, 663–73. BETL 142. Leuven: Leuven University Press, 1999.
Geldenhuys, Norval. *Commentary on the Gospel of Luke*. NICNT. Grand Rapids: Eerdmans, 1977.
Genette, Gérard. *Seuils*. Paris: Seuils, 1987.
Gerber, Daniel. *"Il vous est né un Sauveur". La construction du sens sotériologique de la venue de Jésus en Luc-Actes.* Le Monde de la Bible 58. Geneva: Labor et Fides, 2008.
Giles, Kevin N. "Church." In *DNLT*, edited by Ralph P. Martin and Peter H. Davids, 194–204. Downers Grove, IL: InterVarsity, 1997.
Godet, F. *Commentaire sur l'Evangile de saint Luc.* Vol. 1. 3rd ed. Neuchatel: Attinger Frères, 1888.
Göllner, Reinhard. "Der 'Weg' als christlichen Glaubens: Perspektiven lukanischer Theologie." In *Dreieine Gott und die eine Menschheit*, 199–215. Freiburg: Herder, 1989.
Green, Joel B. *The Theology of the Gospel of Luke.* Cambridge: Cambridge University Press, 1995.
———. *The Gospel of Luke*, NICNT. Grand Rapids: Eerdmans, 1997.

Bibliography

———. Review of *The Assumed Authorial Unity of Luke and Acts: A Reassessment of the Evidence*, by Patricia Walters, *Review of Biblical Literature* (December 2009). n.p. Online: http://www.bookreviews.org/pdf/7084_7695.pdf.

———. "Luke-Acts, or Luke and Acts." In *Reading Acts Today: Essays in Honour of Loveday C.A. Alexander*, edited by Steve Walton et al., 101-19. LNTS 427. London: T&T Clark, 2011.

Gregory, Andrew. "The Reception of Luke and Acts and the Unity of Luke-Acts." *JSNT* 29:4 (2007) 459-72.

Gros, André. *Je suis la route. Le thème de la route dans la Bible*. Thèmes bibliques. Bruges: Desclée De Brouwer, 1961.

Haenchen, Ernst. *Die Apostelgeschichte*. 14th ed. KEK 5. Göttingen: Vandenhoeck & Ruprecht, 1965.

Hartsock, Chad. *Sight and Blindness in Luke Acts: The Use of Physical Features in Characterization*. BIS 94. Leiden: Brill, 2008.

Hawthorne, Jeremy. *A Glossary of Contemporary Literary Theory*. 2nd ed. London: Edward Arnold, 1994.

Hedrick, Charles W. "Paul's Conversion/Call: A Comparative Analysis of the Three Reports in Acts." *JBL* 100:3 (1981) 415-32.

Hengel, Martin. Review of *Der 'Weg' als Selbstbezeichnung des Urchristentums eine traditionsgeschichtliche und semasiologische Untersuchung*, by Eero Repo. *Theologische Literaturzeitung* 92 (1967) 364.

Hengel, Martin, and Anna Maria Schwemer. *Jesus und das Judentum*. Geschichte des frühen Christentums Band I. Tübingen: Mohr Siebeck, 2007.

Herman, David. *Basic Elements of Narrative*. Chichester: Wiley-Blackwell, 2009.

Herman, David, et al. *Routledge Encyclopedia of Narrative Theory*. London: Routledge, 2008.

Hughes, John H. "John the Baptist: The Forerunner of God Himself." *NovT* 14:3 (1972) 191-218.

Hur, Ju. *A Dynamic Reading of the Holy Spirit in Luke-Acts*. JSNTSup 211. Sheffield: Sheffield Academic, 2001.

Jacoby, Adolf. "ἀνατολὴ ἐξ ὕψους." *ZNW* 20 (1921) 205-14.

Jervell, Jacob. *Luke and the People of God: A New Look at Luke-Acts*. Minneapolis: Augsburg, 1972.

———. *The Theology of the Acts of the Apostles*. Cambridge: Cambridge University Press, 1996.

———. *Die Apostelgeschichte*, KEK 3. Göttingen: Vandenhoeck und Ruprecht, 1998.

Johnson, Luke Timothy. *The Gospel of Luke*. SP 3. Collegeville, MN: The Liturgical Press, 1991.

———. *The Acts of the Apostles*. SP 5. Collegeville, MN: The Liturgical Press, 1992.

Jost, François. "Introduction." In *Dictionary of Literary Themes and Motifs*, edited by Jean-Charles Seigneuret, xv-xxxiii. New York: Greenwood, 1988.

Juel, Donald. *Luke-Acts*. London: SCM, 1984.

Klein, Hans. *Das Lukasevangelium*. KEK 3. Göttingen: Vandenhoeck & Ruprecht, 2006.

Kodell, Jerome. "Luke's Use of *Laos*, 'People', especially in the Jerusalem Narrative (Lk 19,28—24,53)." *CBQ* 31 (1969) 327-43.

Köppen, Hans-Bernd, et al. *Anfang ist jetzt. Junge Christen lesen die Apostlegeschichte*. Freiburg: Herder, 2009.

Bibliography

Kuhn, Karl Allen. *Luke: The Elite Evangelist. Paul's Social Network: Brothers & Sisters in Faith*. Collegeville, MN: Liturgical Press, 2010.
Kurz, William S. *Reading Luke-Acts: Dynamics of Biblical Narrative*. Louisville: Westminster/John Knox, 1993.
Kuschke, Arnulf. "Die Menschenweg und der Weg Gottes im Alten Testaments." *ST* 5:1 (1952) 106–18.
Labov, William. *Language in the Inner City: Studies in the Black English Vernacular*. Philadelphia: University of Pennsylvania Press, 1972.
Lagrange, M.-J. *Évangile selon saint Luc*. 8th ed. Collection Études bibliques. Paris: Gabalda, 1948.
Lake, Kirsopp, and Henry J. Cadbury. *The Beginnings of Christianity*, edited by F.J. Foakes-Jackson and Kirsopp Lake, Part I, The Acts of the Apostles, Vol. 4, English Translation and Commentary. London: Macmillan, 1933.
Larivaille, Paul. "L'analyse (morpho)logique du récit." *Poétique* 19 (1974) 368–88.
Larkin, William J. "The Recovery of Luke-Acts as 'Grand Narrative' for the Church's Evangelistic and Edification Tasks in a Postmodern Age." *JETS* 43:3 (2000) 405–15.
Levinskaya, Irina. *The Book of Acts in Its Diaspora Setting*. Vol. 5 of *The Book of Acts in Its First Century Setting*. Grand Rapids: Eerdmans, 1996.
Lindijer, Coert H. "Two creative encounters in the work of Luke. Luke xxiv 13–35 and Acts viii 26–40." In *Miscellanea Neotestamentica (SNT XLVIII)*, edited by F.J. Lijn et al., 77–85. SNT XLVIII. Leiden: E.J. Brill, 1978.
Litwak, Kenneth Duncan. *Echoes of Scripture In Luke-Acts: Telling The History of God's People Intertextually*. JSNTSup 282. London: T&T Clark, 2005.
Löning, Karl. "Lukas Theologe der von Gott geführten Heilsgeschichte (Lk, Apg)." In *Gestalt und Anspruch des Neuen Testaments*, edited by J. Schreiner, 200–228. Würzburg: Echter Verlag, 1969.
Lyonnet, Stanislas. "'La voie' dans les Actes des Apôtres." *RSR* 69 (1981) 149–64.
Mack, Burton L., and Vernon K. Robbins, *Patterns of Persuasion in the Gospels*. Sonoma, CA: Polebridge, 1989.
Maddox, Robert. *The Purpose of Luke-Acts*. SNTV. Edinburgh: T&T Clark, 1982.
Malina, Bruce J., and Jerome H. Neyrey. "First-Century Personality: Dyadic, Not Individualistic." In *The Social World of Luke-Acts: Models for Interpretation*, edited by Jerome H. Neyrey, 67–96. Peabody, MA: Hendrickson, 1991.
Marguerat, Daniel. "The Enigma of the Silent Closing of Acts (28:16–31)." In *Jesus and the Heritage of Israel: Luke's Narrative Claim upon Israel's Legacy*, edited by David P. Moessner, 284–304. Harrisburg, PA: Trinity, 1999.
———. "Luc-Actes: Une unité à construire." In *The Unity of Luke-Acts*, edited by J. Verheyden, 57–81. BETL 142. Leuven: Leuven University Press, 1999.
———. "Luc, metteur en scène des personnages." In *Analyse narrative et Bible*, edited by Camille Focant and André Wénin, 281–95. BETL 191. Leuven: Leuven University Press, 2005.
———. *Les Actes des apôtres (1–12)*, CNT 5a. Geneva: Labor et Fides, 2007.
Marguerat, Daniel, and Yvan Bourquin. *Pour lire les récits bibliques: Initiation à l'analyse narrative*. 3rd ed. Geneva: Labor et Fides, 2004.
Marguerat, Daniel, and André Wénin. *Saveurs du récit*. Geneva: Labor et Fides, 2012
Marshall, I. Howard. *Luke: Historian and Theologian*. Exeter: Paternoster, 1970.
———. *The Gospel of Luke: A Commentary on the Greek Text*, NIGTC. Exeter: Paternoster, 1978.

———. *Luke: Historian and Theologian*. 3rd ed. 1988. Reprint, Exeter: Paternoster, 1992.

———. "Acts and the 'Former Treatise.'" In *The Book of Acts in Its Ancient Literary Setting*, edited by Bruce W. Winter and Andrew D. Clark, 163-82. BAFCS 1. Grand Rapids: Eerdmans, 1993.

———. "How does One Write on the Theology of Acts?" In *Witness to the Gospel: The Theology of Acts*, edited by I. Howard Marshall and David Peterson, 3-16. Grand Rapids: Eerdmans, 1998.

———. "'Israel' and the Story of Salvation: One Theme in Two Parts." In *Jesus and the Heritage of Israel: Luke's Narrative Claim upon Israel's Legacy*, edited by David P. Moessner, 340-57. Harrisburg, PA: Trinity Press International, 1999.

Marshall, I. Howard, and David Peterson. *Witness to the Gospel: The Theology of Acts*. Grand Rapids: Eerdmans, 1998.

Martens, Allan. "Salvation Today: Reading Luke's Message for a Gentile Audience." In *Reading the Gospels Today*, edited by Stanley Porter, 100-126. Grand Rapids: Eerdmans, 2004

Maxwell, Kathy. *Hearing between the Lines: The Audience as Fellow-Worker in Luke-Acts and Its Cultural Milieu*. LNTS 425. London: T&T Clark, 2010.

McCasland, S.V. "The Way." *JBL* 77:3 (1958) 222-30.

McKnight, Scot. "Gentiles." In *DJG*, edited by Joel B. Green and Scot McKnight, 259-65. Downers Grove, IL: InterVarsity, 1992.

Metzger, Bruce M. *A Textual Commentary on the Greek New Testament*. 2nd ed. Stuttgart: Deutsche Bibelgesellschaft, 2002.

Meynet, Roland. *L'Evangile de Luc. Rhétorique sémitique*. Paris: Lethielleux, 2005.

Michaelis, Wilhelm. "ὁδός." In Vol. 5 of *TWNT*, edited by Gerhard Friedrich, 42-117. Stuttgart: W. Kohlhammer, 1954.

Minear, Paul S. *Images of the Church in the New Testament*. NTL. 1960. Reprint, Louisville: Westminster John Knox, 2004.

———. "Luke's Use of the Birth Stories." In *Studies in Luke-Acts*, edited by Leander E. Keck and J. Louis Martyn, 111-30. London: SPCK, 1968.

———. "Dear Theo: The Kerygmatic Intention and Claim of the Book of Acts." *Interpretation* 27:2 (1973) 131-50.

Minguez, Dionisio, "Hechos 8,24-40. Análisis structural del relato." *Biblica* 57 (1976) 168-91.

Moessner, David P. "*Two* Lords 'at the Right Hand'? The Psalms and an Intertextual Reading of Peter's Pentecost Speech (Acts 2:14-36)." In *Literary Studies in Luke-Acts*, edited by Richard P. Thompson and Thomas E. Phillips, 215-32. Macon, GA: Mercer University Press, 1998.

Moles, John. "Luke's Preface: The Greek Decree, Classical Historiography and Christian Redefinitions." *NTS* 57:4 (2011) 461-82.

———. "Time and Space Travel in Luke-Acts," In *Reading Acts in the Second Century*, edited by R. Dupertuis and T. Penner, n.p. Bible World. Sheffield: Equinox, forthcoming.

Morgan, James M. "*derek YHWH*: A Study of the Divine Way in the Old Testament." Master's thesis, Evangelische Theologische Faculteit, 2004.

———. "The Thoroughfare Motif in Luke-Acts: Its Poetic Value and Theological Implications." PhD diss., Evangelische Theologische Faculteit, 2010.

———. "Luc-Actes: un tour de force littéraire et théologique . . . pour nous." *Hokhma* (forthcoming).

Bibliography

———. "Emplotment, Plot, Explotment: Refining Plot Analysis of Biblical Narratives from the Reader's Perspective." *Biblical Interpretation* 21:1 (2013) 64–98.
Moyise, Steve. *The Old Testament in the New: An Introduction*. CBSS. London: Continuum, 2001.
Navone, John. "The Way of the Lord." *Scripture* 20 (1968) 24–30.
———. "Three Aspects of the Lucan Theology of History." *BTB* 3 (1973) 115–32.
———. "The Way and the Journey in Luke-Acts." *Bible Today* 44:2 (2006) 99–105.
Nolland, John. *Luke 1—9:20*. WBC 35a. Dallas: Word, 1989.
———. *Luke 18:35—24:53*. WBC 35c. Dallas: Word, 1993.
Nolli, Gianfranco. *Evangelo secondo Luca*. Vatican City: Libreria Editrice Vaticana, 1983.
Nötscher, Friedrich. *Gotteswege und Menschenwege in der Bibel und in Qumran*. BBB 15. Bonn: Peter Hanstein, 1958.
O'Neill, J.C. *The Theology of Acts in its Historical Setting*. 2nd ed. London: SPCK, 1970.
Pao, David W. *Acts and the Isaianic New Exodus*. BSL. Grand Rapids: Baker Academic, 2002.
Parsons, Mikeal C. "'Short in Stature': Luke's Physical Description of Zacchaeus." *NTS* 47:1 (2001) 50–57.
Parsons, Mikeal C., and Richard I. Pervo. *Rethinking the Unity of Luke and Acts*. Minneapolis: Fortress, 1993.
Pathrapankal, Joseph. "Christianity as a 'Way.'" In *Les Actes des Apôtres: traditions, rédaction, théologie*, edited by Jacob Kremer, 533–39. BETL 48. Gembloux: Duculot, 1979.
Pereira, Francis. *Ephesus, Climax of Universalism in Luke-Acts: A Redaction-Critical Study of Paul's Ephesian Ministry (Acts 18:23—20:1)*. Jesuit Theological Forum Series. Anand, India: Gujarat Sahitya Prakash, 1983.
Pervo, Richard I. *Acts: A Commentary*. Hermeneia. Minneapolis: Fortress, 2009.
———. Review of *The Assumed Authorial Unity of Luke and Acts: A Reassessment of the Evidence*, by Patricia Walters, *Review of Biblical Literature* (December 2009). n.p. Online: http://www.bookreviews.org/pdf/7084_7696.pdf.
Pesch, R. *Die Apostelgeschichte. 1. Teilband (Apg 1–12)*. EKKNT. Neukirchen-Vluyn: Neukirchener Verlag, 1986.
———. *Die Apostelgeschichte. 2. Teilband (Apg 13–28)*. EKKNT. Neukirchen-Vluyn: Neukirchener Verlag, 1986.
Petersen, Norman R. *Literary Criticism for New Testament Critics*. GBS. Philadelphia: Fortress, 1978.
Peterson, David. "The Motif of Fulfillment and the Purpose of Luke-Acts." In *The Book of Acts in Its Ancient Literary Setting*, edited by Bruce W. Winter and Andrew D. Clark, 83–104. BAFCS 1. Grand Rapids: Eerdmans, 1993.
Phelan, James. "Narrative Progression." In *Routledge Encyclopedia of Narrative Theory*, edited by David Herman et al., 359–60. London: Routledge, 2008.
Plummer, Alfred. *The Gospel according to S. Luke*. 5th ed. ICC. Edinburgh: T&T Clark, 1922.
Powell, Mark A. *What is Narrative Criticism?* GBS. Minneapolis: Fortress, 1990.
Powell, Mark A., et al. *The Bible and Modern Literary Criticism: A Critical Assessment and Annotated Bibliography*. BIRS. New York: Greenwood, 1993.
Prince, Gerald. *A Dictionary of Narratology*. Revised ed. Lincoln: University of Nebraska Press, 2003.

Bibliography

Pritz, Ray. *Nazarene Jewish Christianity: from the End of the New Testament Period until its Disappearance in the Fourth Century.* 1988. Reprint, Jerusalem: Magnes, 1992.
Radl, Walter. *Das Evangelium nach Lukas 1,1—9,50.* Freiburg im Breisgau: Herder, 2003.
Reicke, Bo Ivar. "The Risen Lord and his Church: The Theology of Acts." *Interpretation* 13:2 (1959) 157–69.
Repo, Eero. *Der 'Weg' als Selbstbezeichnung des Urchristentums eine traditionsgeschichtliche und semasiologische Untersuchung.* AASF. Helsinki: Suomalainen Tiedeakatemia, 1964.
Resseguie, James L. *Spiritual Landscape: Images of the Spiritual Landscape in the Gospel of Luke.* Peabody, MA: Hendrickson, 2004.
———. *Narrative Criticism of the New Testament: An Introduction.* Grand Rapids: Baker, 2005.
Ricoeur, Paul. *Temps et récit.* Vol. 1. L'intrigue et le récit historique. Paris: Éditions du Seuil, 1983.
———. *Temps et récit.* 3 vols. Paris: Éditions du Seuil, 1983-1985.
Riesenfeld, Harald. "La voie de charité: Note sur I Cor. XII, 31." *ST* 1 (1948) 146–57.
Robertson, A.T. *A Grammar of the Greek New Testament in the Light of Historical Research.* 3rd ed. London: Hodder & Stoughton, 1919.
Robinson, William C. "The Theological Context for Interpreting Luke's Travel Narrative." *JBL* 79 (1960) 20–31.
———. "The Way of the Lord: A Study of History and Eschatology in the Gospel of Luke." Ph.D. diss., University of Basel, 1962.
———. *Der Weg des Herrn. Studien zur Geschichte und Eschatologie im Lk-Evangelium.* TF 36. Hamburg: Reich, 1964.
Roloff, Jürgen. *Die Apostelgeschichte.* NTD. Göttingen: Vandenhoeck & Ruprecht, 1981.
Ropes, James Hardy. *The Beginnings of Christianity,* edited by F.J. Foakes-Jackson and Kirsopp Lake, Part I, The Acts of the Apostles, Vol. 3, The Texts of Acts. London: Macmillan, 1926.
Rothschild, Clare K. *Luke-Acts and the Rhetoric of History: An Investigation of Early Christian Historiography.* WUNT 2. Reihe 175. Tübingen: Mohr Siebeck, 2004.
Rowe, C. Kavin. "History, Hermeneutics and the Unity of Luke-Acts." *JSNT* 28:2 (2005) 131–57.
Schneider, Gerhard. *Die Apostelgeschichte.* Vol. I. HTKNT 5. Freiburg: Herder, 1980.
———. *Die Apostelgeschichte.* Vol. II. HTKNT 5. Freiburg: Herder, 1982.
Scholes, Robert, et al. *The Nature of Narrative.* Rev. and expanded ed. New York: Oxford University Press, 2006.
Schürmann, Heinz. *Das Lukasevangelium.* Vol. 1, Kommentar zu Kap. 1,1—9,50. HTKNT 3. Freiburg: Herder, 1982.
———. *Das Lukasevangelium.* Vol. 2, Kommentar zu Kap. 9,51—11,54. HTKNT 3. Freiburg: Herder, 1993.
Sheeley, Steven M. "Narrative Asides and Narrative Authority in Luke-Acts." *BTB* 18:3 (1988) 102–7.
———. *Narrative Asides in Luke-Acts.* JSNTSup 72. Sheffield: Sheffield Academic, 1992.
Shiell, William David. *Reading Acts: The Lector and the Early Christian Audience.* BIS 70. Boston: Brill Academic, 2004.
Snowden, Frank M. *Blacks in Antiquity: Ethiopians in the Graeco-Roman Experience.* Cambridge, MA: Harvard University Press, 1970.

Bibliography

Spencer, F. Scott. *The Portrait of Philip in Acts: A Study of Roles and Relations.* JSNTSup 67. Sheffield: Sheffield Academic, 1992.

———. *The Gospel of Luke and Acts of the Apostles.* IBT. Nashville: Abingdon, 2008.

Spencer, Patrick E. "The Unity of Luke—Acts: A Four-Bolted Hermeneutical Hinge." *Currents in Biblical Research* 5 (2007) 341–66.

Squires, John T. *The Plan of God in Luke-Acts.* SNTSMS 76. Cambridge: University Press, 1993.

Standaert, Benoît. "Luc, maître narrateur de la rencontre." In *Raconter, interpréter, annoncer,* edited by Emmanuelle Steffek and Yvan Bourquin, 282–95. Geneva: Labor et Fides, 2003.

Stenschke, Christoph. "The Need for Salvation." In *Witness to the Gospel: The Theology of Acts,* edited by I. Howard Marshall and David Peterson, 125–44. Grand Rapids: Eerdmans, 1998.

Sternberg, Meir. *The Poetics of Biblical Narrative: Ideological Literature and the Drama of Reading.* Bloomington: Indiana University, 1985.

Strauss, David. *The Promise and Its Fulfilment in Lucan Christology. The Davidic Messiah in Luke-Acts.* JSNTSup 110. Sheffield: Sheffield Academic, 1995.

Talbert, Charles H. *Literary Patterns, Theological Themes and the Genre of Luke-Acts.* SBLMS 20. Missoula, MT: Scholars, 1974.

———. "Prophecy and Fulfillment in Lucan Theology." In *Luke-Acts: New Perspectives from the Society of Biblical Literature Seminar,* edited by Charles H. Talbert, 91–103. New York: Crossroad, 1984.

———. *Reading Luke: A Literary and Theological Commentary on the Third Gospel.* Rev. ed. Macon, GA: Smyth & Helwys, 2002.

———. *Reading Acts: A Literary and Theological Commentary on the Acts of the Apostles.* Rev. ed. Macon, GA: Smyth & Helwys, 2005.

Tannehill, Robert C. "Israel in Luke-Acts: A Tragic Story." *JBL* 104 (1985) 69–85.

———. *The Narrative Unity of Luke-Acts: A Literary Interpretation.* Vol. 1: The Gospel according to Luke. Philadelphia: Fortress, 1986.

———. *The Narrative Unity of Luke-Acts: A Literary Interpretation.* Vol. 2: The Acts of the Apostles. Philadelphia: Fortress, 1990.

Thayer, Joseph Henry, ed. *Greek-English Lexicon of the New Testament,* Clavis Novi Testamenti translated, revised, and enlarged by Joseph Henry Thayer. New York: American Book Company, 1889.

Thompson, Richard P. *Keeping the Church in Its Place: The Church as Narrative Character in Acts.* New York: T&T Clark, 2006.

Trebilco, Paul R. "Paul and Silas—'Servants of the Most High God' (Acts 16.16–18)." *JSNT* 36 (1989) 51–73.

———. *Self-designations and Group Identity in the New Testament.* Cambridge: Cambridge University Press, 2012.

Tuckett, C.M. "The Christology of Luke-Acts." In *The Unity of Luke-Acts,* edited by J. Verheyden, 133–64. BETL 142. Leuven: Leuven University Press, 1999.

Unnik, W.C. van "The 'Book of Acts'—The Confirmation of the Gospel." *NovT* 4:1 (1960) 26–59.

———. "Once More St. Luke's Prologue," *Neot* 7:1 (1973) 7–26.

Urciuoli, Emiliano Rubens, "'Quella ὁδός che chiamano αἵρεσις.' Alle origini dell'autocomprensione filosofica dei seguaci di Gesù." *Annali di Storia dell'Esegesi* 28:1 (2011) 117–36.

Verheyden, Joseph, ed. *The Unity of Luke-Acts*, BETL 142. Leuven: Leuven University Press, 1999.
Vielhauer, Philipp. *Geschichte der urchristlichen Literatur. Einleitung in das Neue Testament, die Apokryphen und die Apostolischen Väter.* Berlin: Väter, 1975.
Völkel, Martin. "ὁδός." In *Exegetisches Wörterbuch zum Neuen Testament*, edited by Horst Balz and Gerhard Schneider, 2:1200–1204. Stuttgart: W. Kohlhammer, 1981.
Wallace, Daniel B. *Greek Grammar Beyond the Basics: An Exegetical Syntax of the New Testament.* Grand Rapids: Zondervan, 1996.
Walters, Patricia. *The Assumed Authorial Unity of Luke and Acts: A Reassessment of the Evidence.* SNTSMS 145. Cambridge: Cambridge University Press, 2009.
Walton, Steve. "Where Does the Beginning of Acts End?" In *The Unity of Luke-Acts*, edited by J. Verheyden, 448–67. BETL 142. Leuven: Leuven University Press, 1999.
———. "The Acts—of God? What is the 'Acts of the Apostles' all about?" *EQ* 80:4 (2008) 291–306.
———. "A Spirituality of Acts?" In *Reading Acts Today: Essays in Honour of Loveday C.A. Alexander*, edited by Steve Walton et al., 186–201. LNTS 427. London: T&T Clark, 2011.
Weiser, Alfons. *Die Apostelgeschichte. Kapitel 1–12.* ÖTKNT 5. Gütersloh: Gerd Mohn, 1981.
———. *Die Apostelgeschichte. Kapitel 13–28.* ÖTKNT 5. Gütersloh: Gerd Mohn, 1985.
White, Hayden. *Metahistory: The Historical Imagination in Nineteenth-Century Europe.* Baltimore: Johns Hopkins University Press, 1973.
———. "Emplotment." In *Routledge Encyclopedia of Narrative Theory*, edited by David Herman et al., 137. London: Routledge, 2008.
Wilcox, Max. *The Semitisms of Acts.* Oxford: Clarendon, 1965.
Wingren, Gustaf. "'Weg,' 'Wanderung' und verwandte Begriffe." *ST* 3:I–II (1950–51) 111–23.
Witherington, Ben, III. *The Acts of the Apostles: A Socio-Rhetorical Commentary.* Grand Rapids: Eerdmans, 1998.
Wolter, Michael. *Das Lukasevangelium.* HNT 5. Tübingen: Mohr Siebeck, 2008.
Würzbach, Natascha. "Motif." In *Routledge Encyclopedia of Narrative Theory*, edited by David Herman et al., 322–23. London: Routledge, 2005.

Subject Index

analepsis (flashback), 51, 118–19, 141, 145–46, 167
antagonist, 32, 57, 128, 134, 165
associational cluster, 17, 20, 22–23, 192
avoidability (unlikelihood), 21–22, 190
characterization, 10, 29–30, 52, 57, 76, 103, 134, 138–39, 155, 177, 184, 187–89, 191, 193
Christocentric, 131–32, 158, 171–72, 195, 204–6, 208, 216
closure, 6, 31, 37, 46, 49
coda, 55
complication, 101, 131, 146, 156–57, 165
concrete, 5, 16, 19, 28, 164, 192, 197
correlation (symbolic), 22, 23, 190, 192–93
counterplot, 52, 55–56
disciples
    false ("spies"), 111
    Jesus' followers, 11, 13, 14, 27, 31, 54–55, 57, 69, 76–77, 79, 81–82, 85–86, 96, 100, 102, 106, 108–9, 115, 117, 121–23, 126, 136–40, 152, 166, 168, 184–85, 187, 191, 194, 196, 208, 212–13
    would-be, 27, 29, 31, 82–85, 89, 95, 97, 111, 186, 216
emplotment, 37–38, 44, 50, 191, 198, 201–2, 218, 228
encounter
    reader's, 4–5, 17, 18, 23, 26, 33, 35–38, 40, 43, 46, 49–51, 53–55, 61, 68–69, 72, 76, 78, 82, 87, 89, 96, 101, 107–8, 115, 123, 134–35, 137–38, 142, 152, 160–61, 175–76, 179, 183–84, 186, 195, 197–98, 217, 219

"on the road," (thoroughfare), 9, 13–14, 29, 31, 70, 81, 84, 88–89, 94–98, 101–6, 109, 117–19, 121, 123, 128–34, 136, 141–45, 167, 170, 175, 177, 186–88, 211, 213, 216
evaluation (final), 50, 106, 203–4, 216
explotment, 37–38, 198, 217–18
expressive (research, value), 7–8, 12, 15, 17, 199
figurative, 5, 7, 9–10, 16, 18, 20, 23, 26–30, 33, 62, 67–68, 72, 78, 82, 98, 110, 114, 118, 120–21, 125–26, 130–31, 135–36, 138, 144, 147, 149, 160, 164, 166–67, 169, 178, 180, 187, 190–92, 194, 197, 211, 216, 218
frequency, 7, 21–22, 33, 190
hedgerow path, 25, 89–91, 103, 190
hero, 5, 31, 39, 49, 52–57, 61, 68–71, 74–79, 83–84, 87–88, 95, 98, 109, 113, 115–17, 126, 145–46, 148, 154, 177, 184–88, 191–92, 194–95, 197, 199, 205
Jewish people (Jews), 3, 5, 9–10, 14, 40–42, 47, 52–54, 56, 73–74, 86–88, 93–94, 96, 104, 112, 123, 126, 132–34, 137–39, 146, 148, 150, 154–56, 159, 161–64, 167, 169–71, 173–75, 177, 179–80, 184–89, 191, 192, 200, 205–8, 212, 215, 219
level of action, 28–29, 31, 36, 39, 47–49, 52, 74, 76, 79, 94–95, 98, 100, 116, 158, 169, 185, 187, 190, 192, 212, 217
level of reader (discourse), 15, 36, 43, 48, 198, 212, 217

233

Subject Index

Luke-Acts, 3–7, 9, 12–18, 23–26, 29, 32–33, 35–40, 42–43, 45–52, 54–57, 61, 64–71, 73, 75, 77, 79, 81, 92, 94–98, 118, 124, 126, 128, 130, 132–34, 136, 140, 143, 149, 154, 162, 166, 168, 170, 176–77, 183, 188, 190–92, 194–219

mandate, 3, 5, 31–32, 47–48, 52–57, 62, 68–69, 71, 74–76, 78–79, 81–84, 87–88, 91, 94, 98–100, 102–3, 105–6, 109–10, 114–15, 117, 119, 121, 123, 127–32, 134, 138, 143–44, 146, 148, 154, 157, 160, 169, 173, 176–77, 184–88, 191–94, 197, 206, 209, 211–15

meaningful (motif), 4, 17–18, 32, 34, 125, 194, 203, 215, 218–19

metaphor, 10, 30, 65–66, 73, 113, 160, 162–63, 165, 177, 189, 210

mimetic (research), 7–8, 12

mise en abyme, 121, 160

mise en intrigue, 44, 201

mise en scène, 107

motif, 3, 4–6, 12–15, 17–26, 28, 31–36, 39, 45–47, 49, 57, 61, 64, 67, 69–70, 74–77, 79, 82, 94, 96–98, 113, 115–16, 120–23, 128–29, 132–33, 139, 143, 148, 154, 164, 166–67, 170, 175–80, 183–97, 198–201, 203–4, 206–9, 211–14, 216, 218–19

narrative theory (narratology), xi, 6, 18–19, 35–36, 184, 195

nations (Gentiles), 3, 13–14, 27, 30–31, 41–42, 46–48, 52, 54–56, 69, 73–75, 91–93, 96, 99–100, 123, 128, 133–35, 139, 145, 148–51, 153–54, 161, 164, 166, 169, 173, 176–80, 185–89, 191–92, 200, 203, 205–10, 212, 215–16, 219

normalization, 44–45, 57, 150, 160, 203, 212

objective (research, value), 7–8, 14, 17, 75, 126,

opposition, 3–4, 26, 48, 52, 54–55, 74–77, 79, 83–84, 98, 102, 105, 108–9, 114–15, 126, 140, 145–48, 150–51, 161–62, 164, 166–67, 177, 180, 185, 189

orientation
final, 26–28, 50–51, 54–56, 107, 179–80, 189–90
initial, 26–30, 50–51, 54–55, 57, 61, 69, 74, 113, 126, 184–85, 191

path, xii, 5, 7, 10, 17, 24–25, 61, 68, 70–72, 80, 89–91, 103, 121, 137, 142, 148, 150, 152, 177, 188, 190, 216, 218

pattern, 3, 5, 15, 26, 31–32, 51, 55, 67, 78, 94, 96–99, 119, 133, 140, 144, 161, 164, 169, 180, 186, 188–89, 191, 195, 215–16

performance (narrative), 5, 17–19, 22–23, 32, 39, 122, 183, 189, 194, 197–98

pivot, 26–29, 31, 50–51, 53, 55, 57, 94–96, 105, 115, 117–18, 121, 123, 175–76, 186–87, 195–96

plot, xi, 4–6, 18, 21–23, 26, 28–29, 31–33, 35–39, 43, 46–47, 49–51, 55–57, 62, 64, 69–71, 75–76, 83, 87, 94–99, 115, 117, 120, 122–23, 127, 132–33, 137, 144–45, 154–55, 161, 163–64, 169, 174, 177, 180, 183–89, 191, 194–95, 197–209, 212, 217–18

plot synopsis, 47, 49, 56, 195

poetic (research, value), 8, 14, 44, 67, 70, 199, 201–3

point, 4, 22, 114, 200, 203–4, 206–8, 210, 212, 219

point of view, 32, 77, 96, 115, 121, 139, 146, 150, 167, 191–92, 216

potentiality, 68, 154, 209

pragmatic aim, 4, 15–17, 44, 46, 57, 105, 194, 203, 213

pragmatic (research, value, force), 4, 6–8, 13, 15–19, 22–23, 33–35, 38–39, 44–46, 52–55, 57, 70, 75, 88–90, 94, 99, 114, 120, 126, 132, 159–60, 163, 166, 174, 183, 189, 194–95, 197, 203

Subject Index

programmatic, 75, 145, 184, 200, 209–11
prolepsis (flash-forward), 48, 51, 65, 70, 92, 114, 168, 179, 186
proleptic portrait, 52, 54, 57, 62, 65, 69, 71, 74, 76, 94, 96, 108–9, 122, 184, 191
prophecy, 63, 121, 167, 200, 209, 213, 216
protagonist, 30, 32, 39, 49, 56–57, 62, 66, 69, 105, 115–16, 135, 144–45, 157, 160, 177, 185, 187, 189, 191–92, 194
quinary scheme (on action and discourse levels), 49–50,
raveling, 26–31, 50–52, 54–57, 62, 74–76, 84, 99, 103, 110, 114–15, 122, 148, 175, 185–87, 191
reader
  implied, 17, 33, 39, 51–52, 55, 66, 184, 195, 198–99
  real, 39–40, 199
  sympathetic, 5, 35, 40, 50, 139, 157, 164, 194, 219
reality, 4, 55, 68, 137, 154, 209, 216
reception, 3, 36, 43, 47, 51, 53, 55–56, 70, 72, 74–75, 79–82, 84, 86, 92, 94–99, 101–4, 106–10, 114–15, 118, 120–22, 128–34, 138, 140–44, 146, 148, 151, 154, 157, 159–61, 164, 175, 177, 180, 186–89, 191, 215–16
referential (research, value), 7–8, 43, 199
rejection, 3, 40, 46–47, 51–56, 70, 75, 82–84, 86–87, 89, 94–97, 99, 101, 103, 107, 109–11, 115–16, 120, 146, 148–51, 161, 164, 167, 169, 174, 177, 180, 185–86, 188–89, 205, 207–8, 211, 215–16
repetition, 14–15, 19–20, 22, 34, 69, 133, 144, 159, 188, 190, 203, 211
resistance, 54, 102, 140
rhetoric(al), 4, 23, 35–36, 39–41, 44, 46, 90, 98, 136, 139, 147, 151, 163, 176, 201–2

road, xii, 5–7, 10, 13–17, 24, 28, 53, 72–73, 76, 79, 81–87, 89–91, 94–95, 101, 103–5, 107–8, 115, 117–21, 123, 128–32, 134, 138, 141–45, 147, 163, 169, 174–75, 185–87, 213, 216
salvation
  agent, 15, 52, 69, 201, 206–7
  beneficiaries, 69, 90, 98, 184, 192, 201, 206–8, 212–13
  messengers, 207, 212–13, 215
sequence (narrative), 26–28, 32, 51, 56, 74, 184
significance, 22, 69, 134, 190–91, 202
spiritual landscape, 5, 70, 126
street
  narrow, 7, 24–25, 89, 190
  wide, 25, 86, 89–90, 127, 176, 188
symbol, 11, 15, 91, 142, 218
syncrisis, 128, 130
synecdoche (function), 33, 162, 218
teacher, 18, 41, 109–15, 129, 138, 146, 156, 160, 174, 177, 186, 188–89, 193, 207, 211, 214, 216
tension (narrative), 22, 26, 47, 52–56, 71, 73, 75–76, 101, 116, 122, 157, 167, 177, 185, 187, 189, 192, 194
theme, 5–6, 12–15, 17–19, 22, 34–36, 48, 62, 67–69, 73, 75, 79, 94, 97–98, 101, 103–4, 106, 138, 140, 148, 168, 176, 180, 184, 192, 195, 204, 209–11, 214, 218–19
thoroughfare reception scenes, 84, 94–96, 98–99, 101, 103–4, 107, 109–10, 115, 118, 121–22, 128–29, 131–35, 141–44, 175, 177, 186–88, 191
transformation (spiritual), 3–6, 39, 49, 52–56, 63, 69–71, 73, 83, 86, 96, 99–100, 106–7, 118–23, 126–27, 129, 131, 133, 140–42, 144, 148, 155, 159, 175–76, 184, 186–88, 191–92, 194, 196–97, 203, 205, 209–12, 218

Subject Index

transforming action, 49, 51, 55–56, 102, 117, 123–24, 126, 130–31, 158, 160, 176, 188, 195

turning point, 53, 102, 121, 161, 187, 191

unity (narrative), 3, 21, 51, 56, 122, 130, 187, 195

unraveling, 26–32, 50–51, 54–57, 94, 114–15, 121–23, 127, 133, 144, 174–77, 187, 189, 191

way
- way, xii, 5–8, 10, 12–13, 15, 68–69, 71, 81, 152, 163
- divine way, xi, 113, 163, 215, 217
- "the Way," xi, 5, 7–11, 14–16, 43, 48, 54, 80–81, 99, 114, 123, 128, 133–39, 141–42, 144–45, 148, 156–57, 159–75, 177–80, 188–89, 191, 193–94, 196, 200, 211–19
- "the way of God," 5, 9, 18, 110–15, 124–25, 129, 137–39, 149–50, 155, 158–60, 162–65, 171, 177, 186, 188–89, 194, 196, 200, 211, 214, 216–18
- "the ways of/to life," 9, 124–25, 138, 176, 188, 210, 214
- "the way of/for the Lord," 9–10, 12–13, 28, 71–73, 79, 112, 125, 136–39, 149, 154–56, 159–60, 165–66, 168, 177, 180, 184, 188, 200, 215, 217
- "the way of peace," 5, 9, 62, 65, 67–70, 74–75, 86, 92, 100, 103, 106, 109–10, 113, 120–21, 124, 126, 131, 133, 137, 139, 142, 148, 154, 166, 176–78, 180, 184, 186–89, 192, 209–10, 213, 218
- "the way of salvation," 5, 9, 124–25, 136, 151–54, 177, 188, 210, 214, 216

www.ingramcontent.com/pod-product-compliance
Lightning Source LLC
Chambersburg PA
CBHW071941240426
43669CB00048B/2551